AN INTRODUCTION TO COMPUTER-AIDED ENGINEERING

AN INTRODUCTION TO COMPUTER-AIDED ENGINEERING

Andrew Tizzard

Middlesex University

McGRAW-HILL BOOK COMPANY

London · New York · St Louis · San Francisco · Auckland
Bogotá · Caracas · Lisbon · Madrid · Mexico · Milan
Montreal · New Delhi · Panama · Paris · San Juan
São Paulo · Singapore · Sydney · Tokyo · Toronto

Published by
McGRAW-HILL Book Company Europe
Shoppenhangers Road, Maidenhead, Berkshire, SL6 2QL, England
Telephone 0628 23432
Fax 0628 770224

British Library Cataloguing in Publication Data
Tizzard, Andrew
  Introduction to Computer-aided
  Engineering
  I. Title
  620

  ISBN 0-07-707974-4

Library of Congress Cataloging-in-Publication Data
Tizzard, Andrew,
    An introduction to computer-aided engineering/Andrew Tizzard.
      p. cm.
    Includes bibliographical references and index.
    ISBN 0-07-707974-4:
    1. Computer-aided engineering.   I. Title.
  TA345.T59   1994
  670′.285–dc20   93–46759
                                                             CIP

1234 BL 97654

Typeset by TecSet Limited, Wallington, Surrey
and printed and bound in Great Britain by Biddles Ltd, Guildford, Surrey

To my wife, Julia
Without whose love, encouragement, patience and support, this book would not exist.

CONTENTS

PREFACE

Computer-aided engineering or CAE is a wide-ranging, multi-disciplinary subject which has initiated much excitement in the engineering profession in recent years, particularly within the last two decades. A common initial reaction at first encounter with the subject, whether it be by student or professional engineer, is that here is yet another new subject which one needs to study. It is not, however, a new subject in its own right; its various elements have been used and taught since the fifties. CAE is a well-established field but until recently it has been poorly formalized and very fragmented. The traditional approach to teaching the subject is by delivering separate topics or modules each covering the elements which go to make up the field of computer-aided engineering. This, in itself, is not a bad approach, but there is a need to ensure that the integration of areas such as computer-aided design (CAD), analysis, manufacture, production planning and control is taught and stressed to students, particularly as common practices in manufacturing industry these days demand a more holistic treatment of the product development process from concept to delivery by the use of concurrent engineering methods. This is an important theme which runs throughout this book.

There are many books which the student of computer-aided engineering could acquire and use, and that in itself presents a problem when attempting to deal with the subject in a formalized and unfragmented manner. There are texts on engineering drawing and design which discuss computer-aided draughting and design (CADD), there are those covering computer graphics in great depth as well as those dealing with computer-aided manufacture (CAM), production planning and control, computer-integrated manufacture (CIM) and flexible manufacturing systems (FMS). There are also a number of training manuals for various CADD, CAM and CADCAM packages available. All of these texts are useful to the student studying computer-aided engineering and the booklist for such a course can be lengthy.

The modern professional or incorporated engineer is expected to have a broader and more multi-disciplinary knowledge base. Recent changes in the approach to engineering design, for example, have brought about the existence of multi-disciplinary teams working on projects. While these teams may have members with specialist knowledge in mechanical, manufacturing, electrical or electronic engineering, as well as specialists in areas such as marketing, each member needs to have some appreciation of the various disciplines. The material presented in this text is mainly intended for undergraduates undertaking studies in mechanical or manufacturing, electrical or electronic engineering at Higher National Certificate, diploma and degree levels. It is not, however, for the majority of cases, to be considered the only exposure that students will have to the application of computers to engineering. The introductory nature of the material is intended to lead in to more specialized study, more relevant to the field in which the student expects to gain an award.

The approach taken in the book is to build on existing knowledge of the activities of an engineering enterprise by explanation of how and why computers are applied to the specification, design, manufacture and launch of a product. As the range of material covered is wide, any one aspect cannot be covered to a great depth and an attempt is made to give sound appreciation of each area without being over-superficial. While the complete text presents an introduction to the whole field of computer-aided engineering, each chapter can be considered an introduction to one aspect of the subject in its own right and, as such, tutorial problems and example assignments are given for each chapter where appropriate, and in addition a booklist is provided to aid further study.

The material is covered in ten chapters and though the order in which they appear is logical, the reader can adopt a less structured approach to the study of the subject. I recommend that, particularly for absolute newcomers to engineering or computing, Chapters 1 to 3 are read first as they introduce general concepts and explain general computing and hardware from first principles. Chapters 4 to 8 can be read in almost any order depending upon the reader's previous learning and experience. Chapters 9 and 10 summarize and define integration of CAE activity both at the conceptual level and at the physical level with the explanation of electronic transmission of data within the automated factory, and though these can be studied in isolation and provide some detailed knowledge in the areas covered, it may best if they are left until last.

Andrew Tizzard

GLOSSARY OF ACRONYMS AND ABBREVIATIONS

ACSL	Advanced continuous simulation language
ADC	Analogue to digital converter
AGV	Automated guided vehicle
ALU	Arithmetic and logic unit
AM	Amplitude modulation
ANSI	American National Standards Institute
APT	Automatically programmed tools
ASCII	American Standard Code for Information Interchange
B-Rep	Boundary representation
BEM	Boundary element method
BIOS	Built-in operating system
BOM	Bill-of-materials
BSI	British Standards Institute
CAD	Computer-aided draughting computer-aided design
CADCAM	Computer-aided design and manufacture
CADD	Computer-aided draughting and design
CAE	Computer-aided engineering
CAI	Computer-aided inspection
CAM	Computer-aided manufacturing
CAPP	Computer-aided process planning
CD ROM	Compact disk read only memory
CDF	Cumulative density function
CGA	Colour graphics adapter
CIM	Computer-integrated manufacturing
CLDATA	Cutter locating data file
CMM	Coordinate measuring machine
CNC	Computerized numerical control
CPU	Central processing unit
CRT	Cathode ray tube
CSG	Construction solids geometry

CSMA/CD	Carrier sense multiple access with collision detection
DAC	Digital to analogue converter
DFA	Design for assembly or Design for automation
DFE	Design for the environment
DFM	Design for the market or Design for manufacture
DNC	Direct or distributed numerical control
DOGS	Design office graphics system
DVST	Direct view storage tube
DXF	Drawing exchange format
EDD	Earliest due date
EGA	Enhanced graphics adapter
EEPROM	Electrically erasable programmable read only memory
FAS	Flexible assembly system
FDA	Finite difference analysis
FE	Finite element
FM	Frequency modulation
FMS	Flexible manufacturing system
FSK	Frequency shift keying
GM MAP	General Motors manufacturing automation protocol
GNC	Graphical numerical control
HOCUS	Hand or computer universal simulator
IGES	Initial Graphics Exchange Specification
IP	Internet protocol
ISO	International Standards Organization
IT	Information technology
JANET	Joint academic network
JIT	Just-in-time
LAN	Local area network
MAC	Medium access control
Mbps	Mega-bits per second
MFLOPS	(Megaflops) millions of floating point operations per second
MIPS	Millions of instructions per second
MPS	Master production schedule
MRPI/MRP1	Materials requirements planning
MRPII/MRP2	Manufacturing resource planning
MSDOS	Microsoft Systems disk operating system
MTBF	Mean time between failures
MTTR	Mean time to repair
NC	Numerical control
OSI	Open Systems Interconnection
PC	Personal computer
PDES	Product Data Exchange Specification
PDF	Probability density function
PIGS	Pictorial interactive graphics system

PLC	Programmable logic controller
PM	Phase modulation
PROM	Programmable read only memory
PSK	Phase shift keying
RAM	Random access memory
ROM	Read only memory
SCARA	Selective compliance assembly robot arm
SDRC	Structural Dynamics Research Corporation
SPC	Statistical process control
SPT	Shortest processing time
STEP	Standard for Exchange of Product Data
TCP	Transmission control protocol
TCP/IP	Transmission control protocol/Internet protocol
TDM	Time division multiplexing
TPDU	Transport protocol data unit
VGA	Video graphics array
WAN	Wide area network
WIP	Work in progress

TRADEMARKS

CADKEY is developed and supported by CADkey Inc. USA.

CATIA is a general-purpose CAE package developed by Dassault Systèmes, France, and supported by IBM.

DOGS (Design Office Graphics System) is part of the design and analysis suite of programs by PAFEC.

I-DEAS is a fully-integrated package developed and marketed by SRDC Inc., USA.

ONE

THE WHAT AND WHY OF COMPUTER-AIDED ENGINEERING

The meaning of the term computer-aided engineering or CAE is very simple: it is the performance of engineering tasks or functions with the aid of a computer. The emphasis is very much on the word 'aided' as, by and large, these tasks are still administered and controlled by the engineer. Engineering, by definition, requires application of ingenuity to the solution of a problem and ingenuity requires the use of intelligence, rationality and expertise. We hear much about artificially intelligent computer systems these days but these merely apply the observed rules of the working of natural intelligence and use them to draw upon stored knowledge and expertise. They are, in effect, still computer-aided systems. Engineering is a wide-ranging multi-disciplinary subject area and, consequentially, so is the subject of computer-aided engineering. In order for us to cover the area in its entirety, we must examine the ways in which a computer can assist the mechanical, manufacturing, electrical, electronics and civil engineer. This, however, would produce a lengthy text, a majority of which would be largely irrelevant to any one reader. This book will therefore concentrate mainly on those areas of mechanical and manufacturing engineering which can benefit from computer-aided engineering techniques, though many of the principles described, particularly those for design, draughting, modelling and analysis, can easily be carried over to the other engineering disciplines.

1.1 THE CATEGORIZATION OF COMPUTER-AIDED ENGINEERING

Before examining the need for computer assistance in engineering, we need to look at the scope of the subject. Engineering, even when its study is confined to one discipline, covers a very broad spectrum of activities and this is also true for computer-aided engineering. The mechanical or manufacturing engineer will, at some point in his or her career, have studied, used or been exposed to a variety of activities such as engineering drawing, design, numerical methods and analysis techniques, manufacturing techniques and organizational planning and control. There is a computer-assisted means for all of these, and all fall into the definition of computer-aided engineering, which can be broadly categorized into four main areas as shown in Fig. 1.1.

While it is helpful to separate out the areas in this way it must be understood that there are strong links and, in many cases, overlaps between them. In many respects it can be misleading to segregate the areas totally as the tendency is then to develop systems within the areas largely in isolation from each other; in fact there is a history of this practice taking place in the early years of computer-aided engineering software development. The effect of this is a reproduction of effort during the development of systems in different areas which employ similar graphical or numerical and hence programming techniques.

Additionally there should be strong links between the departments which use techniques within any one area; for example it would be inconceivable that a design and development department could carry out its work effectively without reference to the manufacturing or production planning departments. The department would, in effect, be working blindly, not knowing the company's manufacturing abilities, procedures

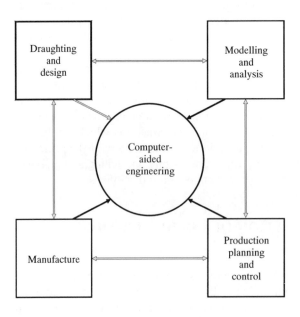

Figure 1.1 Areas of computer-aided engineering

and strengths with the possible result that the components and products could not be produced in-house. This 'over the wall' approach to engineering has been common practice until quite recently; the trend now, however, is to adopt a *concurrent engineering* strategy to design and development where product ideas are realized by a team made up of members of many departments. The principles and benefits of concurrent engineering will be discussed later in this chapter.

The link between the area of draughting and design and modelling and analysis is very strong. In fact modelling and analysis are very important parts of the design process even when computer assistance is not employed. Within a non-computer-aided environment, modelling is carried out by the production of physical models of a component, assembly or product and analysis by the production and use of prototypes in laboratory tests. The results of analysis provide an important feedback path in the design process as they will dictate changes in the current design which meet shortfalls in expected or desired performance. Computer-aided draughting and design (CADD) systems provide the means to generate three-dimensional models within the computer and from those models generate drawings for manufacturing purposes. More complex forms of three-dimensional design systems allow analysis of the computer model to take place, for example, checking for interference between parts of an assembly, calculation of surface area and mass properties as examined in detail in Chapter 4. The computer model definition could be developed yet further to provide analysis of the stresses in a component under load. Manual methods for stress analysis on complex components are generally difficult to apply with speed and accuracy except by the use of numerical methods, such as finite element or boundary element analysis. Complex modelling can be carried out in this way to produce useful results without the need to destructively test expensive prototypes in the laboratory. The methodology of these techniques is explained in Chapter 5.

As there is a need for dialogue between departments and areas of commonality in the computer-aided engineering software systems in each of the four areas described, there is the possibility of electronic communication between the computer systems in different departments. In other words, the model of a component produced on a computer-aided design system (CAD) will be stored on the computer system in a form which can be transferred to or accessed by the manufacturing department so that a program can be produced for a CNC machine to make the component. The use of a computer to assist in the manufacturing process is called computer-aided manufacturing or CAM. There are computer-aided manufacturing systems available for a wide range of activities, such as material removal, moulding and casting, fabrication and assembly and materials handling, and these are the subject of Chapter 6. Thus the commonality between computer-aided design, modelling and analysis and computer-aided manufacture involves common component models for material removal and mould design, finite element analysis for mould design and assembly, and three-dimensional modelling techniques to simulate materials handling systems.

A subassembly or complete product design can be defined in terms of its components and materials for production planning and control purposes. Production planning involves a variety of activities such as machine and process scheduling and materials requirements planning (MRP), and production control requires monitoring and inspection techniques and these will be discussed in Chapter 7. This cannot be successfully carried out without data from the CAM process and also investigations into how manufacturing facilities, for example an assembly flow line, operate under certain situations. Chapter 8 describes how manufacturing systems can be modelled, simulated and tested under various conditions before a new facility is built or major changes made to existing systems. There is also an examination into how some forms of simulation can be valuable in the design, modelling and analysis of control systems.

Any company adopting a strategy to implement computer-aided engineering techniques in its activities must consider the need for intercommunication of data between departments. This is so even if the introduction of computer-aided engineering is carried out piecemeal, for example if the design department implements a computer-aided draughting system to ease the normal bottleneck of drawing production, issuing and storage. The choice of system should be made with the possibility of expansion to three-dimensional modelling and computer-aided manufacture in mind. The eventual aim of the strategy would be to integrate all computer-aided engineering activities so that data can flow electronically between departments and the whole operation can be monitored and controlled. This is the basis for computer-integrated manufacturing or CIM which is discussed in Chapter 9. The physical means by which the activities are integrated by electronic communication methods is described in Chapter 10.

1.2 THE ELEMENTS OF COMPUTER-AIDED ENGINEERING

We have seen that the many of the functions within an engineering company can be carried out with the assistance of a computer and that these aids or tools can be categorized into four main areas. We have also examined the commonality between these areas which can be further understood by exploring in a little more detail what kinds of tools exist to assist engineers and managers within a company in carrying out the company's activities. Figure 1.2 shows the flow of activity for the development of a product from its initial specification to its final delivery to and use by the customer. The kind of tools available for each stage is shown and reveals that the field of computer-aided engineering is strewn with acronyms and jargon.

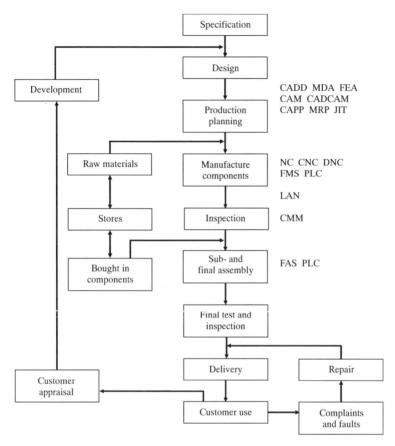

Figure 1.2 CAE in the product development process

If all the software and hardware tools were applied to every possible stage and if they were linked together within a computer-integrated manufacturing environment then the concept of the totally automated factory could be realized. The actual occurrence of this in modern industry is rare, though there are cases where large parts of the manufacturing process are carried out with very little human intervention.

The specification stage requires a large amount of human intervention as it is here that an idea for a product is conceived. This is normally the result of either a specific customer's request for a solution to their problem or that of market research. The application of computing technology at this point is usually limited to the use of word processing or desktop publishing systems to create the specification. The design of the product to the specification can then take place and, in an ideal situation, this is carried out by a team of specialists made up of design and manufacturing engineers, marketing and sales personnel. This is essential not only to ensure that the product fulfils the specification, and hence market requirements, but also to ensure that it can be efficiently manufactured by the company. This team approach to the design of a product is called *concurrent or parallel engineering*; the traditional alternative to this is often referred to as *over the wall engineering* as illustrated in Fig. 1.3.

The use of the concurrent engineering technique means that no longer do departments work in isolation by preparing information only relevant to the next stage and then throwing that information over what seems like a solid brick wall to the department who will take the development to the next stage. To describe the communication between departments in this way is, perhaps, a little extreme, as some intercommunication does need to take place. However, this is normally in the form of feedback to a previous department, often when the development has gone much farther than it needs to have done. The concurrent engineering strategy ensures that incorrect assumptions made by one department can be corrected very early on and is valid and desirable even when computer assistance is not employed at any or even all stages of the product development process.

After the product has been through the design stage, which is further explained in Chapter 4, its manufacture needs to be planned batch by batch according to the quantities required. The methods and processes used for manufacture will have, for the most part, already been established as part of the design and development. The scheduling of the production, the acquisition of raw materials and bought-in components and the control of quality could all be carried out using computer-aided production planning techniques. The actual manufacturing processes could be computer assisted and the production line and all its elements such as automated assembly and machining cells could be designed and analysed for efficiency by simulation techniques. Thus there are computer-based tools which can be used in the stages from production planning through to delivery. Even then the product is not complete, as customer use resulting in possible complaints and need for repair will invoke further development and design changes, which may have significant effect on the whole manufacturing procedure. Computer-

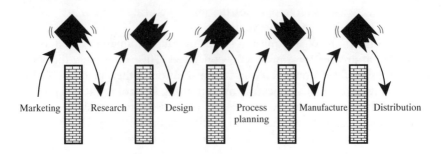

Figure 1.3 Over the wall engineering

aided engineering techniques, when implemented and used correctly, can reduce the effect of these changes on the productivity of a company.

The many elements of computer-aided engineering can therefore be identified more specifically in terms of how they fall into the four main areas and, to some extent, where there is overlap and commonality between them as shown in Fig. 1.4. Draughting and design incorporate three-dimensional design techniques, the end result of which is normally a working drawing. In addition to this such techniques as design for assembly or design for automation may be needed. There is no specific computer-aided tool for these methods as they are concepts which ensure that components are designed in such a way as to ease methods of manufacture. The link to computer-aided manufacture is provided by a CADCAM tool. Modelling and analysis includes tools such as finite element and finite difference analysis, mechanism design, which is a feature of some CADD systems, and simulation techniques, including continuous and discrete event simulation and dynamics analysis.

Computer-aided manufacturing techniques are used to produce programs for CNC machines, robot manipulators and automatic inspection devices such as the coordinate measuring machine, which are included in the basic building blocks of flexible assembly or manufacturing systems. These machines and systems being in their own right computer controlled, are also

Draughting and design		Modelling and analysis	
CADD DFA CADCM	Draughting and design Design for assembly/automation Link to computer-aided manufacture (CAM)	FEA	Finite element analysis Finite difference analysis Mechanism design Continuous simulation Discrete event simulation Dynamics analysis
Computer-aided engineering			
Manufacture		Production planning and control	
CAM CADCAM CNC DNC PLC CMM FAS FMS	Computer-aided part programming (CNC) Computer numerical control Direct/distributed numerical control Programmable logic controllers Coordinate measuring machines Flexible assembly/ manufacturing systems	CAPP MRP BOM JIT	Production planning and control Scheduling Quality control Material requirements planning Bill-of-materials Just-in-time

Figure 1.4 Elements of computer-aided engineering

classified as computer-aided engineering systems and are described as such in Chapter 3. Production planning and control requires the use of shopfloor scheduling and control of the manufacturing process. The acquisition and control of resources and quality control are significant features of this area which may also involve the application of advanced manufacturing strategies such as the 'just-in-time' philosophy.

1.3 THE NEED FOR COMPUTER-AIDED ENGINEERING

The need to develop computer-assisted techniques in engineering has arisen largely because of modern market demands. Western culture, in particular, is consumer based; its people require consumer goods of high quality and functionality and to meet this demand there is a need for increased productivity in industry, as depicted in Fig. 1.5. Indeed this demand does not only impinge on the engineering industry but also the service industries such as banking which has, in particular, been very prompt in applying computing technology to its activities.

The implementation of computer-aided techniques which, in a large number of cases, implies automation and hence a reduction in human resources, raises a large number of social issues. Although this is somewhat outside the scope of this text, it must be stressed that managers and engineers should be aware of the problems of automation. Our society still has a long way to go before it can cope with the changes in lifestyle required

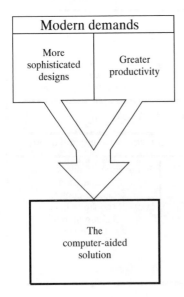

Figure 1.5 The need for computer-aided engineering

for large-scale automation in manufacturing industry, while still maintaining a fair standard of living for all concerned. There are also ecological considerations to be taken into account, particularly regarding the mass production of consumer goods. Some companies have begun to demonstrate an awareness of this by employing *design for the environment* strategies which recognize, among other things, the need to incorporate recyclable components in their product range.

The main issue under examination here, however, is how computers can meet the demands placed on modern industry. The sophistication required in many domestic products can be seen by visiting any local electrical goods retailer or car showroom. There are varying degrees of complexity and functionality in the goods on offer which give the consumer a wide choice depending on personal preference and budget. Before computers were used in the manufacturing process it was difficult to provide this kind of variety, as mass production techniques tended to dictate to the customer that they could have 'any colour as long as it is black'. With modern production techniques it is possible to introduce variety in the product range as the complexities involved in the control of flexible manufacturing facilities can be handled with far greater ease by the data processing abilities of a computer.

The development of computing technology over the last 40 years has been so rapid that it is often referred to as a second industrial revolution. This has come about as computers have been utilized more and more to assist in the design and manufacture of goods and in the provision of services. The growth of the computing industry has meant that computing equipment has rapidly fallen in price and reduced in physical size while at the same time increased in performance, as illustrated in Fig. 1.6.

This trend is dealt with more specifically in Chapters 2 and 3. Chapter 2 describes the development of computing to date, the fundamentals of computer operation and the hardware typically in use in the modern

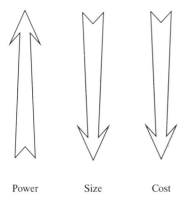

Power   Size   Cost

Figure 1.6 Evolution of computing technology since the late 1950s

engineering design or planning office. Chapter 3 describes the hardware and operation of functionally dedicated computing facilities currently used on the modern factory floor such as CNC machines, programmable logic controllers, robots and other materials handling systems.

1.4 THE COMPUTER AND THE ENGINEER

The advent of computer-assisted techniques in engineering is bringing about a change in the capabilities of the engineer. An engineer, by definition, must be creative and ingenious in solving problems using technology particular to his or her specialism. For example, a mechanical engineer will apply the use of mechanical systems and technology to solving a problem, and an electronic engineer will be involved with the design of electronic circuits to fulfil a purpose. This, in many instances, not only requires the generation of new ideas but also the application of tried and tested techniques. Traditionally this means that the engineer must be equipped with the knowledge necessary to apply, for example, complex numerical techniques to problem solving, and this can be time consuming to the point that ingenuity often takes second place. The computer-aided engineer, however, should be largely relieved of those aspects of problem solving which can be carried out with a computer leaving more time for the generation and development of ideas.

To illustrate this let us examine the different capabilities of a human and a computer to see how the computer can be used as a problem solving tool. Figure 1.7 highlights those capabilities of the human required to carry out an engineering task. Within the execution of a task such as, for example, the

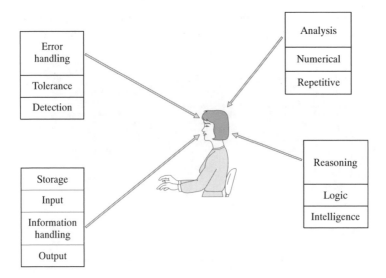

Figure 1.7   Human capabilities

design of a component or the planning of a manufacturing procedure, the engineer will need to call upon his or her abilities in four main areas: analysis, reasoning, information handling and error handling.

Figure 1.8 illustrates that a computer does have, by and large, abilities in the same four areas but these abilities vary in proportion, mode of operation and speed. It is the purpose of any computer-aided engineering technique to ensure that the abilities of both the engineer and the computer are well matched to produce an effective problem solving environment.

An engineer needs to employ both intuitive and numerical analysis, which correspond closely to ingenuity and the application of numerical methods, respectively. For complex situations numerical analysis can be lengthy and repetitive and it is for this reason that many computer-aided engineering systems are numerical analysis tools. The computer is particularly apt at carrying out complicated numerical analysis or 'number crunching'; provided that the methods are accurately defined in the program then the computer will faithfully apply the formulae to the data very much quicker than can be done by a human. This of course still places an important responsibility on the engineer to ensure that the method carried out is accurately defined and that the data to be used in the numerical analysis is also accurate.

Intuitive analysis is best carried out by the engineer as the ability for this is based on the amount of reasoning that can be applied. Reasoning is the ability to evaluate conditions and circumstances and, based on that

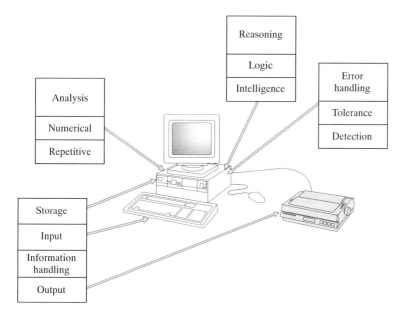

Figure 1.8 Computer capabilities

evaluation, decide on a course of action. This decision may, in many cases, just be the result of simple logic: if it is dark and you wish to read then turn on the light; but for more complex cases there is a need to draw on a wide range of experience much of which seems to be unrelated to the activity in question. The computer cannot be said to have any real intelligence or rationality and any attempts to make it so would be artificial. The computer is capable of applying logic to a problem but will do so with a very limited and inflexible precision. Artificial intelligence uses the computer's logical capabilities to draw on a very large database of knowledge and a set of rules for applying it. These rules are formulated from observing how human experts respond to situations. The resulting system is still unable to replace the engineer but can be a valuable tool in increasing the speed of problem solving.

Thus any ability that a computer has to simulate human intelligence is based on its ability to store, manage and access large amounts of data. Computer systems are particularly apt at doing this; large amounts of data can be stored on a variety of different media, and programs written which enable that data to be accessed and made available to the user. The human brain tends to be inconsistent in recalling memorized facts at any particular time; they are sometimes remembered inaccurately and at other times completely forgotten. The computer's 'memory' is as reliable as the data storage equipment used and the care taken in ensuring adequate backups are made to alternative media. An application of this ability in design is that all solutions to design problems, that is components or assemblies fulfilling particular purposes, can be stored for use for inclusion for subsequent and similar designs. Much doubling of effort is saved or, in other words, the quite common practice of 'reinventing the wheel' is eliminated. Another important application is that the data handling ability of the computer is a key to successful operation of a computer-integrated manufacturing (CIM) system.

Much of the success in using a computer as an engineering tool involves the formulation of accurate analysis techniques and the input of accurate data. The responsibility to ensure this accuracy is still very much with the engineer, as a computer will always faithfully carry out the instructions with which it is programmed and on the data given to the program. The only error handling and recovery that a computer has is programmed into it by the hardware manufacturer and the software suppliers, and this only covers those errors which occur with the operation of the computer and its software and not those related to the application of the software. That is a computer can detect and possibly recover from an error in the format of data in its memory but not from an engineer applying an incorrect load to a component under stress analysis. The computer's error handling abilities are therefore based on logic rather than intuition. An example of this is the use of a spelling checker in a word processor. The program will scan a document and check every word against a dictionary and suggest any necessary corrections; a program could even be devised to highlight simple grammatical errors but to check for poor style, which is largely based on opinion and intuition, is beyond the capabilities of even the most sophisticated word processing systems. Even so, the computer's logical and systematic approach to error detection and recovery can be an important asset in the quest for quality.

One of the key factors that affect the efficiency of any engineering process is communication and the computer's capabilities in this area can provide an excellent productivity tool. Humans accept and pass on information via the senses, mainly in spoken and visual forms, which is stored for later use. These communication media are generally slow and subject to unreliabilities particularly in the area of personal interpretation. The computer's capacity for communication is based on the abilities for information handling and systematic error detection already discussed. A computer can acquire information via a variety of different devices and is highly intolerant to any deviations in format from that which it is programmed to receive. A computer system can output written and graphical data electronically or in human-readable format rapidly and with consistent accuracy. Thus, depending on the functionality of peripheral devices such as printers or plotters, a computer system can produce high quality reports, documents and engineering drawings as well as transmit such information rapidly around the factory to the departments or processes requiring it. This electronic factory communication system is another vital key to the successful computer integration of manufacturing.

In this chapter we have discussed the scope and need for computer-aided engineering and also how the functional attributes of a computer can be used as an effective tool to assist with a wide range of engineering activities. We can summarize the need for CAE and hence answer the question 'Why computer-aided engineering?' as follows:

> Computer-aided engineering techniques provide the means to cope with the demand for increased productivity of more sophisticated and reliable product design and manufacture in today's market.

We can also reiterate how this is achieved by summarizing the abilities of the computer as in Table 1.1.

The key to all these benefits is good systems design which includes efficient and reliable hardware and effective usable software. Subsequent chapters of this book explain hardware and software of various types. Computer-aided engineering software can be described in general terms by a universal model as shown in Fig. 1.9. At the heart of every CAE software package is a database made up of entities or elements relevant to the application. For computer-aided draughting the database consists of geometric or detail entities such as lines, circles, arcs, text, dimensions, etc., for a solid modeller there are 3D geometric entities defining a solid such

Table 1.1   Computer abilities for CAE

Analysis	Powerful, rapid and accurate numerical analysis of engineering problems
Data handling	Storage, management and rapid access of large amounts of engineering data
Error handling	Logical and systematic approach to error detection
Communication	Rapid and accurate reproduction and transmission of data in human-readable and electronic forms

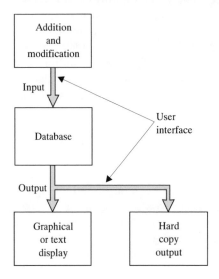

Figure 1.9   Universal CAE software model

as vertices, edges, surfaces, etc. In a simulation package the data is a mathematical model of the system under investigation. The software has facilities to manipulate and to carry out numerical and other analysis techniques on the contents of the database under control of the user. The software also provides the means to add to the database for design or model synthesis and to modify the existing contents for editing. The user can control this process by a direct visual display of the data which, in many cases such as draughting and 3D modelling, is graphical; in other cases, for example material resource planning and scheduling, the display may be in text format. In either case the user should be able to make changes to the model or system and immediately see the effects of that change.

There will inevitably be some time in the use of the software in a particular situation where the engineer will need to generate a report or drawing and so the software will also provide a means of providing a hard copy version of the data on a printer or plotter. The software functions which enable additions or modifications to be made to the database and those which facilitate the output to peripheral devices form part of the *user interface* to the package. The design of the user interface should be such as to make communication between the user and the software tool as simple as possible and it is the effectiveness of this user interface which can make the difference between a usable (or user-friendly) system and an unusable one.

EXERCISES

Class and Group Activity

In groups of about four or five, discuss the following questions:

(a) What changes in the product development process, as you understand it, would the implementation of computer-aided engineering impose?
(b) What is the possible social impact of complete automation? What changes in the working practices and lifestyles of individuals would need to take place to accommodate it?

Each group should note down their responses and a spokesperson invited to present them.

Assignment

From notes taken of the responses of all groups in the above activity and by literature survey write an essay of not more than 1500 words on the role and impact of the application of computing technology to manufacturing.

Questions

1.1 Draw a block diagram showing the four main areas of CAE. How definitive are the boundaries between the areas?

1.2 With the aid of a flow chart describe the product development process from specification to delivery to the customer. At each stage state the CAE or IT tools which can be used to increase productivity, and into which area(s) described in question 1.1 they can be categorized.

TWO

CAE HARDWARE 1:
THE ENGINEERING OFFICE

Computing has developed into a complex and wide-ranging subject area, far too wide, in fact, for the mechanical or manufacturing engineer to be able to delve too deeply into it. The engineer's study of computing is therefore restricted to the type of equipment that can be used to assist his or her job function. In this chapter we shall begin to examine the fundamentals of computing applied to engineering and specifically the hardware available for carrying out engineering tasks. Computer facilities and services can be divided into two areas, namely software and hardware. *Hardware* is used to describe the actual physical equipment, that is the computer itself from the electronic circuitry to the case in which it is housed and its peripherals such as printers, plotters. The term *software* refers to the computer programs which are run or executed by the computer. Specific types of computer-aided engineering software will be described in later chapters. The computer-aided engineer will meet essentially two types of computer hardware: that which is encountered in an office environment, that is in the design or manufacturing offices, and that which is used to control machinery and processes on the shopfloor. The latter is, generally speaking, more rugged in construction and more limited as to what it can achieve, and a more detailed treatment of this type of equipment is given in Chapter 3.

2.1 A BRIEF HISTORY OF COMPUTING

The roots of the modern computer date back to the mid-nineteenth century when Charles Babbage (1792–1871), a Cambridge mathematician, devised his analytical engine. It was a machine designed to undertake laborious calculations more quickly than by hand; but more than that it was also to be capable of storing the results of those calculations for further use. This would have been the first stored program computer provided that the manufacturing technology of that era were up to the task of producing it—but sadly it was not. The next major advance in technology which was to inspire the development of today's computers occurred in 1904 when Ambrose Fleming invented the first diode: a device based on the thermionic principle which allowed current to flow in one direction only and could therefore be used to rectify alternating currents. This principle was developed further by Lee de Forest who devised the triode valve which controlled the flow of current through the device by the application of a small current on the grid—a third electrical connection to the device. At last there was a means of providing an electronically controlled switching system, a system upon which all modern computers are based.

The first electronic computers realized in the forties used thermionic valves as switching devices to store and manipulate binary numbers. The valves themselves were large and because of the large numbers of them required to make a system of any usable power, the computers themselves were enormous; in many cases filling large rooms and generating large amounts of heat. In the early fifties computers began to become commercially available, engendering much public concern which was thoroughly nurtured by the science fiction writers of the day who fantasized profusely about societies dominated by intelligent but unfeeling machines. We have already considered in the previous chapter the fact that computers are not really intelligent in the same sense that humans are; they only perform those tasks for which they are programmed and only have access to information given to them. It follows then that if the information is incorrect, the results produced by the computer will also be incorrect.

Alongside the commercial development of valve computers the first steps towards the introduction of solid-state technology were being made. In 1947, at the Bell Laboratories in the USA, the first transistor was developed. This technology was to advance so rapidly that over the following 10 to 20 years, the transistor was introduced commercially and used in what have been called 'second generation computers', which were soon followed by a third generation of computers based on small-scale integrated circuits. Integrated circuits were first available in the early sixties and, at that time, were fairly simple electronic circuits consisting of many transistors and other components produced on one small silicon chip. As the complexity of this technology increased then so did that of the circuits, so that today an integrated circuit can contain many thousands of transistors and have all the functions of a complete processing unit for a computer. This is the microprocessor, the introduction of which has given rise to the fourth generation of computers. The advancement of computing technology in this way has bought about the general reduction in size of computers and hence an increase in performance of large computers. The improvements in the manufacturing processes involved in the production of integrated circuits means that computers are effectively becoming cheaper year by year. For example, a personal computer (PC) purchased one year may be many times faster than an earlier model bought the previous year for a similar price.

Up to the latter part of the seventies two types of digital computer had emerged: the *mainframe* and the *minicomputer*. The former was a large installation normally occupying a fair-sized room which had to be temperature and humidity controlled because of the large amount of heat generated by the electronics and the sensitivity of all the equipment to moisture. A mainframe involved, and still does, a large capital investment and was therefore only accessible to large companies or computer bureaux who sold computing services to companies who could not justify their own outright purchase. They were mainly used for such data processing applications as payroll calculation and accounting. Minicomputers were somewhat smaller and less powerful than a mainframe and tended to be used by research establishments and smaller companies. The meaning of the term 'minicomputer' has become rather vague now as what some people refer to as a mainframe is, in fact, a minicomputer. This is true for such computers as the DEC VAX range which are, in effect, minicomputers but if a number of them are 'clustered' in one installation they could provide the power and services of a mainframe. Workstations, which will be discussed in more detail later, are also often referred to as minicomputers.

2.2 FUNDAMENTALS OF COMPUTING

As the microcomputer is far simpler than a mainframe we shall use it to examine some fundamentals of the structure and operation of computers. Many of the principles described can be applied on a larger scale to mainframe installations; the major difference in operation being that the mainframe is capable of allowing greater numbers of people to use the computer at the same time owing to its ability to execute programs much faster. Hence mainframe installations are generally known as multi-user systems. The various users scattered throughout the building, or even other buildings in other towns, cities or countries, gain access to the services of the mainframe via a local area network or a wide area network such as the standard telephone system. This is depicted in Fig. 2.1.

The facilities provided by a typical mainframe installation include processing, that is the ability to execute the programs required by the users, storage facilities for those programs and the data used and produced by them, and hard copy services such as printing and plotting. Users communicate with the mainframe using a number of different devices such as text or graphics terminals or graphics workstations. The operation of program and data storage methods, hard copy devices and terminals will be explained later. It is not until more recently that microcomputers have been able to support more than one user and even then it is the more

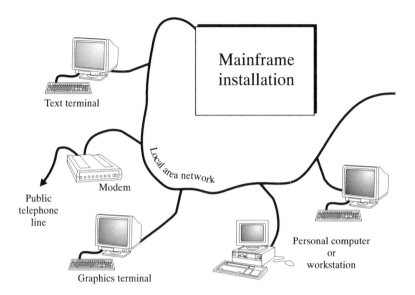

Figure 2.1   Mainframe installation and access

sophisticated 'workstations' which are capable of doing so. This is why the microcomputers developed for industry and commerce have been named personal computers or PCs. Home computers were also developed alongside personal computers, being far cheaper and of lower performance. The term 'home computer' has largely disappeared now as personal computers of quite high performance are now within the budget of the typical home user.

The basic function of any computer is that of data processing, which can be modelled using Fig. 2.2. Input is given to the computer by the user for processing into a usable output. The type of input depends on the application and can include numerical data for calculations, a common application in engineering, or lists of data for storage, manipulation and calculation, such as employee pay details in a payroll application. The output would be the results of the calculations or manipulation which, in the case of the payroll program, would be the actual pay slips for the employees. This model is expanded in Fig. 2.3 to show that there are a number of

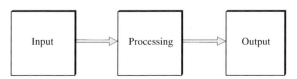

Figure 2.2   Basic function of a computer

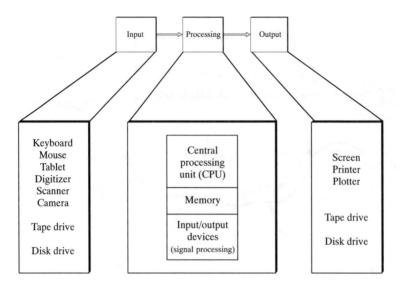

Figure 2.3　Basic computer function expanded

different methods of providing input to and retrieving output from the processor.

These pieces of equipment such as keyboards, screens, printers and tape and disk drives, are known as *peripherals*. A typical processor system, that is the actual computer, typically consists of a *central processing unit* (CPU), *memory* and *input/output devices* which provide the communications channels between the peripherals and the processor. The CPU is the heart of any computer and in a microcomputer this is the microprocessor.

2.2.1 The Microprocessor

A microprocessor is a complex integrated circuit containing all the elements of the central processing unit of a computer. In the early seventies the INTEL Corporation of America was commissioned to design a series of integrated circuits for use in electronic calculators. What was actually developed was a single integrated circuit capable of use in any of the required calculators as it was a general purpose device which could be programmed to perform a variety of tasks. It was essentially a central processing unit—a microprocessor. The first to be available on the market was the INTEL 4004, and was a 4-bit microprocessor, that is it could perform single operations on numbers or data consisting of 4 binary digits (bits). Binary or base 2 is the number system used by all digital computers and a 4-bit number can represent any decimal value between 0 and 15. The 4004 processor could also access 4096 of these 4-bit numbers stored in memory connected to the processor. Technology has progressed at a high pace since then as INTEL introduced 8-bit, 16-bit and 32-bit processors from the early seventies to date. Other manufacturers, namely Motorola, National Semiconductor, Zilog and Texas Instruments, also began developing microprocessors and many microcomputer manufacturers used these in their personal and home computers.

The transistors integrated in the microprocessor are arranged as logic gates or electronically controlled switches which, under certain circumstances, either allow current to flow or not. This is why the microprocessor uses binary as its arithmetic medium; a binary digit can only have two values, 1 or 0, and the presence of a voltage or a current flowing is used to represent binary 1 and the absence of a voltage or current represents a binary 0. The binary number system is explained in some detail in a number of texts, e.g. Scanlon (1985), Stern and Stern (1990) and Khambata (1987). The logic gates in a microprocessor make up a number of circuits which can perform certain tasks on binary numbers such as the movement of numbers to and from memory connected to the CPU, arithmetic and logic functions such as addition, subtraction, AND, OR and many more, as well as the ability to store numbers for use in the arithmetic and logic operations. These circuits can be categorized into three main types which make up two distinct units: the *control unit* and the *arithmetic and logic unit* or ALU, as well as a number of internal *registers*. This arrangement is depicted in the block diagram of a typical microprocessor shown in Fig. 2.4.

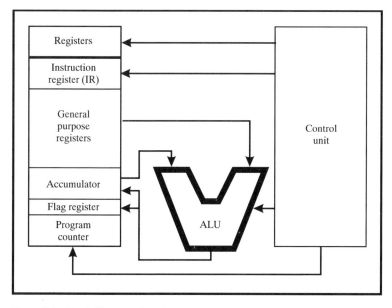

Figure 2.4   Block diagram of a microprocessor

The control unit mainly contains the circuitry which moves data between the CPU and memory and within the CPU itself. Data to be moved is of two types, the first being instructions stored in memory which form part of the program currently being run by the microcomputer, the other being data which the program is processing. A powered up and functioning micro-computer is always running a program even though to the user it just seems to be waiting for an instruction; even the act of waiting for an instruction involves the execution of a program. In this case the program is a simple loop which is checking the keyboard to see if a key is pressed, and if so a further part of the program ascertains which key it is and stores the code for the character in memory. When a complete instruction has been typed in another part of the program decodes the instruction which will cause it to be carried out. These simple areas of program or *routines*, which are available when the computer is first switched on, form part of what is known as the *operating system*. Whenever the control unit sends or fetches any data from memory it does so by specifying to the memory the address of that data so that it can read or write a value from or to a particular memory location. Each memory location can be viewed as a pigeon hole where a byte of data can be stored and each pigeon hole is uniquely identified by its address which is in the form of a binary number. In the case of data used within a program the control unit can either read the contents of a memory location into the CPU or can write a binary value from the CPU to memory. In the case of program instructions the control unit only reads the values into the CPU.

The arithmetic and logic unit (ALU) contains the circuitry which can perform certain arithmetic and logic operations on two binary numbers. Most microprocessors contain instructions to add and subtract two numbers; multiplication and division normally require a simple program to perform, though some processors do have implicit multiplication. These arithmetic operators only work on signed binary integers and so extra programming is required to carry out arithmetic on real or floating point values. Logic operations include NOT, AND, OR and XOR (exclusive OR) which have particular uses in control applications and programming.

The registers in the CPU can store binary numbers for use in a program. Some of these registers have particular functions such as the *program counter*, which keeps a track of where the processor is when executing a program, or the *accumulator* to which the results of all arithmetic and logic operations are returned. There are also some general purpose registers which are used to temporarily store numbers for subsequent and current program operations. The programming of microprocessors is described in greater detail in a number of texts, e.g. Brey (1984).

2.2.2 Memory

The main memory of a microcomputer is outside the CPU. It consists of an array of memory locations and each of these can store an 8-bit number; that is a binary number consisting of 8 digits. Each memory location has a unique address so that any 8-bit number can be accessed and fetched into the CPU or any value can be written from the CPU into any desired location. The number of memory locations that a computer has depends on the type of CPU or microprocessor. For example, the INTEL 8085 can access as many as 65 535 (64 Kbytes) memory locations, as can the National Semiconductor 6502 microprocessor, upon which the famous Acorn BBC microcomputer was based. The INTEL 8088 and 8086 processors, which form the heart of the early IBM PCs and compatibles, are capable of accessing up to 1 048 567 (1Mbyte), while the later 80286 processor can access up to 16 Mbytes of memory. An example of how microcomputer memory is configured is shown in Fig. 2.5. The example shows a 64K memory system as used by the earlier microprocessor types.

The address is shown in hexadecimal (base 16) because in this case it is represented in the microcomputer as a 16-bit number and it is easier to write this in its hexadecimal form than to show it all as ones and zeros. The numbering of the addressing starts at zero and proceeds through to the highest allowable address which, in the case of Figure 2.5, is FFFF hexadecimal or 65 535 in decimal. The memory in any microcomputer is made up from two distinct types: ROM or *read only memory* and RAM or *random access memory*.

Memory address (hex)	Memory contents (binary)
0000	0011 1010
0001	0000 1011
0002	0101 1010
0003	1111 1111
0004	1011 0000
.	.
.	.
.	.
FFFB	1101 1101
FFFC	1000 0001
FFFD	0011 0011
FFFE	1001 0101
FFFF	0101 1000

Figure 2.5 Microcomputer memory configuration

ROM, as its name suggests, can only be read from. The programs or data stored in this type of memory are placed there during the manufacture and are of a type which is required to be present when the microcomputer is switched on. In a personal computer this is normally what is known as the BIOS or *built-in operating system* or *boot ROM*. When a computer is switched on it does not 'know' how to do anything and needs a program in order to load and run the operating system. This program will be stored in the boot ROM or BIOS and will simply instruct the computer to run some tests on the hardware and load the operating system from a disk. This process is known as *booting up* or *bootstrapping* and the term is derived from the idea that the computer is attempting to pull itself up by its boot laces. There are different types of ROM, namely PROM or *programmable read only memory*, EPROM or *erasable programmable read only memory* and EEPROM or E^2PROM or *electrically erasable programmable read only memory*.

A PROM is programmed by the manufacturer of the microcomputer and can be programmed only once. If the programs in the PROM need to be updated then the device is discarded and replaced by the updated version. This is the type most commonly found supporting the BIOS of most personal computers and workstations. The contents of an EPROM, however, can be erased after which the device can be reprogrammed. Erasure is carried out by shining ultraviolet light through a transparent window of quartz or similar material on top of the device as shown in Fig. 2.6. The ultraviolet rays fall upon the silicon chip which contains the array of circuitry for the EPROM and this has the effect of resetting all the bits in the device to zero.

The EEPROM, or E^2PROM as it is sometimes called (said E squared PROM), is erased by electrical signals applied to the device or in some cases the memory contents can be changed just by normal writing to a location. This potentially allows programs created in the microcomputer itself to remain even when the power is turned off.

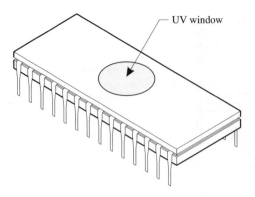
UV window

Figure 2.6 A 28-pin EPROM

Random access memory is that which is used during the normal operation of the microcomputer to store the user's data and programs. It can be read from and written to and its contents are lost when the computer is switched off. The majority of a microcomputer's memory is made up of RAM and the amount of RAM supplied in a computer system is an important factor in determining its suitability for an application. Many CAE packages, particularly CADD systems, require large amounts of RAM as the programs are normally complex and therefore large. They also tend to generate large amounts of data, most of which needs to be stored in RAM before writing it onto a disk or other backing storage system.

2.2.3 Programming Languages

The processor itself only operates using the most basic of computer programming languages or codes—*machine code*. Machine codes or languages are often referred to as the *first generation* of programming languages. Each instruction that the processor uses to carry out its data processing has a unique binary code and all programs, however complex, are made up of these simple instructions. Very few programmers ever create programs directly using these codes as to do so would be a very laborious task unless the program was very simple. Also different processor manufacturers tend to use different codes for the instructions in the devices they supply, and so, in order for any program to be able to operate on any type of computer, it will need to be completely rewritten for the different processors. In some situations, however, it is desirable to produce a program for a particular processor in machine code. To achieve this effectively a programmer will normally use the *assembly language* for that processor. Assembly languages—the *second generation* of programming languages—define each machine code instruction as a mnemonic to ease program writing and a separate program, called an assembler, will convert the mnemonics and the other symbols and tools available in the language into a machine code program for that processor type.

Most CAE applications which are used in the engineering office such as computer-aided draughting, design, manufacture, etc., are too complex to write in machine code or with assembly language. In many cases suppliers of these packages produce versions of the software for different types of computer so that the user is not restricted in choice of hardware. In this case the software is created and developed using any one of a number of *high level languages* available. A high level language enables the programmer to define a program or solve a problem using a code which is more similar to human language than the machine code to which the program will be eventually converted. A program using a high level language is produced using an editor and stored in a file and then converted into an executable machine code program by a procedure of compiling and linking as shown in Fig. 2.7.

A special program known as a *compiler* converts the program into an intermediate *object code* for the particular computer. The programmer is often assisted in creating a program by a library of standard procedures or subroutines, that is small segments of high level language code, which carry out commonly required functions. Examples of such routines are those to draw lines, circles and other geometric shapes on a graphics screen or complex mathematical functions. This library will also exist in a file as object code and the required routines from the library are *linked* with the programmer's code to produce a final working machine code program in a file which can be loaded into memory and executed. The compiler and linker are specific to the computer on which the final program will execute but if the language format or *syntax* is standardized for all computers, and hence independent of computer type, then the program can be transferred to another computer for compilation, linking and execution. This principle of complete program portability is an ideal never quite achieved in practice because in a number of cases, particularly where computer graphics are used, the way the software is written to achieve certain functionality is dependent on how the hardware operates and is driven by the software. Therefore a complex program written in a high level language and compiled

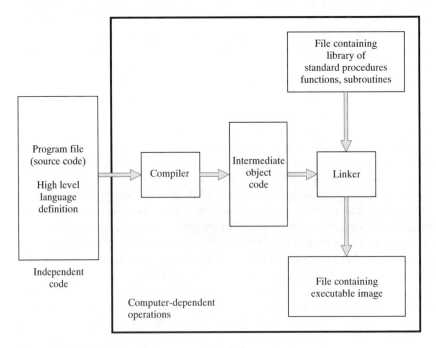

Figure 2.7 High level language program compilation

for one processor will almost certainly need some modification before it can be compiled to operate on another, unless the standardization is taken further to include hardware and software interaction. Most modern high level languages are referred to as *third-generation programming languages* (3GLs) but more recently fourth and fifth generations have emerged which define a completely different way of solving problems using a computer. Whereas a third-generation language will instruct the computer step by step how to solve a problem, fourth- and fifth-generation languages state the solution and a set of rules for achieving it. They have particular applications in querying and managing databases and because of this are used in the development of systems exhibiting artificial intelligence.

The first widely available 3GL was FORTRAN (*FO R*mula *TRAN*slation) which enabled the programmer to write mathematical formulae in algebraic form for solution by the computer. It was developed in the fifties for use by computer scientists, mathematicians and engineers who formed the majority of computer users, and it is still used extensively by engineers for CAE applications today. By 1960, particularly as computers were being used more and more for business and financial applications, it was realized that FORTRAN was not the ideal tool for all program development projects. Business applications require more input and output functions and only simple arithmetic procedures and so a language more suited to this type of operation was needed. COBOL (*CO*mmon *B*usiness *O*riented *L*anguage) was therefore developed to meet these needs and is still used extensively in the services sector today. PL/1 (*Programming Language 1*) was then developed as a language which combined the major advantages of both FORTRAN and COBOL for those programmers wishing to combine both business and scientific type functions in one application.

The languages FORTRAN, COBOL and PL/1 were designed by computer scientists for use by trained programmers and they were deemed by many scientists and engineers to be to difficult to use. In 1964 a new simpler to use programming language emerged which was designed to enable those not formally trained in computing to be able to create quick and simple programs for their needs. This language, BASIC (*B*eginner's *A*ll-purpose *S*ymbolic *I*nstruction *C*ode), attempted to do just that. The syntax, that is the way in which instructions are structured, was far simpler than other high level languages. The problem with BASIC, however, was that the code was never compiled and linked—it was an *interpreter*. An interpreter scans the high level code line by line and converts each line to machine code and executes it before moving on to the next. After the execution of each line the machine code is essentially discarded so when a section of a program is run many times in a *loop* then the conversion has to be repeated each time. This means that interpreted code executes much slower than compiled code, which is restrictive for complex applications where high speed is an important factor. BASIC compilers have become available more recently but are not very popular as other compiled, simple to use languages have emerged to take its place.

One of these languages is *Pascal* which was developed in the late sixties and early seventies. Older style 3GLs did not allow programs to be well structured for easy modification and documentation. Pascal was the first development in structured languages and was designed as an aid to teaching good programming practice. It has gained wide acceptance, not only in education but also in business and industry even though it has been expanded and improved to generate *Modula-2*—but this still tends to be used far less than Pascal itself. A more difficult to learn structured programming language is *C* which combines high level language syntax with lower level assembly programming. Its use is engineering applications is extensive as it was used in the development of a popular operating system *UNIX*. C is particularly defined and standardized to allow easy program portability from one type of computer to another.

2.2.4 Operating Systems

An operating system is a program or suite of programs which provides the user or programmer of a computer with basic facilities to control and manage the computer system environment. In other words the operating system is the basic interface between a user and a computer. It enables the user to run applications programs (e.g. word processors etc.) and to manage files and the disks on which those files are stored. It also enables a programmer to carry out the basic functions of the computer such as reading a key pressed on the keyboard or displaying a character on the screen.

MSDOS is the most common operating system used by IBM PCs and compatibles and will be used as an example to explain the principles of operating systems. There are many different operating systems available for different computers. Two common operating systems found on mainframes and workstations are UNIX and VMS. MSDOS stands for Microsoft Systems disk operating system and is called thus because the user of a PC has more control over the use of the disk drives than that of the mainframe user. The operating system of a PC can be said to be divided into three parts.

1. *The BIOS*. The built-in operating system is not part of MSDOS but is built into the PC on ROM. MSDOS makes use of all the routines found in the BIOS to carry out its basic tasks. The BIOS contains a number of basic routines which can be called from any program. These include routines to read a key pressed, read a line of text typed on the screen, output characters to the screen, output graphics to the screen, open files on disks, read and write characters and other data from and to files on disks, etc.

2. *The operating system command shell.* This is a program which is loaded and executed at the end of the boot up process. In MSDOS it is called *COMMAND.COM* and resides on the hard disk, if the PC has one, or on the boot up floppy disk if not. When a PC is switched on and booted up then it is COMMAND.COM which is loaded and running and displays the prompt:

   C: > _

   if a hard disk is fitted or:

   A: > _

   if no hard disk is present. It then waits for the user to type in a command. It also contains a number of routines for management of files and disks which are carried out when the appropriate command is typed in.

3. *The command library.* In addition to the program COMMAND.COM there is a suite or library of programs which carry out file, disk and environment management tasks. To fit all of these tasks into COMMAND.COM would make it too big and when loaded will not leave sufficient memory to run applications programs. The suite of DOS programs resides on the hard disk or on a set of disks supplied with the PC. If they are on the hard disk they are normally stored in a *directory* called DOS or MSDOS. Figure 2.8 gives a list of the programs which form part of MSDOS.

COMMAND	COM	MEM	EXE
DISKCOPY	COM	MORE	COM
FDISK	EXE	SHARE	EXE
FORMAT	COM	SORT	EXE
KEYB	COM	SUBST	EXE
REPLACE	EXE	TREE	COM
SYS	COM	XCOPY	EXE
ASSIGN	COM	LINK	EXE
ATTRIB	EXE	PRINT	COM
CHKDSK	COM	APPEND	EXE
COMP	COM	FASTOPEN	EXE
DEBUG	COM	GRAFTABL	COM
DISKCOMP	COM	GRAPHICS	COM
EDLIN	COM	MODE	COM
FC	EXE	NLSFUNC	EXE
FILESYS	EXE	RECOVER	COM
FIND	EXE	BACKUP	COM
JOIN	EXE	RESTORE	COM
LABEL	COM	VALIDATE	COM

Figure 2.8 MSDOS command library

Some of the more commonly used commands in the COMMAND.COM shell are listed in Table 2.1.

Table 2.1   MSDOS shell commands

Command	Function
chdir (cd)	Changes the current working directory
cls	Clears the screen
copy	Copies specified files
del	Deletes specified files
mkdir (md)	Makes a directory
prompt	Sets the MSDOS prompt
rmdir	Removes specified directories
type	Displays specified files on the screen
ver	Displays MSDOS version number

Files and directories   A program or some data generated or used by a program is stored on a disk in a *file*. Each file has a unique name so that it can be accessed from the disk by another program. Program files are accessed by the operating system when invoked for execution at which point the operating system loads the file from disk into the computer's memory and begins execution. The full name for a file in MSDOS is of the form:

$$< drv > :\backslash < dir > \backslash < dir > \backslash .. \backslash < dir > \backslash filename. < ext >$$

where:

$< drv >$ is the disk drive on which the file is stored. If this is the current drive then it need not be stated;

$< dir >$ is the directory in which the file is stored on the disk. Directories may be nested several deep and so many references to these may need to be made unless the directory in which the file is stored is the current directory, in which case they need not be stated;

filename   is the name of the file; and

$< ext >$ is the file extension which specifies the type of file and consists of up to three characters. A filename or directory name can be up to eight characters in length.

A directory is a subdivision of a disk in which more files and directories can be stored. This allows the user to subdivide programs and files for easy management. A newly formatted disk has only one directory called ' \ ' — the root directory and the user can create a new directory using the *mkdir* or *md* command. The current working directory can be changed using the *chdir* or *cd* command. This means that any files referenced or created will or should be stored in that directory unless the filename specifies another directory.

Other shells, e.g Windows There are a number of software packages available for PCs which make the use of the operating system more friendly to users. Some PC operating systems already incorporate a 'desktop' type of environment; an example of this is available for and used on the Apple Macintosh PC. The system makes full use of the computer's graphics capability to select commands from the screen using a mouse. Directories and commands can appear as icons in windows which pop up in the screen area and they are executed by pointing at them with the mouse and clicking or double-clicking the mouse button. MSDOS used on IBM PCs is historically a text-based operating system but there are software packages which convert MSDOS to graphics or window-based environments. The most common of these is Microsoft Windows but there are others such as GEM, DOSSHELL and an inexpensive text version from Logitech called PopDOS.

Microsoft Windows enables the user to define all the applications programs (e.g. CAE programs, word processing, spreadsheets, etc.) as icons on the screen so that they can be run simply by 'double clicking' with the mouse on the icon. Many of the MSDOS commands are available via menus selected from the screen. Windows comes complete with a notebook, diary, word processor and painting package all of which can be popped up as windows on a simulated desktop. The idea of these types of user interfaces is that the user has a desktop on the screen upon which these applications can be placed and used in much the same way as a normal desk can be used.

UNIX Whereas MSDOS was specifically developed for IBM PCs and compatibles the UNIX operating system has been implemented on a wide range of computers from PCs to mainframes. It was originally developed as a simple operating system for use on minicomputers by a AT&T's Bell Laboratories and written in the C programming language. It provides multi-user and hence multi-tasking capabilities, that is a number of different programs can be run concurrently by one or more users. Like all operating systems it provides the user with a number of commands and utilities to manage the computing environment. The commands themselves are often described as being too cryptic and hence not so user friendly as other systems such as MSDOS or VMS. Examples of this are given in Table 2.2 which shows some common MSDOS commands and their UNIX equivalents. In some cases the UNIX command is quite similar but with others such as *ls* or *list* and *rm* or *remove* the command is less self-explanatory.

UNIX is, however, becoming increasingly popular at all levels of computing, being the main system supplied with such minicomputers and

Table 2.2   MSDOS/UNIX command equivalents

MSDOS command	UNIX equivalent
chdir (cd)	cd
copy	cp
del	rm
dir	ls
mkdir (md)	mkdir

workstations as MicroVAX, Sun, HP Apollo, Silicon Graphics, IBM RS6000 and others. Microsoft has developed a version of UNIX for PCs called XENIX.

2.3 PERSONAL COMPUTERS AND WORKSTATIONS

There are many factors affecting the performance of a computer system and hence its ability to carry out certain CAE functions. CAE applications normally require good graphics capabilities, numerical analysis or both and so the choice of platform, that is PC, workstation or mainframe, is highly dependent on the functionality required from the software. Table 2.3 gives a brief summary comparison between mainframes, workstations and personal computers for primary storage, processor speed and cost.

Table 2.3   Summary comparison of computer types

Type	Category	Primary storage (Mbytes)	Processor speed (MIPS)	Cost range (£k)
Mainframe	Mainframe or Supermini	> 64	> 20	> 20
Workstation	Minicomputer	4–64	10–100	5–20
Personal computer	Microcomputer	1–8	1–10	0.5–5

Apart from performance, the most distinguishing feature of a mainframe is the fact that it is multi-user. Although a minicomputer workstation can support more than one user it is best used as a powerful single-user resource. Only rarely are personal computers suitable for multi-user environments. There is, in some cases, a grey area in the distinction between mainframe and minicomputer. For example the VAX 6000 series is classified as a minicomputer but is capable of delivering a performance close to that of a mainframe. Such computers are also referred to as superminis. A mainframe type computer needs a large internal or primary storage to cope with the numbers of users and it also has a high processor speed. This processor speed, however, is shared among the concurrent users of the system and so the speed perceived by any one user may be slow when the mainframe is running at high capacity. Processor speed is measured mainly in two ways: one is the rate of normal instruction execution, that is MIPS or millions of instructions per second; and the other is the rate at which the processor can carry out mathematical manipulations with floating point or real numbers, that is MFLOPS (pronounced megaflops) or millions of floating point operations per second. Both give a good indication of how fast the computer will execute programs but the latter is particularly relevant to many computer-aided engineering applications which rely on complex numerical analysis.

Workstations and personal computers are increasingly becoming the most popular platforms for CAE applications. This is because they can provide a powerful computing resource at relatively low cost. Many CAE software packages use graphics as the means of communication between the user and the software, and workstations in particular have highly sophisticated graphics capabilities. Many have high resolution displays capable of displaying millions of colours for visual realism when displaying rendered images of designs or manufacturing situations. A typical workstation or personal computer configuration is depicted in Fig. 2.9.

As a workstation or PC is designed for a single user each unit has all the facilities of a computing system, either built in or accessible over a network. The system unit houses the processor and means of communicating to the peripherals. It may also contain mass storage systems such as a hard or fixed disk and a floppy disk drive. In some cases a system may be supported by a remote hard disk of high capacity called a *file server* which is accessed via a

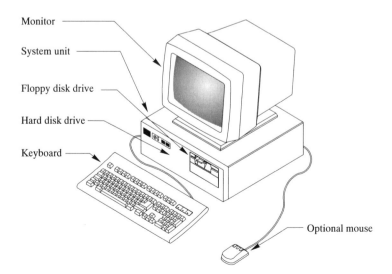

Figure 2.9 Typical workstation/PC configuration

local area network (LAN) and shared by a number of workstations. A floppy disk drive is useful for those users wishing to port data from one system to another, though on a networked system this is not absolutely necessary.

A monitor capable of supporting graphics is normally supplied as standard even on the cheapest PCs. This may display monochrome or colour images and, even though more expensive, a high resolution colour monitor will give better results. The graphics subsystems on PCs are generally less sophisticated than those supplied with workstations though the Super VGA system available for IBM PC compatibles is capable of displaying 1280 by 1024 pixels of resolution with a choice of up to 256 colours with the right type of monitor.

A number of input devices are available for the personal computer or workstation. The keyboard is standard equipment for any computer or terminal and should have the standard key layout similar to a manual typewriter (QWERTY keyboard) as well as additional keys for cursor movement, screen editing and additional functions. In a graphics system it is important that the user can move a pointer on a screen to select functions and indicate positions. For this a pointing device is required and the most common of these is the mouse.

2.4 GRAPHICAL INPUT (POINTING) DEVICES

As many computer-aided engineering applications make use of computer graphics then one of the most important hardware facilities which provides an interface between the user and the software is the graphics pointing device. The user must have the means to point to menus, features, positions and areas on the graphics screen to carry out the basic functions of the software. The four most common hardware devices which have been used for this function are: the *mouse*, the *tablet or digitizer*, the *joystick* and the *light pen*. The latter two are seldom used in modern computer graphics systems but are included mainly for historical interest. In all cases, except that of the light pen, movement of the devices causes a corresponding movement of a graphically displayed pointer or *cross-hair* on the screen with which a menu item, feature or position can be selected or an area of the graphics screen defined. The way in which the pointing device is used in conjunction with the functionality of the software forms part of what is known as the *user interface*. The principles of a good user interface are described in more detail in Chapter 4.

2.4.1 Mouse

The mouse, so called because of its rodent-like shape, is shown in Fig. 2.10.

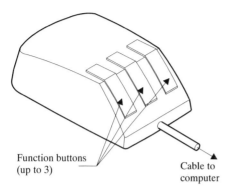

Function buttons (up to 3)

Cable to computer

Figure 2.10   A three-button mouse

Movement of the mouse over a flat surface such as a desk top causes a corresponding movement of the pointer or cross-hair on the graphics screen. It is the most commonly available pointing device mainly because of its low cost and ease of use. For the majority of mice available on the market, the principle of operation is based on a rubber ball, a small part of which protrudes from the underside of the mouse, which revolves as the mouse is moved over the desk. A cut-away view of the underside of a typical device is shown in Fig. 2.11. The rotation of the ball revolves two digitizer disk assemblies mounted at right angles to each other to give signals to the computer to move the graphics pointer on the monitor screen in 'x' and 'y' directions. The digitizer disks have an arrangement of slots around the

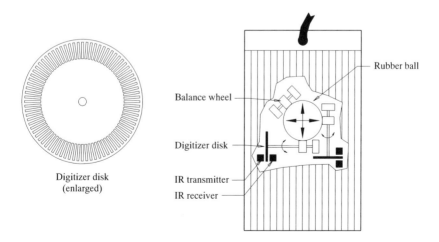

Digitizer disk (enlarged)

Balance wheel

Digitizer disk

IR transmitter

IR receiver

Rubber ball

Figure 2.11   Principles of mouse operation

circumference and as they rotate an infrared light beam is cut by the material between the slots. The resulting interrupted beam is detected by a light-sensitive receiver which produces electrical pulses. The number and frequency of the pulses is interpreted by the mouse driver software running in the computer to evaluate distance moved and speed. A typical mouse has two or three function buttons; pressing any combination of the function buttons may be interpreted by the software to take certain actions. The mouse has a number of advantages and disadvantages as a graphics pointing device. Advantages include low cost and ease of use as already mentioned. The size and amount of desk area required to operate the mouse is also quite small compared with that of the tablet as shall be seen later. One disadvantage is that the mouse produces a relative movement, that is the screen pointer only moves while the mouse is in contact with the desk top. This can be helpful in reducing the desk area required but sometimes it is difficult to determine what movement is required to position the screen pointer to a desired position, particularly if it is at one edge of the screen. Another disadvantage is the fact that the rubber ball tends to pick up dirt and other foreign matter from the desk top and deposit it in the internal mechanism of the mouse causing jamming and poor response.

2.4.2 Digitizer Pads and Tablets

One of the most recent innovations in interactive graphics pointing devices is the tablet or digitizer pad shown in Fig. 2.12. They can cost anything from around £250–£2 000 and vary in size from 30 cm square to that of an A0 size sheet of paper. The tablet itself consists of a flat surface over which the user moves a cursor or puck. The cursor or puck can have any number of function buttons which are interpreted by the software.

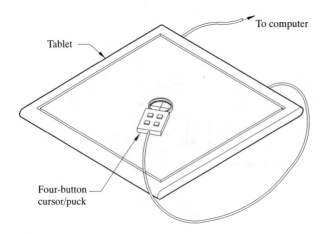

To computer

Tablet

Four-button cursor/puck

Figure 2.12 Tablet/digitizer and cursor/puck

In a typical device there is an electromagnetic communication between a coil in the puck and an accurately arranged grid of wires in the tablet such that the coordinate position of the cross-hairs in the puck can be sent to the computer. In many cases a coil in the puck is energized with a current and the resulting magnetic field induces current in the grid of wires. The intensity of the current in the grid wires can be used to evaluate the position of the puck. The digitizer or tablet can be used for any combination of three tasks in a computer-aided engineering environment:

1. As a pointing device to the screen. As the puck is moved over the surface of the tablet a corresponding cursor on the monitor screen will track its position.
2. As a menu selection device. A preprinted menu card can be laid on the tablet and the puck used to select individual software functions when used in conjunction with the function buttons.
3. As a means of digitizing manually produced drawings. If a large enough tablet is used, a manually produced drawing can be laid on the tablet, and with a specifically designed piece of software the drawing can be converted into a CAD model by digitizing key points on the drawing. This mode of operation is particularly employed by those companies wishing to transfer manually produced drawings onto a newly acquired CADD system. The resulting drawing, however, is only as accurate as the tablet, the original drawing and the user's skill in positioning the puck.

The fact that a tablet can be used for a preprinted menu card can be an advantage, as many commonly used functions in a software package can thus be accessed very rapidly just by pointing and clicking on the tablet. The downside of this approach is that if a complex software package relies entirely upon a tablet menu for function selection then the resulting menu card may be difficult to read and functions hard to find quickly. Using the tablet as a pure pointing device can be more effective than using a mouse as a tablet is an absolute positioning device, that is the position of the puck on the tablet surface is directly related to the position of the graphics pointer on the screen enabling very rapid positioning to a desired screen position. However, the use of a tablet simply for this purpose is a little like 'using a sledge hammer to crack a nut' in that not only is the device over four times as expensive as the mouse but it also takes up significantly more desk or office space.

2.4.3 Joystick

The joystick has been used for many years as a graphics pointing device for CAE software but is used very rarely nowadays as the mouse offers a far more efficient means at around the same price range. The movement of the joystick in a combination of '*x*' and '*y*' directions causes the graphics pointer or cross-hair to move in a corresponding direction. At its central position the joystick produces no movement and the amount of displacement from the central position controls the speed of pointer movement. The basic internal construction of the joystick device is shown in Fig. 2.13. The movement of the stick causes rotation of two potentiometers mounted at right angles to each other. A voltage is placed across the potentiometers and as they rotate a signal of varying voltage is read from the wiper of each potentiometer. These signals are converted to a digital value by *analogue to digital converters* (ADC) in the computer such that the speed of cross-hair or pointer movement on the screen can be evaluated. One major advantage of a joystick is that the simple construction makes it an inexpensive means of providing a graphical user interface. Further examination of the construction and operation, however, shows that the potentiometers are heavily used over a small proportion of their range of movement. This, in time, will produce excessive wear of the carbon tracks in the potentiometers and they will eventually become unreliable. Also extra hardware in the form of analogue to digital converters is required, though these devices are generally cheap and reliable. Another disadvantage of such a device is based on the fact that moving the joystick controls the speed of the graphics pointer rather than its actual position and this requires greater control in pointing to the desired position or area on the graphics screen.

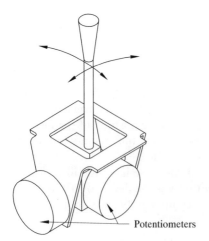

Potentiometers

Figure 2.13 Internal view of a joystick

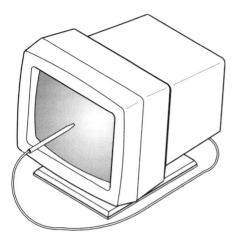

Figure 2.14   Light pen as used with a monitor

2.4.4 Light Pen

The light pen is the oldest of all pointing devices and was used with the very first computer-aided draughting systems. It is used to indicate features or menus from the screen as shown in Fig. 2.14. It is a very simple device consisting of a light-sensitive tip or fibre optics bundle which 'sees' lit areas on the graphics screen. The actual position pointed to on the screen is determined by measuring the amount of time elapsed from the start of the screen image being drawn to the point when the area beneath the light pen is activated. It is a very low-cost device and, if used infrequently, simple to operate. If used frequently and for long periods of time, however, it can be very tiring for the operator as the device has to be picked up and aimed at the screen, which is a very unnatural mode of operation for a pen-type device.

2.5 GRAPHICS DISPLAYS

As well as being able to communicate by providing input to a system and because most software packages available nowadays are interactive, the computer-aided engineer must also have a good visual display of the work being undertaken. The development of graphics displays over many years has had a very strong influence on how effective CAE techniques have become in increasing productivity. We shall briefly examine the development of graphics display technology which can be studied in greater depth in Foley and Van Dam (1984).

2.5.1 Early Graphics Displays

The first graphics display devices were based on the cathode ray tube (CRT) which has much earlier roots in the development of television, radar and oscilloscopes. The principle of operation of any CRT is that electrons are fired at the inside of the screen surface which is coated with phosphor. When bombarded with electrons in this manner phosphor emits light for a short period of time, which is what the viewer sees when looking at an image on the screen. The electrons are generated and fired as a beam by an electron gun, focused so that they converge to a point on the screen, and deflected so that the beam is directed to a specific point. In an oscilloscope this deflection is provided by a time base in the horizontal direction and the waveform being measured in the vertical direction.

The first graphics displays, known as *refresh displays*, used a similar technique. The electron beam was deflected to draw or trace the graphics image on the screen and this had to take place very quickly in order that the complete image could be seen by the user. In fact the human eye cannot detect a movement which is faster than about 40 ms (0.04 s) and so, if the display could trace out a complete drawing in less than that time, it would appear instantaneous to a human viewer; if it were repeatedly drawn in this way then the image would appear stable on the screen. The very first CAD packages used this technique to display drawings but if the drawings were large enough such that they could not be refreshed in less than 40 ms then the image would be noticeably unstable and present the user with viewing difficulties.

This problem was overcome by a further development known as the *direct view storage tube* or DVST which allowed an image to remain on the screen without the need to be continuously refreshed. Electron beam production, focusing and deflection are similar to that of a refresh display but the addition of an extra flood gun, collector grid and storage surface allows an image to be traced once and retained. The image can be erased and redrawn by applying a positive voltage to the storage surface to erase the image and after restoring it to its normal voltage a new image can be retraced.

2.5.2 Raster Scan Displays

Modern high definition display technology is based on the raster scan method. This method is that employed in the domestic television, where the image is made up of a series of horizontal lines. The standard European television picture is made up of 625 such lines and the rectangular shape generated in this way is known as the raster. For a computer graphics display the number of lines depends on the resolution of the display, so for a standard VGA display of resolution 640 by 480 pixels the raster is comprised of 480 lines. A pixel (picture cell) is one indivisible spot on the screen, and so in this case each line of the raster is subdivided into 640 pixels.

Colour is achieved by the presence of three electron guns, one for each of the three primary colours: red, green and blue. On the screen surface each pixel area has three dots, known as a triad, and each dot emits light of a different colour when excited by electrons; the intensity of emitted light is proportional to the rate of electron bombardment. A shadow mask behind the surface has an arrangement of holes identical to the arrangement of the triads on the surface and this allows only the electrons emitted from the red, green and blue guns to strike the respective spots in the triad. Thus all colours can be displayed in a pixel by varying the intensity of each of the primary colours.

The image on a raster scan display is therefore made up of a grid of pixels and this image is stored in the computer in an area of random access memory (RAM) known as the refresh buffer. Figure 2.15 shows a block diagram of how a raster scan image display system operates. The refresh buffer is accessed by the computer's image display system which scans the refresh buffer and recreates or rasterizes the image stored there onto the display. It must do this in less than 40 ms or the time taken for the display to produce the raster to avoid any noticeable flicker on the screen. The graphics software writes the memory version of any graphics entities such as lines, circles, text, etc., into the refresh buffer to be continually interpreted and displayed on the monitor.

The size or number of bytes in the refresh buffer depends on the resolution of the screen and the number of colours that the system can display as each pixel on the display is represented in the refresh buffer by a number of bits of memory. For a monochrome display one bit can represent one pixel which is either 1 for the pixel lit or 0 for dark. If two bits represent

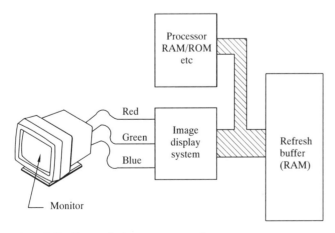

Figure 2.15 Raster display system operation

a pixel then four colours can be displayed as in the old IBM CGA system on early personal computers, and so 1 byte of refresh buffer RAM can represent four pixels. The image display system knows which bytes map to which physical pixels on the monitor. The EGA standard for personal computers was able to display 16 colours with a resolution of 640 by 350

Table 2.4   IBM EGA colour combinations

Number	Binary value	RGB	Intensity	Displayed colour
0	0000	none	low	black
1	0001	B	low	blue
2	0010	G	low	green
3	0011	GB	low	cyan
4	0100	R	low	red
5	0101	RB	low	magenta
6	0110	RG	low	amber
7	0111	RGB	low	light grey
8	1000	none	high	dark grey
9	1001	B	high	light blue
10	1010	G	high	light green
11	1011	GB	high	light cyan
12	1100	R	high	light red
13	1101	RB	high	light magenta
14	1110	RG	high	yellow
15	1111	RGB	high	white

pixels. Each pixel here is represented by four bits and so two pixels could be represented in a byte. Three of the bits indicate which of the three primary colours were active and the fourth determined whether the colours were at high or low intensity. This is illustrated in Table 2.4 which shows the binary value of any four bits representing a pixel and the resulting colour of that pixel.

The size of the refresh buffer in bytes can be calculated using the general expression:

$$S = \frac{R_h \, R_v \, N}{8} \tag{2.1}$$

where R_h is the horizontal resolution (number of pixels per line), R_v is the vertical resolution (number of lines) and N is the number of bytes representing one pixel's colour. For the EGA screen this evaluates to

$$S = \frac{640 \times 350 \times 4}{8} \tag{2.2}$$
$$= 112\,000 \text{ bytes}$$
$$\simeq 109 \text{ Kbytes.}$$

This memory is not part of the main memory of the computer but forms part of the circuitry of the display system printed circuit board. Pixel information is written to the memory by using specific BIOS instructions. In display systems which give a wider range of colours the number of bits required to represent a pixel is reduced by employing a look-up table. A common arrangement is to allow a display to simultaneously show 256 colours from a possible 4096 or more. In this case each pixel is represented by one byte and the contents of the byte do not directly map to the intensities of the colour guns but contain a colour number. This number refers to an entry in a table of 12-bit words which contain the actual colour gun intensities as illustrated in Fig. 2.16.

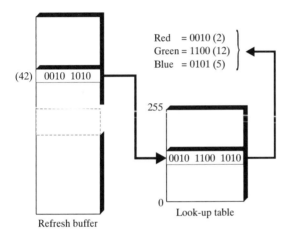

Figure 2.16 256-colour display using look-up table

The choice of 256 colours represents a wide range of shades which can be displayed on the screen while at the same time reducing refresh buffer memory size by a third. If a particular byte in the buffer, which maps to one pixel on the screen, contains the value 42_{10} or $0010\,1010_2$ then that pixel will be lit with colour number 42 which from the look-up table is an actual value $0010\,1100\,0101_2$. The actual colour of the pixel will therefore have a red intensity of 3, a green intensity of 12 and a blue intensity of 5 where 0 represents no intensity for the colour and 15 (1111_2) represents the brightest.

2.6 HARD COPY DEVICES

The end result of any computer-aided engineering task is nearly always some form of human-readable output. This could be a report, drawing, parts list, stock inventory, etc. The quality of the output will vary according to its use;

for example a parts list will be in text form and needs to be legible but not necessarily of publishable quality. A report or technical manual, however, will need to be of a professional quality in order to be suitable to present to the customer. An engineering drawing needs to be clear and precise to avoid errors during manufacture.

2.6.1 Printers

Text output, or documents which are mainly text, will require a printer to produce. Printers can be categorised into two main types, dependent on whether they reproduce text, graphical images or both:

- text-only printers;
- dot matrix printers.

The *daisy wheel printer* is a text-only printer of very similar construction to a manual typewriter. Its operational speed is very slow compared with other types of printer but the output is of very good quality. Another type of text-only hard copy device is the *line printer*. The quality of output is generally quite low but it reproduces text at very high speeds. This is particularly useful for large amounts of text in non-publishable form, for example a complete stock inventory or computer program listings.

Dot matrix printers can reproduce both text and graphics and there are three main types:

- 9 or 24-pin dot matrix printers;
- ink jet printers;
- laser printers.

The first dot matrix printers which could reproduce graphics comprised a print head of nine pins vertically arranged, which sweeps the paper horizontally one line at a time as shown in Fig. 2.17. The combination of pins firing at the paper through an ink ribbon as the head is moving produces the text characters or part of a rasterized graphics image. The text can be of varying quality and type and the arrangement of dots which make up each character is stored in the internal memory of the printer. Graphics images are created in a manner similar to a raster scan graphics display: the graphics image is broken up into strips the height of the print head vertically down the page and then further divided into eight or nine lines to correspond to each of the pins. For greater speed of reproduction a lower quality text style or graphics resolution can be chosen. By using a ribbon with several colour bands some models can produce text and graphics in colour.

A 24-pin dot matrix printer operates in a similar manner except that there are 24 pins arranged in three vertical lines of eight pins on the print head such that the resulting dots produced on the paper overlap. This produces

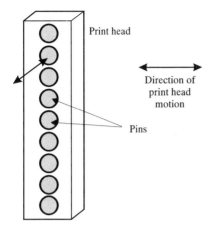

Figure 2.17   9-pin dot matrix printer operation

far higher resolution graphics much quicker than a 9-pin model: 24-pin graphics can be emulated with a 9-pin printer but it does so by making three passes of the print head per line.

Another type of dot matrix printer is the ink jet printer. The principle of operation is similar to that of the pin type except that instead of pins the print head has a vertical arrangement of fine nozzles through which liquid ink is ejected onto the paper. As the nozzles are very small, more of them can be arranged in a vertical line and such printers are available with heads having 48 nozzles in the same height as a 24-pin printer has its pin arrangement. The resulting resolution is very high being of the order of 360 dots per inch or around 14 dots per mm—this represents a dot spacing of 0.07 mm which is barely noticeable by the human eye.

The laser printer represents the latest development in high quality text and graphics reproduction technology. The principle of operation is similar to that of a photocopier; a full page image is represented as a dot matrix arrangement of electrostatically charged areas on the paper. The page is then passed through a toner bath or mist and the toner is attracted to the electrostatically charged dots which dry black, or any desired arrangement of colours in a colour printer, to produce the final image. Most laser printers can reproduce images with a resolution of around 300 dots per inch (12 dots per mm), which is a dot spacing of 0.08 mm, with speeds varying from 4 to 12 pages per minute.

The pin-type dot matrix printers are generally low-cost devices, the 24-pin types being naturally more expensive, but they are noisy when operating, the main source of noise being the pins striking the paper through the ribbon. As the print head involves precision moving parts it can be unreliable; the pins can become clogged with ink and may jam, which is easy to rectify, but in some cases they can actually break off which involves an expensive replacement of the head. The most frequently required maintenance, however, is the replacement of the ribbon. The printers are available for normal A4 size paper, continuous feed or single sheet, as well as for wider paper such as that normally found on line printers. Ink jet printers are generally more expensive than the pin type but are far quieter in operation. The ink nozzles in the print head tend to become clogged with dry ink, particularly when the printer is not used for some time. This is easily rectified as many printers have cleaning functions which flush the head with ink to remove obstructions. The ink is normally available in cartridges which need to be replaced regularly as does the ribbon in a pin printer. Laser printers are the most expensive graphics printing devices. They are extremely quiet when operating, the only real noise being the motorized paper feed for each sheet of printout.

2.6.2 Plotters

Although engineering drawings and other graphics can be reproduced on a dot matrix printer, they generally require the use of a plotter, particularly for larger drawings such as A3 or greater. There are many types on the market varying greatly in price depending on quality and size. Choosing a plotter depends on the space considerations in the design office, the size of paper to be used, speed of reproduction, mode of operation (single drawing or batch) and the variety of different line widths or colours required. There are two basic methods of plotting:

- pen plotting;
- electrostatic plotting.

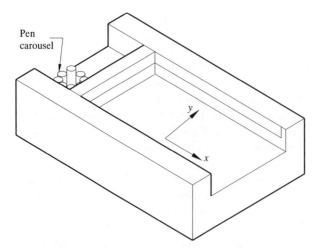

Figure 2.18 A flatbed plotter

Pen plotters are available in two configurations, namely flatbed plotters and drum plotters. Figure 2.18 shows a flatbed plotter. As its name suggests, the paper is in single-sheet form and placed on the flat bed. Pens are selected from a carousel or bank in the corner or at one edge of the drawing area. The pen currently in use is moved over the paper on a gantry system in 'x' and 'y' directions. For small paper sizes up to and including A2 this type of plotter is ideal if large numbers of drawings are not required. The main disadvantage is with loading the plotter with paper. For each new drawing a new sheet has to loaded and the plotter restarted. This can be a lengthy process for the production of a large numbers of drawings. Another disadvantage is that for large paper sizes up to A0, the plotter bed is large and cumbersome and requires a lot of physical space and special handling procedures.

The drum plotter, like that shown in Fig. 2.19, has the paper normally supplied on a roll. This gives an advantage over the flatbed plotter when producing a large number of drawings, though, conversely, single drawings, particularly those produced on smaller paper sizes, can be very wasteful. With older drum plotters the paper was fed off the supply roll over a drawing roller and onto a take-up roller.

The pens are moved in one direction along the length of the roller on a gantry, while movement in the other direction is provided by a backward and forward rotation of the drawing roller itself. The operation of this type of plotter is rather slower than that of a flatbed because of the need to move the rollers, which provide extra inertia. An advantage is that the roller construction makes the plotter more compact than its flatbed counterpart. Later designs replaced the large roller with a more compact arrangement of

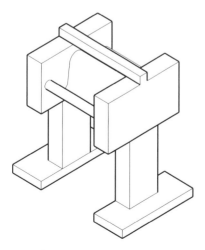

Figure 2.19 A drum plotter

pinch rollers along its width resulting in much faster operation and the possibility of single-sheet operation.

The electrostatic plotter, which is becoming more common, also has paper fed from a roll. It is passed under an electrostatic head which operates on a similar principle to that of a laser printer; the head covers an area across the width of the paper but only a small section along its length. The image is rasterized along the length of the paper and each line of the raster is laid down on the paper as it is fed under the head. An advantage of this type of plotter, like the drum type, is that it can produce large quantities of drawings without a paper change. Also, because of the technology deployed, it takes approximately the same time to do a drawing of any size regardless of its complexity. This is because the drawing is 'rasterized' in the memory of the plotter and it is only this small overhead and the length of the drawing which gives any variation in plotting time.

EXERCISES

Assignment

Carry out a survey of currently available UNIX-based work stations with high resolution colour graphics capability. Produce a report comparing the devices with respect to cost, performance, maximum internal memory capacity, hard disk expansibility and graphics performance in terms of resolution, colour range and speed.

Questions

2.1 State three differences between a mainframe and a personal computer.
2.2 Draw a block diagram of a CPU of a typical microprocessor showing the basic elements that make up its circuitry.
2.3 What do the terms ROM and RAM mean and what is the major difference between the two?
2.4 Define the term *portability* in the context of computer software and describe the benefits it presents to an engineering manager in the choice of CAE software.
2.5 Describe with the aid of sketches(s) the operation of a mechanical (non-optical) mouse.
2.6 Discuss the advantages and disadvantages of the mouse compared with the tablet as a pointing device for interactive graphics.
2.7 Describe the three main types of plotting device available for producing hard copy output of graphical data and discuss their advantages and disadvantages.

REFERENCES

Brey, B. B. 1984, *Microprocessor/Hardware Interfacing and Applications*. Merrill, Columbus, OH.

Foley, J. D. and A. Van Dam. 1984, *Fundamentals of Interactive Computer Graphics*. Addision Wesley, Reading, MA.

Khambata, A. J. 1987, *Microprocessors/Microcomputers. Architecture, Software and Systems*, 2nd edn. Wiley, New York.

Scanlon, L. J. 1985, *IBM PC & XT Assembly Language*. Brady, New York.

Stern, N. and R. A. Stern. 1990, *Computing with End-User Applications*. Wiley, New York.

THREE

CAE HARDWARE 2:
THE FACTORY FLOOR

In the previous chapter we examined the fundamentals of computing hardware and operating systems and how these were used in the engineering office. In general the computing systems found in this environment are general purpose, that is the software that can be used in the systems covers a wide range of applications which are not just restricted to those involving computer-aided engineering. Mainframes, minicomputers, workstations and personal computers were discussed and it was realized that, in most cases, all but the personal computer were multi-user systems where many applications, from the user's point of view, could share the processing power of the computer simultaneously. The computing hardware encountered on the factory floor, however, is fundamentally different in nature in that instead of being general purpose and multi-user, the system is dedicated to one type of function. Such systems can be said to be functionally dedicated. This chapter gives details of examples illustrating functional dedication, such as the controller for an automatic machine tool which is designed purely for the purpose of controlling the movement of the component being machined (or in effect the cutting tool). There are functionally dedicated systems to assist in nearly all areas of manufacturing including material removal (cutting) and handling (movement), surface treatment, joining, assembly and inspection.

3.1 MATERIAL REMOVAL

Numerical control (NC) and computerized numerical control (CNC) machine tools provide a programmable automated means of machining components. There are such machines to carry out all types of material removal, shaping and forming including drilling, milling, turning, sheet metal punching and bending. Numerical control machines first appeared in the fifties and CNC machines in the seventies. The essential difference between NC and CNC machines was their ability to store a program to machine a component in internal memory. NC machine control was made up of hard-wired electronic circuitry which could read programmed instructions, one at a time, from a paper tape. These instructions caused straight line movements of the tool table or turret from the current position to a new position at a specified feed rate or controlled other functions of the machine tool such as turning on the spindle or coolant. CNC machine controllers are computer based and as such the program, often still read from paper tape, can be partially or completely stored in the internal memory of the controller and executed from there. These machines also have greater functionality than the older NC machines because the computer control is capable of carrying out the necessary numerical processing required to perform more complex machining operations such as circular motion, automatic tool size compensation and tool changing.

3.1.1 Computerized Numerical Control

A CNC machine such as that illustrated in Fig. 3.1 consists of two parts: the machine tool and the controller.

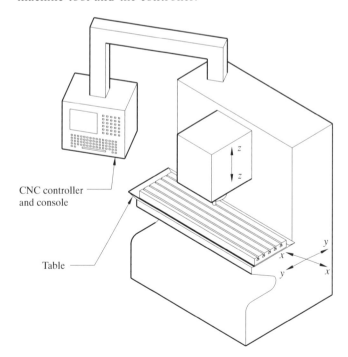

Figure 3.1 A simple CNC milling machine

The design of the machine tool is generally of a similar configuration to its manually operated counterpart; the major differences being that the machine table or slides are driven by some form of motor, and other services such as the spindle and coolant flow are turned on and off via relays and valves. The controller is a microprocessor-based computer which interfaces with the driven and switched components on the machine tool such that they are under complete programmed control. The controller's interface to the machine tool is depicted in Fig. 3.2.

A typical CNC controller is equipped with a user console consisting of a keypad or keyboard and visual display. The keyboard serves as the main user interface between the operator and the machine tool and is used to issue commands to load programs from backing store, to edit the program and begin execution of a program and control its progress. The visual display indicates to the operator the status of the program and in many controllers a graphical image of the tool path can be displayed. The backing store for CNC machines is traditionally paper tape because the harsh conditions on the factory floor are hardly an ideal environment for magnetic media such as tape or disk—paper tape is relatively inexpensive to replace when damaged—though some controllers do use magnetic tape in the form of microcassettes and some even have floppy disk drives. As a CNC program to machine a component is rarely correct first time, particularly if it was written without computer assistance, the operator has the facilities to correct the program in the controller's memory and create a new paper tape image, using a paper tape punch, for future use. Each slide or direction of table or quill movement on the machine tool represents one axis in a Cartesian coordinate system. A vertical machining centre or mill, as shown in Fig. 3.1, has a minimum of three axes: the 'x' and 'y' axes refer to

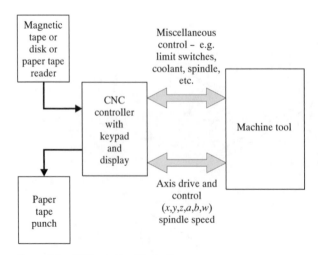

Figure 3.2 CNC machine block diagram

horizontal movement of the table and the 'z' axis normally refers to the vertical movement of the quill. Extra axes may also be available: a 'w' axis may refer to the vertical movement of the table (knee drive), an 'a' axis to a rotary table and a 'b' axis to a tilting table (angle dekker).

Figure 3.3 shows a block diagram of a typical controller for a CNC machine and how it drives a table or slide on the machine tool. The controller itself is similar in structure to a typical microcomputer. The CPU is a microprocessor (Chapter 2) which can access memory which is made up of both read only and random access types. The ROM contains the firmware to provide the control of the machine tool and to interpret operator commands and program instructions into machining operations. The RAM is the internal memory into which the part programs are stored.

The input and output facilities of the microcontroller service the operator's console and backing store (paper or magnetic media) as well as the driven and switched services on the machine tool itself. Figure 3.3 shows the control elements for one axis of the machine tool. The controller provides a signal to the motor driving the table or slide such that it will move to a programmed position at a given feed rate. This signal will begin as a binary number representing the feed rate or the speed of the motor and will be processed into a suitable form to provide the motion. The example shows the table or slide being driven by a servo-motor which requires a

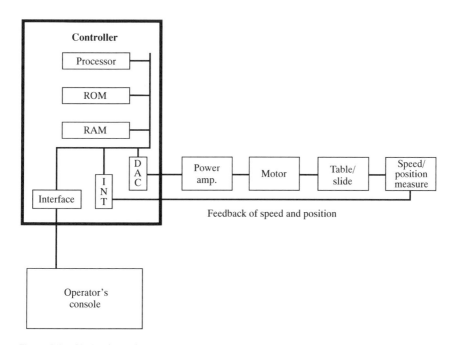

Figure 3.3 CNC schematic

certain voltage input to rotate at a given speed under a given load. The binary number representing the feed rate needs to be converted to a voltage which is proportional to its value and this is achieved by a digital to analogue converter (DAC). The output signal thus produced has insufficient power to drive a heavy duty motor and so it is processed further by a power amplifier. The table or slide is driven by the motor in a similar manner to a manually operated machine, that is via a lead screw or other means to convert the rotary motion of the motor into the desired linear motion. It is an essential design feature of a CNC machine tool that the axis control is precise both in position and speed. The positional precision gives the required dimensional accuracy of machining and the speed precision ensures a constant programmed feed rate being achieved in practice. As the table or slide moves any changes in machining conditions, such as a change in the depth of cut, will alter the load required by the motor to maintain a constant feed rate. The motor control system must respond rapidly by adjusting the value of the signal to the motor in response to these changes and so the speed and position of the machine tool axes are measured and these data are fed back to the controller. The normal method of feedback is from a digitizer disk mounted on the motor which operates in a similar manner to that found in a mouse (Chapter 2) except that it provides a more precise measure of position, and hence speed, and is more robust.

The motorization of the machine tool axes is achieved by a variety of different means, namely DC or AC servo-motors, stepper motors or hydraulic servo motors. Servo-motors always require positional and speed feedback but stepper motors need not. Stepper motors operate on the principle that one electrical pulse to the motor causes a rotation of the motor shaft through a known angle which will correspond to a small known linear movement in the relevant axis. Therefore to move the axis a programmed distance requires a specific number of pulses to be sent to the motor. The need for a digital to analogue converter is therefore also eliminated, but other control techniques are needed to ensure that the motor accelerates gently up to the desired rotational speed so that pulses, and hence positional accuracy, are not lost.

3.1.2 Programming

Most CNC machines are programmed using a very simple language with which movements and services are defined by a combination of different *words* arranged as lines of programming code. Each word is specified by one alphabetic character and is followed by a numeric value in a suitable format; a summary of common CNC programming words is given in Table 3.1.

Some controllers may include other words in their vocabulary to carry out certain functions and the format of the values vary among the many different types from different vendors. A typical line of program code for a

Table 3.1   CNC programming word summary

Word definition	Typical value format	Meaning
N	4 digit integer	Line number in program
G	2 digit integer	Preparatory code—type of motion, units, etc.
M	2 digit integer	Miscellaneous function—switchable utilities, coolant, spindle, etc.
X,Y,Z,A,B,W,I,J,K	real number	Axis position in desired units, e.g. mm, inches
F	4 digit integer	Feed rate value mm/min or in/min
S	4 digit integer	Spindle speed RPM
T	2 digit integer	Tool number and length offset

CNC machine therefore consists of a line number (N word) followed by a sequence of words specifying a combination of one or more miscellaneous functions and one move. There are a number of preparatory commands to define the type of movement, the most common of which are listed in Table 3.2.

The codes are normally modal, that is once they have been programmed their effect remains active until changed or cancelled by another. Each code that specifies a move of any combination of the axes is accompanied by the X, Y, Z, A, B or W words defining the new position and also the F word to specify the feed rate if different from that previously programmed. The codes which specify circular motion also require a combination of two of the I, J and K words to be stipulated which define the centre of rotation relative to the start position of the move in the *x, y* and *z* directions, respectively. The preparatory codes which specify cutter or tool radius compensation

Table 3.2   CNC preparatory moves

Code	Function
G00	Rapid move to specified position
G01	Linear move at programmed feed rate
G02	Clockwise circular move at feed rate
G03	Anticlockwise circular move at feed rate
G40	Cancel cutter radius compensation
G41	Cutter radius compensation—tool left
G42	Cutter radius compensation—tool right
G70	Coordinate data in inches
G71	Coordinate data in metric (mm)
G80	Cancel canned cycle
G81–G89	Canned cycles, e.g drill, peck, bore, etc.
G90	Coordinate data absolute positions
G91	Coordinate data incremental moves

allow the programmer to specify the actual positions of features to be machined as opposed to having to allow for the radius of the tool in the program. The radius or diameter of each cutter can be physically measured and stored in a table in the controller's memory to enable this automatic compensation facility. Preparatory codes also provide options for coordinate data input so that imperial or metric values can be programmed and moves can be specified as absolute values relative to the origin of the coordinate system or incremental relative to the current position. Many controllers also have a series of preprogrammed *canned cycles* to carry out hole generation which include normal drilling, deep hole drilling (pecking), counterboring and thread tapping.

The miscellaneous functions of a CNC machine provide control for machine facilities such as the spindle, coolant, tool changing and program control—some examples of miscellaneous functions are given in Table 3.3, and are largely self-explanatory. The spindle control functions require the use of the S word to specify a change in speed and the M06 command requires the T word to specify which tool to select from the carousel. The use of the commands explained above can be illustrated using the example shown in Fig. 3.4 and Fig. 3.5 which is a simple component requiring the external profile to be machined.

Table 3.3   CNC miscellaneous moves

Code	Function
M00	Program stop
M02	End of program
M03	Spindle on clockwise
M04	Spindle on anticlockwise
M05	Spindle stop
M06	Tool change
M07	Coolant on mist
M08	Coolant on flood
M09	Coolant off
M30	End program and rewind to start

The machine always returns to the coordinate position (0,0) in the x, y plane and at a safe distance above the machining table to change the cutting tool. The first move after changing the tool to that required would be at rapid feed rate to a suitable position (shown dashed) so that an approach can be made to the first edge. The next move is the approach at a suitable feed rate with cutter radius compensation turned on such that the tool will always be to the left of the programmed path. The program given in Fig. 3.5 could be used on some CNC machining centres but it must be stressed that the programming codes defined by different controllers do vary in meaning and the word values in format.

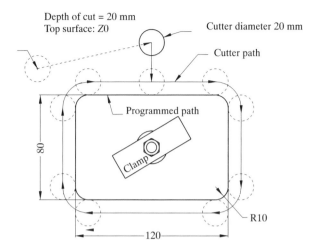

Figure 3.4 CNC programming example

```
N0010G00M06T01X0.Y80.Z-20.
N0020M03M05S1500
N0030G01G41F0100Y40.
N0040X50
N0050G02X60.Y30.I0.J10.
N0060G01Y-30
N0070G02X50.Y-40.I10.J0.
N0070G01X-50.
N0080G02X-60.Y-30.I0.J10.
N0090G01Y30.
N0100G02X-50.Y40.I10.J0.
N0110G01X0.
N0120G00G40Y80.Z0
N0130M05M09
N0140M02
```

Figure 3.5 CNC program for example

3.1.3 Computer-assisted Part Programming

Using the language of CNC machines to produce programs for complex parts can be very time consuming. Over the years that NC and CNC machines have developed, methods of producing part programs using higher level computer assistance have also developed and these systems can be categorized in the area of computer-aided manufacturing. This is a major topic of discussion in Chapter 6 where the history and use of CAM systems and how they link to computer-aided draughting and design are described.

3.1.4 Direct and Distributed Numerical Control (DNC)

The concept of CNC, as opposed to NC, was conceived early on in the development of automated material removal techniques though the technology of the day did not make it viable. In the mid-sixties microcomputer technology did not exist and so the only way to provide CNC was to use a mainframe or minicomputer to control a machine tool. The cost of this approach was extremely high, though some systems were developed where several machine tools were controlled directly and simultaneously by one large computer as shown in Fig. 3.6. This was termed *direct numerical control* and only survived as a usable concept until microcomputer technology allowed sufficiently small and inexpensive controllers for individual machine tools to be produced.

The acronym DNC now has a different interpretation—*distributed numerical control*—which defines a means of central storage and distribution of CNC part programs rather than central control of the machines. This type of DNC system can be applied to existing stand-alone CNC machines by linking them using a local area network and by modifying each controller so that instead of loading programs by paper tape, they are electronically transmitted from the central storage system to the machine as illustrated in Fig. 3.7. To operate most effectively a DNC approach would form part of a computer-integrated manufacturing system (CIM) as described in Chapter 9. It is also particularly efficient if part programs are produced with computer assistance using a CAM package. In this way a part program can be prepared without the need to specify the machine on which it will be produced, as the post processing to generate a program for a particular controller need not be done until it is known which machine is available for the production run. Part program production using CAM and post processing is described in detail in Chapter 6.

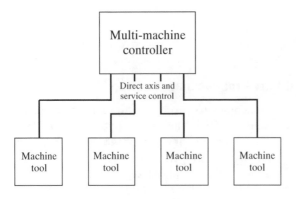

Figure 3.6   Direct numerical control

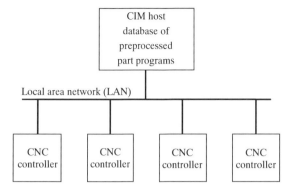

Figure 3.7 Distributed numerical control

3.1.5 Applications

As already mentioned there are many applications for CNC machines in the area of material removal. The very early NC machines were simple drilling machines which just provided point-to-point movement in the horizontal plane and linear movement in the vertical plane. Numerically controlled drilling operations are now generally carried out on milling machines or machining centres. Numerically controlled machining centres are available in two configurations: vertical and horizontal as depicted in Fig. 3.8.

Vertical machining centres allow milling and drilling operations to be carried out on the top face and end milling of profiles and pockets. Horizontal machining centres are particularly suited for drilling, face and end milling of cuboid components as the component can be indexed on the table to present any number of faces to the cutting tools. Both vertical and horizontal machining centres allow automatic programmed selection of

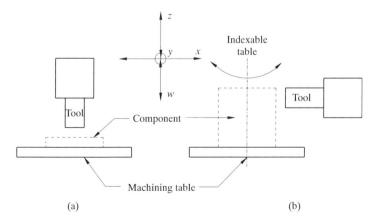

Figure 3.8 CNC machining centres: (a) vertical; (b) horizontal

different cutting tools from a carousel mounted at the side of the machine so that a wide range of cutting operations can be done such as face and end milling, drilling, boring, counterboring and thread tapping.

Turning of cylindrical components can be achieved using numerically controlled lathes or turning centres, which provide an automatic equivalent to manually operated centre or capstan lathes. The turning tool can be moved to cut the component in the x and z directions and drilling and boring operations can be carried out using tools mounted in a tailstock which is normally designated as the w axis as shown in Fig. 3.9.

A number of turning tools, normally up to six, can be automatically selected from an indexable turret to provide cutting operations such as rough and finish turning, facing, undercutting and external thread chasing and also a similar number of tools can be selected from the tailstock turret for centre-drilling, drilling, boring and internal thread tapping. The rotational speed of the chuck or collet is functionally equivalent to the spindle speed in a machining centre and can also be programmed to vary relative to the depth of cut to ensure a constant surface cutting speed for a better finish.

Another common application of numerical control is the removal of material from, and forming of, sheet stock. Historically, manual sheet metal work is slow in both preparation and execution; the sheet material needs to be accurately marked out and positioned for quality results. The use of CNC methods for sheet metal work eliminates the need for marking out and reduces the effort for accurate positioning. Numerical control can be applied to punching simple shapes, cropping more complex shapes and bending

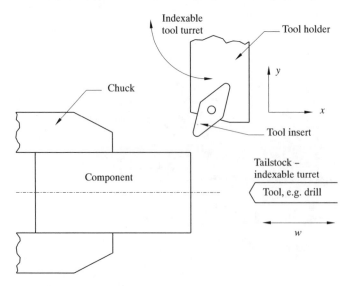

Figure 3.9 Numerically controlled lathe configuration

sheet metal into sections. A CNC punch can move a sheet of material on a flat bed to accurately position a tool of desired shape to produce a profiled hole or component either in one punching action or by cropping with a series of cuts along a programmed path. With computer assistance for producing the program many components can be produced from a sheet or strip with minimum waste. Bending can also be accurately carried out by controlling the positions of stops and the movements of tools to assist the operator in producing quality components by a process which is difficult to use manually.

Other processes which use the functionality of numerical control to profile complex shapes in sheet material incorporate the use of lasers, high pressure water jets and wire erosion. Industrial lasers have developed to the point where they can be used to cut, drill, heat treat surfaces and weld. The use of lasers for any of these processes cannot be safely achieved without some form of automatic control, but when driven by a computerized numerical controller, even though the laser itself represents an expensive investment, they are very effective. A laser beam can pierce and cut, with a diameter of the order of 1 mm, sheet steel up to 10 mm thick or more as the energy in the beam is absorbed in a localized area of the material such that the material burns in air and vaporizes. The process is very quick but the resulting surface finish of the edges is quite poor. Reducing the amount of energy or using different frequencies of light can cause melting for welding purposes or heating for surface hardening. Water jet cutting is still very much in its infancy but when the high pressure water jet is directed at a material surface under numerical control complex shapes can be profiled in very hard materials, for example granite, if the water jet is mixed with abrasive particles. Plain water jets are ideally suited to cutting material where contact with metallic cutters would be undesirable, such as, for example, in the food industry. Wire erosion is a more established means of profiling shapes in sheet metals. A thin stainless steel wire carrying an electrical current is slowly drawn through the material which is being flooded with a saline solution, the result being that the erosion process is accelerated and a fine 'cut' is made. The wire erosion process, as with laser cutting, is only really possible to carry out with accuracy by numerical control; it is, however, significantly slower than laser cutting though it does produce a better surface finish on the edges of the finished profile. A simplified diagram of the wire erosion process is shown in Fig. 3.10.

3.2 MATERIALS HANDLING, JOINING AND ASSEMBLY

The systems dedicated to materials handling, joining and assembly are similar to those for materials removal in that they involve a machine being directly controlled by a microprocessor-based controller. They are different,

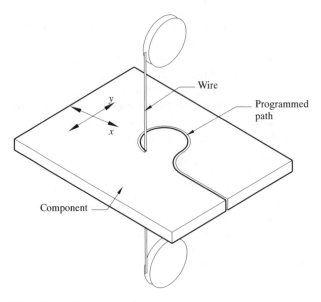

Figure 3.10   The wire erosion process

however, in the fact that the operation of the machine element is more complex and varied in nature. Systems of this nature are mainly robotic manipulators but also include automatic guided vehicles. Robotics, as a subject, is very detailed and extensive and so its treatment here is purely introductory and serves to highlight the requirements of the computers that control them. A very extensive coverage of the subject of robotics and its applications can be studied in Groover *et al.* (1986).

3.2.1 Robot Manipulators

Industrial robots are the most common devices used for handling components and materials in automatic manufacturing processes which involve positioning parts for gluing, screwing and welding and in other forms of assembly. The term *robot* comes from a Czechoslovakian word 'robota' which means servitude or forced worker and was first used to describe android type machines in a play in the twenties. Science fiction writers since then have used robots, which were mainly androids, as key features in their plots. Probably the most notable science fiction writer in this area was Isaac Asimov who, it is believed, first used the term *robotics*. Robots in science fiction have been credited with much more intelligence than real industrial robots and this has caused much misunderstanding regarding the role of robots in modern society. Interestingly though, Isaac Asimov did define three laws of robotics, the first two of which describe how robots ought to be used in industry; these first two laws refer to safety and functionality, respectively.

An industrial robot can be simply defined as a programmable manipulator designed to move and position resources, for example tools and materials, through predefined paths. A robot task is a program defined by a manufacturing engineer and stored in the memory of the controller. This controller is very similar in structure to that of the CNC machine already described, the main difference being that the control program is capable of determining the position in space of the *end effector*, that is the hand or finger of the robot, from the positions of the joints and limbs. This, in most cases, requires a more complex numerical analysis than determining the position of a tool in a CNC machine and this can be better understood by considering a robot as a kinematic chain as shown in Fig. 3.11.

It is relatively simple to determine the position of the end of the first limb, but the position of the end of the second limb can only be determined from that of the first, and so on, until the position of the end effector becomes a complex function of the relative orientations of all the limbs. The actual calculation depends on the type and coordinate system of the robot itself, of which there are essentially four, namely: *Cartesian* or rectangular, *cylindrical* or polar, *spherical* and *jointed arm* or anthropomorphic. The simplest configuration to deal with is the robot with a Cartesian or rectangular coordinate system as depicted in Fig. 3.12 which incorporates three prismatic or sliding joints to move the end effector in *x*, *y* or *z* and, in most cases, one revolute or rotational joint to orientate the end effector about its own axis.

There is little or no difference between this configuration and that of a CNC machining centre; with a machining centre the tool, or end effector, is stationary in the horizontal plane while the table moves, whereas a prismatic robot generally involves a kinematic chain where each link represents one of the orthogonal axes. The reach or working volume of such a robot is limited

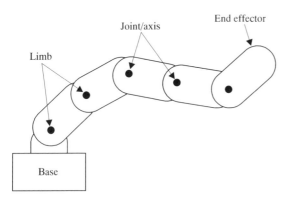

Figure 3.11 A robot as a kinematic chain

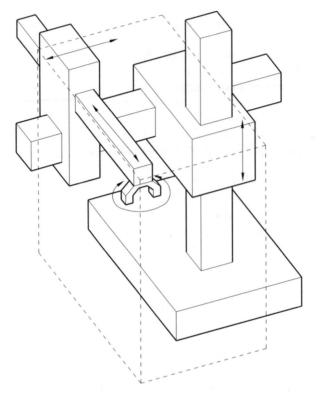

Figure 3.12 Cartesian configuration

to a cuboid and the orientation of the end effector is generally limited to rotation about the vertical axis.

A cylindrical configuration as shown in Fig. 3.13 involves a polar arrangement of axes in one plane, for example the horizontal, and a linear movement in the vertical direction. For the polar coordinates the angle of rotation is set by a revolute joint and the radius generally by a prismatic joint. Therefore at any vertical position the end effector can be orientated by defining this angle of rotation about the vertical axis and a radial distance determined by the extent of the prismatic joint. The end effector can normally be rotated about its own axis.

One type of physical robot which has a similar working volume to the cylindrical configuration is the SCARA robot or *S*elective *C*ompliance *A*ssembly *R*obot *A*rm which is illustrated in Fig. 3.14. It is a jointed arm robot which allows vertical movement of the end effector via a prismatic joint at the end of the arm and radial or lateral movement by a revolute joint at the elbow. It is particularly suited for assembly or *pick and place* tasks as it can rapidly position the end effector to any point and orientation in the horizontal plane at a suitable height, lift a component and move it to the

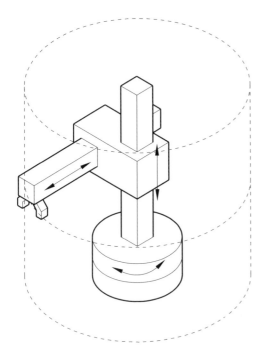

Figure 3.13 Cylindrical robot configuration

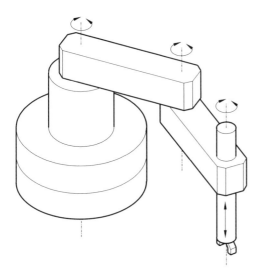

Figure 3.14 The SCARA robot

position where it is to be assembled. The assembly operation thus executed is limited to vertical insertion which accounts for a large number of requirements in manufacturing, an example of which is insertion of electronic components in a printed circuit board.

The spherical configuration depicted in Fig. 3.15 allows for rotation in all three orthogonal planes by revolute joints and radial movement via a prismatic joint. Whereas the Cartesian and cylindrical configurations limit the work of the end effector to the horizontal plane and generally in a downward direction, the spherical system can present the end effector in almost any attitude. Although all three configurations described can position the end effector reasonably freely in any one or more planes and even perform interpolation in a straight line or curve in those planes, there is a limitation on the extent or freedom of movement.

The jointed arm robot as shown in Fig. 3.16, however, has significantly greater freedom of movement within its work volume. The working volume is essentially spherical but the robot's ability to position and move the end effector in any orientation is greater. The configuration can be said to be *anthropomorphic* or 'human like' as it attempts to emulate the structure and hence mobility of the human arm. It has the ability to carry out such tasks as welding or the application of adhesive around the edges of complex surfaces and because of this the control of such a robot is more complicated than any of the other types discussed.

In order to gain an appreciation of the type of control needed for a robot let us consider the kinematics of a polar configuration as shown in Fig. 3.17

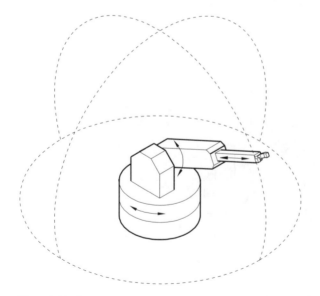

Figure 3.15 Spherical robot configuration

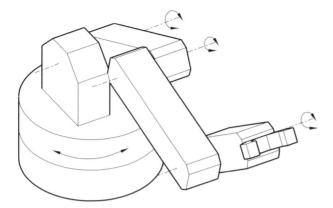

Figure 3.16 Jointed arm robot

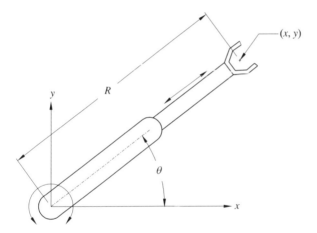

Figure 3.17 Polar configuration kinematics

for a simple two-dimensional case. The robot arm rotates about the origin and extends in length via a prismatic joint. The robot controller measures the position of the end effector (x, y), by knowing the rotation (θ) and length (R) of the arm. The programmer would normally understand the positions required to be serviced by the robot in terms of their Cartesian coordinates. Therefore even though the programmed input for a position will be Cartesian, the robot has to convert it into polar notation in order to move the robot. In this case the conversion is done by simple coordinate geometry; the Cartesian position can be ascertained from the polar coordinates:

$$x = R \sin \theta$$
$$y = R \cos \theta$$

(3.1)

and the polar parameters evaluated from the Cartesian coordinates. The angle could be calculated from

$$\theta = \tan^{-1}\left(\frac{y}{x}\right), \tag{3.2}$$

but this would cause a problem for the case when $x = 0$, whereupon the value of (y/x) is undefined. A more correct method from a programming point of view is to first calculate the length of the extended arm:

$$R = \sqrt{(x^2 + y^2)} \tag{3.3}$$

and therefore:

$$\theta = \sin^{-1}\left(\frac{y}{R}\right)$$
$$\theta = \cos^{-1}\left(\frac{x}{R}\right). \tag{3.4}$$

These conversions require the robot controller to evaluate the trigonometrical functions for sine and cosine and, in cases where the end effector is interpolating in a straight line, it would need to make many such evaluations 'on the fly'. Evaluation of trigonometrical relationships involves the application of the infinite polynomials for these functions which, because the robot is operating in real time, would be too lengthy. To overcome this time constraint a look-up table of sines for key values of θ is stored in the ROM of the controller; evaluation of sine values in between those given in the table are obtained by interpolation in a similar manner to using old-fashioned log tables. Although less accurate than applying polynomials the gain in speed ensures that real-time control of end effector position can be performed. The controller's task to perform real-time control is even more demanding for a jointed arm robot which can be demonstrated by considering Fig. 3.18 and the simplified analysis for the two limbs shown.

In order for such a configuration to position the end effector at (x, y) there are two possibilities for the orientation of the limbs, though both are covered by the analysis of the kinematics. When programming a position the programmer can specify an *above* or *below* position for the elbow. The Cartesian position for the elbow can be evaluated in much the same manner as shown in Eq. (3.1):

$$x_1 = R_1 \cos \theta_1$$
$$y_1 = R_1 \sin \theta_1 \tag{3.5}$$

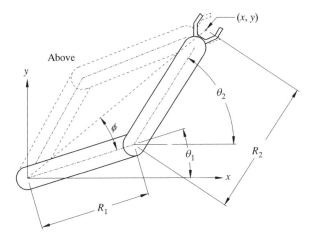

Figure 3.18 Two limbs of a jointed arm robot

The position (x, y) can be evaluated in a similar way relative to (x_1, y_1) such that

$$x = R_1 \cos\theta_1 + R_2 \cos(\theta_1 + \theta_2)$$
$$y = R_1 \sin\theta_1 + R_2 \sin(\theta_1 + \theta_2).$$

(3.6)

The reverse analysis, that is the evaluation of joint angles θ_1 and θ_2 from the desired position in Cartesian coordinates in the robot workspace (often referred to as the *world space*) is rather too complex to include in this introduction, but it can be seen from the preceding development that the more joints, and hence degrees of freedom, that a robot has, the more numerical analysis the controller has to undertake.

In addition to the numerical control complexities of a robot another problem to be overcome is the variation of the geometry of the real robot from that of the ideal robot used as a model by the controller. The ideal robot is completely rigid, is manufactured to precise dimensions and has no backlash in the gears in the joint drive assemblies. A real robot can never be identical in these respects to the ideal robot and even though each robot of any type produced will vary within the tolerances specified for component manufacture, the control program will be basically the same. Therefore each robot needs to be calibrated against the ideal so that in operation it will perform with consistent accuracy and repeatability. The accuracy of a robot defines the tolerance with which a robot will position the end effector to a desired position and the repeatability defines the consistency with which the end effector returns to a position time after time.

3.2.2 Robot Programming

There are essentially three methods of programming a robot to carry out a task:

- taught path programming (leadthrough);
- languages (for the controller);
- CADCAM (task design, simulation and post-processing).

Taught path programming involves physically moving the robot to position the end-effector and recording that position in memory. Taught path programming is also known as *leadthrough* programming as the object of the exercise is to lead the robot through its motions to carry out the task. For a task which involves the robot making simple point-to-point movements to pick up tools or materials for placement elsewhere (pick and place operations), the end positions for each move are arrived at using a *teach pendant*. This is normally a small hand-held device with the necessary controls to steer the robot to a desired position by direct drive of the joint motors. For other tasks which require the robot to interpolate complex paths, such as paint spraying or continuous curve welding, manual leadthrough is used. For this method the programmer physically takes the end effector and, with the robot in teach mode, moves the end effector through its programmed path. When the program is executed the robot will faithfully reproduce the movements within the limitations of its accuracy and repeatability.

Robot controller languages are developing through a series of generations in a similar manner to computer languages (Chapter 2). First-generation languages such as VAL combine taught path programming with a written or textual language control. If a number of taught points are stored in memory then further written instructions can be used to provide a sequence in which those positions are visited. Straight line interpolation, simple sensor reading and end effector control commands are also available. Second-generation languages include many enhancements over first-generation languages in that sensor control can deal with more complex situations than those requiring just on or off states, and better input and output facilities are available to enable interfacing and communication with other computing equipment. An example of a second-generation language is VAL II.

One particular drawback encountered with robot programming is that it nearly always requires some use of the teach pendant and therefore this has to be carried out with the robot itself. This means that the robot has to be taken out of its normal production schedule in order for a new program to be devised, resulting in excessive downtime. CADCAM systems for robots have been devised where the programmer designs a computer model of the robot, its surroundings and the task to be performed. Such software normally uses interactive graphics and so the model can be animated on the screen prior to any program being produced. A post-processing technique similar to that used for CNC part programming can then generate the robot program in its own language which can then be tested with the real system. Even though the likelihood of the program being perfectly correct first time is small the amount of downtime for the robot can be significantly reduced.

3.2.3 Robot Applications

Many applications for robots have been implied in the preceding text. Probably the most common task that robots carry out is automatic assembly which involves picking materials or components from feeders and placing them in their finished positions in the assemblies or subassemblies. The end effector in these situations is nearly always a gripper which seizes the components like a hand. There are many types of gripper, depending on the geometry and fragility of the components they are intended to handle. Fragile components may need complex gripping systems to prevent breakage and much work has been and is being carried out on the development of tactile or force-sensitive grippers. Robot configurations for assembly tasks vary; for vertical insertion situations, a simple Cartesian, cylindrical or SCARA robot can be used but for more complex orientation of components a spherical or jointed arm robot should be considered.

Other robot operations include welding and other forms of joining such as the application of adhesives and in these cases a jointed arm robot is most commonly used. The end effector is the welding torch or adhesive gun and such situations require careful continuous path programming. Another similar task is paint spraying where the end effector is the spray gun which is played over the surface to be painted according to the taught path. In all these situations the robot can provide a more controlled and consistent quality to the finished job and also affords a means of eliminating the need for human operators from potentially dangerous manufacturing processes.

3.2.4 Automated Guided Vehicles

The use of robots as materials handling devices is restricted to a particular locality or process. There is a need, however, to provide automated means of transporting materials and components to these processes from stores or other processes and present them in a manner suitable for automated manufacture or assembly. This is largely met by the use of conveyors or automated guided vehicles or AGVs. Although seemingly a new development for the automated factory, the first AGV systems appeared as long ago as 1958 or earlier. A more detailed survey of AGV development, use and control than is possible here can be found in Hammond (1986). An AGV is essentially a driverless vehicle programmed to convey materials or work in progress through a predefined route or route options. It has greater freedom to select a route than a roller or belt conveyor system and is more flexible in use.

There are many types of vehicle for different applications which include *tuggers and trailers, pallet trucks* and *unit load carriers*. Tuggers can pull a train of wheeled carriers around a factory and are therefore suited to carrying large quantities of materials or parts. Automated pallet trucks are equivalent to manual pallet or fork lift trucks which are also suitable for bulk carriage particularly within stores or from stores to a manufacturing process area. Unit load carriers can be viewed as the equivalent to manually propelled trolleys or conveyors which mainly transport work in progress from one manufacturing or assembly operation to another. In all cases the AGV requires an on-board controller and an off-board controller.

The on-board control of an AGV ensures that the vehicle is moving along the correct path at a suitable speed and is communicating with the off-board control which transmits instructions to the vehicle to carry out its task. There are a number of ways in which a vehicle can be guided so that the off-board control system knows the whereabouts of all the vehicles in the AGV system; these include passive methods such as optical tracking, and active methods such as guidewires, dead reckoning, infra-red beams, gyroscopes and pattern recognition. The passive optical system requires a reflective tape or other substance placed on the floor over which the vehicle will ride. The vehicle shines a light onto the tape and detects the reflection using optical cells as shown in Fig. 3.19. Any deviation from the path is detected by a difference in the amount of reflected light detected in either sensor which must then be corrected.

The most common method of AGV guidance is by a wire embedded in the floor and this wire is energized with a low voltage alternating current. The

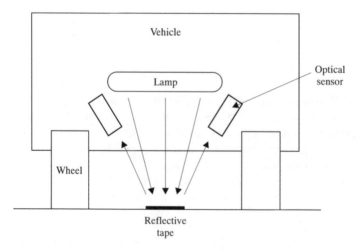

Figure 3.19 Passive optical guidance system

resulting magnetic field generated around the wire is detected by two inductive sensors arranged in the vehicle in a similar manner to passive optical sensors; a comparison of the magnitude of the magnetic field detected will determine whether the vehicle's actual path is off-centre from the desired path determined by the wire.

The dead reckoning method of guidance allows a vehicle to either leave a laid guidance system for a period of time or be completely free-roaming. It requires a more sophisticated on-board control as the position of the vehicle is determined by distance travelled, calculated from measurement of the number of revolutions made by the wheels. This is subject to many inaccuracies and disturbances and is generally only used in conjunction with some form of external guidance if the vehicle's range of movement is wide. Another way of controlling a free-roaming AGV is by the use of an on-board gyroscope which can detect accelerations in all directions and by numerical integration to ascertain incremental distance travelled.

The use of infra-red beams can be either passive or active. Reflective targets placed in key positions *en route* can be used passively by the vehicle as landmarks for determining position or the targets themselves can actively transmit information encoded in the beam so that they act both as a homing beacon and a communications device. A major disadvantage of such a technique is that the communication is highly dependent on a clear line of sight from the vehicle to the target and any obstructions will partially or totally cut off the beam. An alternative method of using key points in the AGV's working environment is *pattern recognition.* This requires the vehicle to have an on-board vision system which 'sees' its surroundings and makes a comparison with a pattern stored in the memory of the controller. There are many problems associated with this technique such as the need for a large memory for the controller and the fact that any alteration in the pattern of the surroundings, such as a machine being moved or objects being moved into the area, will cause a deviation with the expected pattern.

The off-board control is concerned with the whole AGV system which incorporates all automated vehicles of all types in the system and so ideally will be a part of the CIM facility for that factory. The CIM system is concerned with monitoring and controlling the whole manufacturing process and therefore will deploy any AGVs to ensure that raw materials and components are available for the manufacturing processes at the right time for maximum efficiency and hence productivity. There must therefore be reliable means of communication from the materials handling control system to the individual AGVs whatever the means of guidance. The communication must be bidirectional from the control to the vehicles and back so that any vehicle can transmit its status. The communication is either continuous, that is the controller can always communicate with a vehicle regardless of its position or state, or discrete, where communication can take place only if the vehicle is in the vicinity of a communications device.

Continuous communication is possible with inductive techniques, where data is modulated on wires buried with the guidewire or encoded in the guidewire itself, or by the use of radio transmitters and receivers; these however, are subject to interference from some manufacturing processes or other devices such as welding processes and electric motors. Discrete communication is possible using infra-red beams at key stations as already described or by inductive stations embedded in the floor at discrete points on the vehicle's path.

3.3 PROCESS CONTROL

So far in this chapter we have examined the control of manufacturing processes which are largely continuous in nature, such as the movement of machine tools, robots and other materials handling devices. There is, however, the need to control processes or parts of processes which are discrete or digital in nature and these include conveyors in the context of flow lines and the interfacing of materials handling systems and machining or assembly operations. If components or materials are supplied to a CNC machine or mechanized assembly cell by means of an AGV or conveyor then there must be some coordination between the arrival of those materials, their loading to and unloading from the machine and their transport to a further operation or process. This, by and large, involves digital control or on–off instructions signalling the starting and stopping of conveyors and machines and the handling of safety, maintenance and other manually derived conditions. This is commonly achieved by the use of *programmable logic controllers* or PLCs; a detailed introduction to PLCs and their uses in given in Crispin (1990).

3.3.1 Programmable Logic Controllers

The mechanization of manufacturing processes was conceived and used well before the advent of relevant computing technology. Assembly processes, in particular, have been mechanized using mechanically activated electrical switches, solenoids, relays and motors as well as their pneumatically powered equivalents. For example, a product in transport on a conveyor could be stopped and positioned by one or more pneumatic cylinders activated by roller actuators similar in principle to the electrical microswitch. The design and operation of such systems were based on the use of logic and electrically operated systems were designed using *ladder logic*—a means of schematically representing the on–off control of actuators.

Programmable logic controllers were first conceived in 1968 as a more flexible means of implementing mechanization than the hard-wired logic approach. The principle of the PLC was initially to enable the same logic definition methods to be used but using a programming language which meant that the 'program' could be easily modified. PLCs have been designed such that their means of programming is identical to the design tools used for hard-wired logic and so a user interface based on ladder logic has emerged and is still in frequent use today. This has meant that systems engineers have been able to utilize the new computer technology with very little retraining in design tools.

The operation of a PLC can be described by the functional block diagram in Fig. 3.20, which appears as a typical microcomputer functionally dedicated to logic control and sequencing. Like the controller for a CNC machine or robot, the microcomputer system is devised such that there is an amount of RAM (random access memory) for storage of the control program written by the user (which is an interpretation of the ladder logic diagram or other notation) such that the system programs in ROM (read only memory) can carry out the desired control. There is a form of interface to a programming console which is normally detachable because a PLC program, once proven correct, needs very little modification as most applications of PLCs, for example flow line control or flexible manufacturing cells, provide the infrastructure of automated systems and any flexibility required is built into the program. Therefore, in most cases, the RAM in the PLC is of a non-volatile type such as EEPROM, or is backed up by an internal battery so that the program is retained in the event of shut down or failure (Chapter 2).

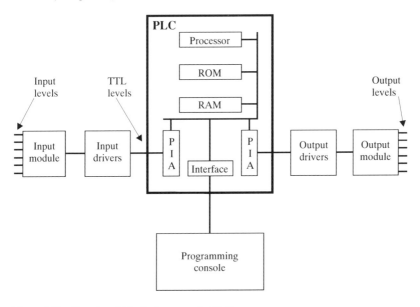

Figure 3.20   Functional block diagram of a PLC

The inputs to and outputs from a PLC vary in voltage levels according to the services being controlled. Input devices include manually activated switches, microswitches, reed switches, pressure switches, light-sensitive devices and proximity sensors. Output devices include solenoids, contactors, relays and motors of various types. The power supplies applied to these devices are normally different (24 V) from that of the microcomputer and so some conversion to an appropriate level for the PLC, normally TTL (transistor–transistor logic: true = $+5$ V, false = 0 V) is required. One way of achieving this is to use an opto-isolator as shown in Fig. 3.21, which can take a a digital input of non-TTL value and couple it to the input of the PLC.

The resulting signal is not only at the right level but is also isolated from any transient electrical noise which may be present owing to the harsh conditions of a factory floor; any rapid variations of light level in the LED caused by fluctuations in the signal applied to it are not readily responded to by the photo-transistor in the device. The input drivers therefore present the digital states of all input devices of the controlled system to the PLC which are read and stored by a digital interface device, such as a *peripheral interface adaptor* or PIA, as a binary number. Each bit of this number represents the state of each input. The outputs to controlled devices are also stored in the memory of the PLC as digits of a binary number and these states power the devices via the output drivers which convert the low power TTL signals into a suitable form. These output drivers can be voltage and power amplifiers or solid-state relays.

The PLC processes the inputs and switches the outputs according to the control program in a cyclic fashion. At the beginning of a cycle it reads the states of all the inputs and stores them as an image in memory. It then uses those input levels and the logic defined in the program to set the states of all the outputs which are also stored as an image in memory and interfaced via the PIA to the output drivers. It then repeats the cycle in a continuous loop until the program is stopped as illustrated in Fig. 3.22.

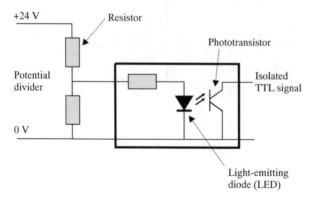

Figure 3.21 Opto-isolator input driver

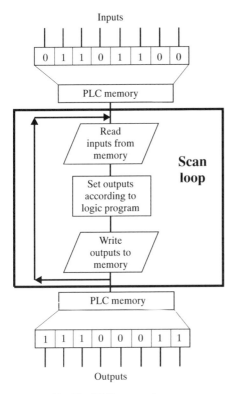

Figure 3.22 The PLC scan cycle

This cycle is known as a *scan* and it is the parameter known as the *scan time* which is an important measure of the performance of a programmable logic controller. The scan time is the period of time taken to read all the inputs and set the corresponding outputs and is a function of the power of the processor used in the PLC, the efficiency of the firmware, the complexity of the user's program and the number of inputs and outputs. Typical scan times may vary from 50 ms to 200 ms.

Programming PLCs Ladder logic is still the most commonly used programming language for PLCs and uses a concept of switches as inputs set high or low by sensors in the controlled process to activate actuators such as motors, solenoids and other internally defined control aids like timers and counters. Figure 3.23 shows some examples of ladder logic programming using direct actuation, internal relays and combinations of inputs to perform logical functions.

Ladder logic derives its name from its schematic representation which resembles a ladder. The two vertical stays are functionally equivalent to power supply lines, the left-hand stay being equivalent to $+V$ and the right

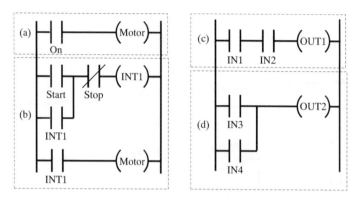

Figure 3.23 Ladder logic examples: (a) single throw switch; (b) on–off latch; (c) logical AND; and (d) logical OR

hand to 0 V. Between these are rungs which represent circuit equivalents. In Fig 3.23(a) the switch ON represents a normally open (NO) contact which when closed will complete the circuit to the MOTOR which is connected to a switched output from the PLC; when the switch is opened again then the motor will be turned off. The example in Fig 3.23(b) shows how a circuit may be *latched* using an internal relay of the PLC. The contacts START and STOP are push switches—START is a normally open, push-to-make switch and STOP is normally closed, push-to-break. If START is pressed the relay INT1 is activated to close its related contact of the same name which, because this bridges the contact START, will hold the relay energized. INT1 can have a second pole to its contact which can turn on the MOTOR, which will remain on until STOP is pressed, breaking the current to the relay which, in turn, turns off the motor. The presence of internal relays is one of the useful tools found in PLCs to enable sequencing in the mechanization of processes. Contacts can be arranged in a number of different ways to perform logic functions such as AND and OR.

Timers and counters are also important features in PLCs. They are represented in ladder logic in a number of ways depending on the PLC manufacturer; some examples are shown in Fig. 3.24.

In some cases timers and counters are shown as blocks as in Fig 3.24(a)(i), where the closure of contact IN1 resets the internal timer T1 to zero after which it will keep time in steps of hundredths or tenths of a second. The value of the timer can then be used to activate an output port or internal relay to represent a delay in the controlled process. Alternatively a timer can be shown as an internal relay with an associated time delay constant as in Fig 3.24(a)(ii). Closing contact IN2 resets timer T2 and after a delay of 10 s will close an associated contact of the same designation to activate other services, in this case an output OUT2. Representation of counters is similar as shown in Figure 3.24(b)(iii) and (iv). With the block representation a

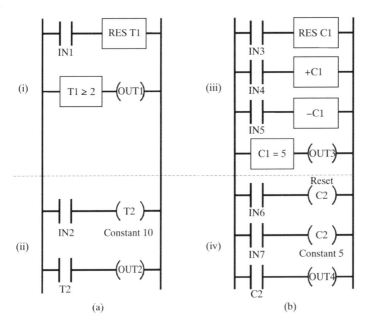

Figure 3.24 Timing and counting: (a) timers and (b) counters

contact arrangement can reset, increment or decrement a counter and the value of the counter used to activate outputs. Figure 3.24(b)(iv) shows a counter C2 as an internal relay with associated value which can be reset (by IN6), incremented (by IN7) and upon reaching the desired value activate the contact of the same name. Many PLCs using ladder logic as their programming medium use block functions for a variety of other facilities including mathematical operations on variables which can be useful when controlling systems with analogue elements.

An alternative PLC language which has emerged in recent years is *Grafcet* which is a graphical function chart programming method. The representation of a Grafcet program is similar to a flow chart where a process is defined by a series of *actions* or *steps* starting and terminating with a *transition* which represents a change of state in the process. Therefore any action cannot take place until the preceding one is complete, which ensures that the operational steps in the controlled process occur in the correct sequence. Consider the motor start/stop action in Fig. 3.23(b). This may provide the means of starting a motor or other machine at the start of an operation and stopping it at the end but the operation requiring the motor must take place in the mean time. The ladder logic rung will allow the motor to be erroneously stopped at any time during the sequence and even though the program could be redefined to prevent this, a Grafcet approach would ensure correct sequencing as shown in Fig. 3.25. Each step or action in the Grafcet program can be defined as ladder logic routines or subprograms

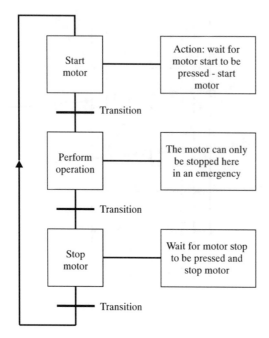

Figure 3.25 Simplified Grafcet example

which have only one entrance and exit point—a condition which computer scientists and software engineers will be quick to tell you is indicative of good program structure. Sequencing of this sort can be done using ladder logic by the use of internal relays acting essentially as transitions but it is less explicit and readable than a Grafcet program.

Another programming method which ensures correct sequencing and good readability and is provided with some PLCs is a high level textual language similar to BASIC. In such a language the states of input and output ports are considered as logical variables which can be used in programming statements of the type:

IF IN1 **AND** IN2 **THEN SET** OUT3

Further advantages of this type of programming are that input and output ports, subroutines and procedures can be given realistic and relevant names to aid programming and subsequent modification.

PLC applications The areas to which PLCs can be applied are many and varied and though mainly involving digital control, some PLCs have the ability to read and provide analogue signals which would be of particular use in such applications as temperature control. The digital control capabilities of PLCs are largely used in areas where sequencing or coordinating the activities of several machines working together is required. Examples of this type of control are assembly stations, where robots carrying out assembly tasks are activated by the arrival of components via some materials handling device, and flexible manufacturing cells where materials arrive at a cell to be processed by one or more CNC machines. The latter case is interesting because such systems may incorporate conveyors to bring materials to the cell and take finished items away to the next process, a robot to load and unload the work to and from the machines and the CNC machines themselves. The arrival of material at the cell will invoke the robot to load it to a machine and start the machining process. When finished the robot will unload the finished item and load it to another machine or to the output conveyor. Such a process needs careful coordination and communication between the machines and the PLC. Inputs to the PLC will include sensors on the input conveyor to signal the arrival of material and signals from the CNC machines and robot to indicate their status. Outputs from the PLC will need to invoke the work cycles of the robot and the CNC machines.

An assembly cell on a flow line like that shown in Fig. 3.26 could be controlled by a PLC to coordinate the movement of the conveyor, the clamping of the product and the operation of the robot with the arrival of the product into the work area, which is detected by a proximity sensor. The robot signalling the end of its assembly operation will be an input to the PLC to deactivate the clamp and restart the conveyor.

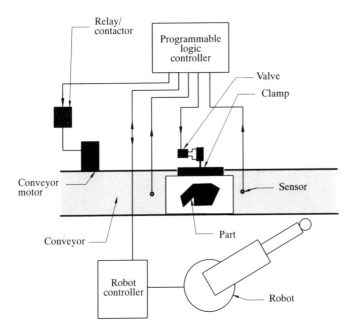

Figure 3.26 FAS cell controlled by a PLC

3.4 AUTOMATIC INSPECTION

Quality assurance is perhaps the most important activity to ensure a company's success in its market area and so much emphasis has been placed in recent years on increasing productivity in this field. The quality of a product is measured and assured at various stages throughout its manufacture by inspection of raw materials, bought in and manufactured components, subassemblies and in its finished form. Much of quality assurance is preventive and involves the inspection of machines and tools and the validation of manufacturing processes. It is therefore a monitoring process which affects the management and control of the whole factory's activities and as such can be used as a key part in a computer-integrated manufacturing system. The main area to which quality assurance can be attributed is computer-aided production planning and control and as such is the subject of further discussion in Chapter 7. The use of computers in quality assurance is therefore extensive and with regard to factory floor equipment it involves machinery for computer-aided inspection or CAI. Examples of techniques adopted in manufacture include the use of coordinate measuring machines for inspecting machined components, in-cycle gauging to check tool wear in machining operations and vision systems for subassemblies and assemblies.

3.4.1 Coordinate Measuring Machines

A coordinate measuring machine or CMM is a computer-controlled device which can be programmed to inspect the dimensions, positions and form of the features of a machined component. The object of any program devised for a CMM is to compare the machined features with the design parameters and produce a report on the variations found. This report may cause a component to be rejected but more importantly, it can be used to monitor the reliability and repeatability of a manufacturing process. A CMM consists of a flat table on to which a component is mounted and a movable head arranged in a rectangular configuration similar to a Cartesian robot or CNC machine though manufactured with greater precision. The head, which holds a sensing probe or stylus, can be positioned within its working volume under motorized control to touch key points on features in the component being inspected. It can also be orientated to measure features in any orthogonal or auxiliary plane. The probe has a hard, accurately dimensioned tip which as it touches a feature moves in the head as depicted in Fig. 3.27.

The slightest movement of the probe in any direction is detected by the head which signals the machine's controller to measure its position; the sensitivity is so great that a very accurate position is determined with negligible measuring force. Thus the head can be programmed to move and

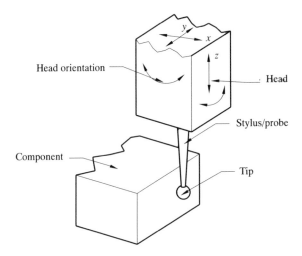

Figure 3.27 Coordinate measuring machine probe

measure the position of one point on a particular feature. The controller can carry out any numerical analysis required to ascertain the position and form of the feature from a number of such points. For example to measure the position, orientation and form of a straight edge the CMM can be programmed to touch a number of points (five or more) along its length and a circular or cylindrical feature, such as a hole, can be likewise measured by touching at points around the circumference and even at various depths. This is illustrated in Fig. 3.28 which shows that the basic geometry of a straight edge can be evaluated from two points and that of a circle from a minimum of three. More points will be needed in both cases to measure geometric tolerances or form such as flatness and cylindricity.

The programming of a CMM is much more complex than a CNC machine and so the language requirements are more stringent. The program needs to position the probe to take sufficient measurements and commands are available to evaluate geometric tolerances of features relative to each other. Programs for complex components take a long time to develop and are best generated using a productivity aid such as a CADCAM system. If a computer-aided draughting and design system were used to design the

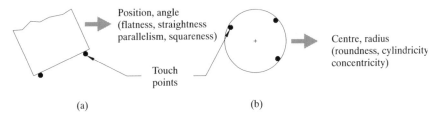

Figure 3.28 Coordinate measurement of features: (a) straight edge and (b) circle

component then all data relevant to inspection would be implicit in the model, that is feature positions and sizes and design tolerances.

3.4.2 In-cycle Gauging

The probing system for the coordinate measuring machine, or a more robust and less sensitive version of it, can also be used to inspect machined components during manufacture so that preventive quality control measures can be taken. The probe mounted in the head of a CNC machine can be positioned in a similar manner as the CMM except that the position will not be as precise and therefore the results of such measurements cannot be used as part of a final inspection report. The method is useful though for determining tool size and wear. In a fully automated system where tools are brought to a CNC machine by an AGV and automatically loaded to the machine, in-cycle gauging can determine when tools have worn excessively and need replacing. The CNC machine communicating within a CIM environment could request that new tools be brought and the old ones removed for resharpening. The new tools may be undersize and so the gauging technique could then be used to adjust tool size offsets in the CNC machine after machining one component and measuring key features. The probe can be used to measure edges and profiles and more robust devices such as air plug gauges, suitably interfaced to the controller, could measure drilled and bored holes.

3.4.3 Vision Systems

A form of automatic inspection to replace manual visual inspection can be achieved by the use of vision systems. A video camera interfaced to a microcomputer can rasterize or digitize the shape of an object and compare it with an ideal master stored in the memory of the computer. This technique is useful for components with fairly relaxed tolerances (of the order of ± 1 mm) and with complex shapes such as car body assemblies. The use of vision systems has its limitations in that the image analysed is generally monochrome and to be of acceptable resolution requires much memory in the controller.

EXERCISES

Assignment

By surveying recent literature, i.e. journals, books, magazines, etc., write a report or prepare a 10–15 minute oral presentation on *one* of the following topics:

The use and control of laser technology in manufacturing
Automatic test and inspection
Direct and distributed numerical control
Automated guided vehicles
Automated stores
The design and use of bowl feeders

Questions

3.1 With reference to hardware used in computer-aided engineering, explain the term *functionally dedicated system* and how this is differentiated from a general purpose system. Give one example of a functionally dedicated system and, by means of a diagram, explain its operation or use.

3.2 Sketch the block diagram of the structure of a typical programmable logic controller and briefly describe its principle of operations. Define the term *scan time*.

REFERENCES

Crispin, A. J. 1990, *Programmable Logic Controllers and their Engineering Applications*. McGraw-Hill, London.

Groover, M. P., M. Weiss, R. N. Nagel and N. G. Odrey. 1986, *Industrial Robotics. Technology, Programming and Applications*. McGraw-Hill, Singapore.

Hammond, G. 1986, *AGVs at Work*. IFS Publications, Bedford, UK.

FOUR

COMPUTER-AIDED DRAUGHTING
AND DESIGN

During the years from its first appearance until recently the term CAD has been used to mean either computer-aided draughting or computer-aided design. This has often caused design office management to suffer some confusion when investigating a CAD system for potential use; a draughting system may offer much less functionality than expected and hoped for, while a more complex design system may contain too much, if only assistance with the production and management of engineering drawings is required. Computer-aided draughting is a technique where engineering drawings are produced with the assistance of a computer and, as with manual drawing, is only the graphical means of representing a design. Computer-aided design, however, is a technique where the attributes of the computer and those of the designer are blended together into a problem-solving team. When the term CAD is used to mean computer-aided design it normally refers to a graphical system where components and assemblies can be modelled in three dimensions. The term design, however, also covers those functions attributed to the areas of modelling and analysis as discussed in Chapter 1. The acronym CADD is more commonly used nowadays and stands for computer-aided draughting and design; a CADD package is one which is able to provide all draughting facilities and some or all of those required for the design process.

4.1 HISTORY AND BACKGROUND

The first important step in the development of computer-aided draughting was made at the Massachusetts Institute of Technology (MIT) in 1963 where a system called *Sketchpad* was developed and demonstrated. It consisted of a cathode ray tube (CRT) driven by software running on a Lincoln TX2 computer which was able to create, modify and graphically display a drawing on the screen using a light pen as a pointing device. CAD systems today are still based on this approach but rarely use light pens as the technology in terms of hardware and software has improved considerably. The configuration of the hardware for the Sketchpad system is shown in Fig. 4.1 and this type of arrangement, where graphically displayed data can be manipulated and modified, is known as *interactive graphics*.

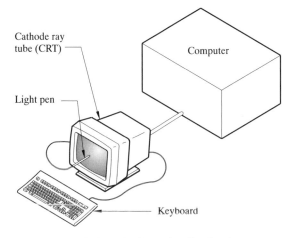

Figure 4.1   Early CAD hardware, i.e. Sketchpad

In modern systems the light pen has been replaced by more effective pointing hardware like that discussed in Chapter 2, that is a digitizer tablet, a mouse or both as shown in Fig. 4.2. The design of hardware is a key factor in easing the communication between the user and the software functions and a vital part of the software which makes use of the peripheral hardware to give the operator a usable interface to the functionality of the software is

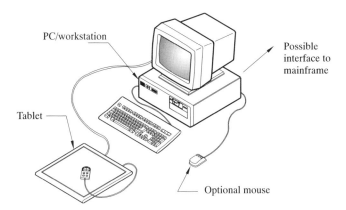

Figure 4.2   Typical modern CAD hardware configuration

called the *user interface*. The effectiveness of the user interface of any CAE system, whether it employs interactive graphics or not, should be a very important consideration when selecting a system for purchase as user interface design very much affects the efficiency of the system in terms of how easy it is to learn and use.

Draughting systems are available for personal computers, workstations, minicomputers and mainframes all of which are discussed and compared in Chapter 2. The modern personal computer is more than capable of handling the relatively simple tasks demanded by two-dimensional draughting and three-dimensional line or wireframe modelling. The latter is the simplest form of three-dimensional computer-aided design allowing the production of geometric models of a component or product for spatial and visual analysis. A personal computer is, however, limited when other forms of analysis need to be carried out such as the evaluation of mass properties or stress analysis. Design systems produced for personal computers therefore have limitations as to the complexity of the tasks undertaken. The restrictions are the amount of internal memory and performance or speed of the processor or computer. Design techniques such as finite element stress analysis, surface or solid modelling involve more complex calculations than required for simple line modelling. Personal computers are becoming more powerful as more sophisticated processors are developed which are faster and can access more internal memory. The difference between the performance of what is termed a personal computer and a workstation is fast becoming small.

The workstation, which is similar in appearance to a personal computer, is generally of higher performance and typically four to five times more expensive. Computer-aided engineering software available for workstation platforms is normally capable of carrying out the more demanding numerical analysis required of sophisticated design systems with acceptable performance in speed. A mainframe computer system is capable of supporting the functional demands of complex software packages, and for CADD systems these are accessed and presented to the user via a graphics terminal. The mainframe performs the relevant mathematical modelling and sends the results in graphical form to the terminal, which has some computing power to interpret the data received, manipulate it and display it in graphical form.

4.1.1 CADD Software Structure

In Chapter 1 we viewed the basic structure of a typical CAE software package as being a means of adding to and modifying a database under user control. Figure 4.3 shows this structure for a CADD system.

The database for a CADD package contains data defining the two- or three-dimensional geometry of the drawing or design. It can be viewed as a

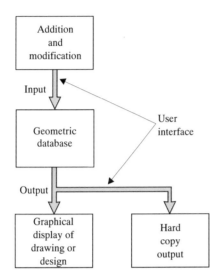

Figure 4.3 CADD software structure

mathematical model which is a precise geometrically accurate representation of the component or assembly. The input to this is the addition to and modification of the model by the designer or draughtsman and includes the addition of geometric and detail entities such as lines, curves, points, notes or dimensions and modification to correct errors and enhance productivity. These additions and modifications should immediately be seen on the graphical display, which is the main interactive output medium of the software and therefore needs to be very effective. In the case of draughting one needs to be able to add a drawn feature with as much or greater ease than one would be able to do on a drawing board.

4.1.2 User Interface Design

The design of the user interface to a CADD package, or indeed any interactive computer software, is vital to its effectiveness in increasing productivity in the activity for which it is a tool. There are a number of rules which should be adopted in designing a user interface the adherence to which should be investigated when choosing a software package for a particular task. The most important of these rules are:

- A clear, well presented screen layout.
- Easy function selection by a well-structured menu system.
- Meaningful function names.
- Meaningful and helpful prompts to the user.
- Easily accessible and clearly written help information.

A clear screen layout ensures that the user can see immediately the effects of the use of the software functions, the status of the software and any messages that the software is communicating to the user. Many graphics packages divide up the screen into a number of areas each containing different information relating to the use of the system. An example of this is shown in Fig. 4.4 which is the graphics display screen for CADKEY version 1.55. This is a 2D/3D draughting and line modelling package for use on IBM PC compatibles and its use can be studied in Goss (1990).

The menus of available functions appear at the left-hand side of the screen and are selected by moving the cursor to the desired function and pressing one of the buttons on the pointing device. It is inadvisable that any graphics package be used without one of the input pointing devices described in Chapter 2, that is a mouse or tablet or, in rare situations nowadays, a joystick or light pen. As the menu functions are selected the menu area is normally refreshed with a submenu giving the different options available for the function. In the case of CADKEY the user can see the sequence of functions selected from the main menu through the many associated submenus on the history line. A graphics-based CAE package such as a draughting, design or manufacturing system will have a large number of

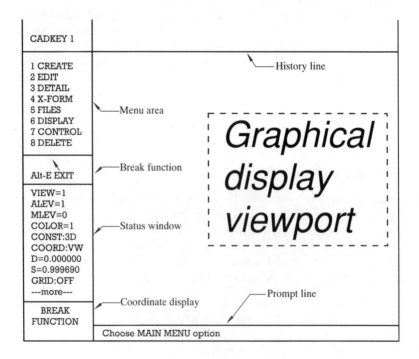

Figure 4.4 CADD graphics screen layout example: CADKEY

functions each with many options. For example, there may be many options for drawing a line by defining it by its end points on the screen, parallel or perpendicular to an existing line or tangential to one or more curves and these options would be displayed after the selection of the line draw function. The breaking down of the command repertoire of the software into many smaller menu groups eases the use of function selection and a facility like the history line in CADKEY allows the user to see the development of menu selection. Another way of displaying the sequence of menu and submenu selection is by the use of *cascading menus* which are incorporated into the user interface of a number of CADD system such as I-DEAS level VI. A cascading menu structure is illustrated in Fig. 4.5.

An advantage of cascading menus over a fixed menu area like that used in CADKEY is that all the menus selected are still displayed on the screen and so selection from a preceding menu is still possible by directly pointing to a function still partially visible. In the system used in CADKEY the user can only select previous displayed functions by using the Escape key or BACK-UP or ESC commands in the *Break function* area. A problem with cascading menus is that if the menu tree has many branches then the large number of menu windows displayed may encroach on another areas of the graphics screen.

An alternative means of selecting software functions is by means of a tablet menu system. A card with printed areas containing function names or *icons*, as illustrated in Fig. 4.6, is secured to a tablet and a function is selected by moving the puck over the desired area and pressing one of the function buttons. Most tablet menus also incorporate an area to move the puck which will allow the position of the graphics pointer on the screen to be controlled. A well-designed tablet menu system can be advantageous over a

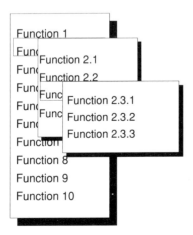

Figure 4.5 Cascading menu structure

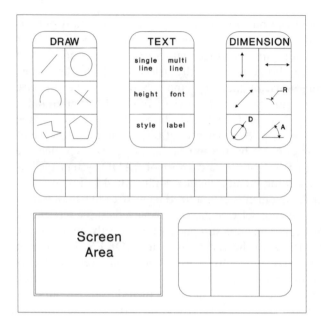

Figure 4.6 Example tablet menu card

screen menu because those areas of the screen used for the menus can be given over to displaying the drawing or design thereby increasing the visibility. This benefit has to be balanced, however, by the extra expense of a tablet which may seem unnecessary if a large monitor is used. A complex CADD system may have too many functions to fit onto one menu card, in which case a number of cards may be provided which can be placed on the tablet as needed. The initial problem encountered by many users of tablet menu systems is that it takes some practice to know where certain functions are situated on the card. Much time can be lost scanning a menu card for a function which may be vaguely described by a small icon. Some CADD systems allow the tablet menu facility to be optional so that the user can choose to select functions from the screen, the menu card or a combination of both.

As well as an easily accessible and well structured approach to function selection the actual names of the functions need to be meaningful to the intended user. A draughting and design package is intended to assist the draughtsman or designer in carrying out his or her work and the transition that needs to be made from using manual to computer-aided methods needs to be made as easy as possible. Mechanical or manufacturing engineers, having become experts in their respective fields, do not want to devote a great deal of time to becoming computer scientists as well! Therefore the functionality of a software package needs to be presented in terms with which they are familiar and so the naming system used to describe the software functions needs to be based on the relevant terminology. Consider the CADKEY example in Fig. 4.4: the first item in the main menu displayed is **CREATE** which, when investigated further, is found to be the function which allows geometry such as lines, circles, arcs, points and polygons to be drawn. Perhaps a better name for the function would be **DRAW** or **GEOMETRY** as most draughtsman understand well the concept of drawing and most know what geometry is! In this particular example the problem can hardly be considered serious as it will not take many engineers long to accustom themselves to 'creating' instead of 'drawing' geometric entities. The learning difficulties of software of this type can become serious, however, if instead of written menus the functions are described by means of icons or small symbols depicting the nature of the function. Such a system is used by the draughting package DOGS version 4.3, the screen layout of which is shown in Fig. 4.7. The intention here is not to single out any one package for criticism but to demonstrate the various ways in which commercial CADD packages present their user interfaces. DOGS has developed over many years, being one of the earliest commercially available draughting systems in the UK, and the addition of the icon menu system is an effective enhancement to the package. Icon menu systems are generally becoming more popular with CADD users and many vendors are

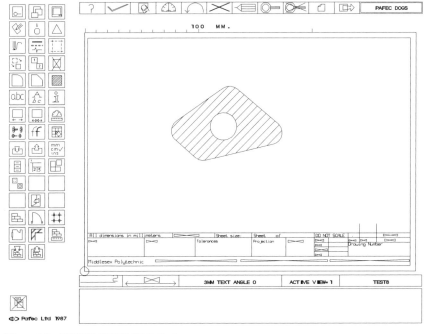

Figure 4.7 PAFEC DOGS V4.3 display screen

responding to this market demand by giving the user the option of displaying menus in this fashion as opposed to normal text. The advantage of an on-screen icon menu is that many more functions can be displayed in a given area but if the icons are too small to be easily recognizable or graphically too vague then the learning process and the software's productivity benefits can be significantly impaired.

In addition to the presentation of the functionality of the software by well-structured menus the user needs to be guided through the steps leading to the creation of modification of geometry or details. Most systems have an area on the screen dedicated to providing the user with prompts and instructions relating to the function being carried out and the clarity of these prompts are important to the usability of the software. They need to be concise for quick reading and so as not to take up too much space on the display but they also need to be meaningful, particularly for new and inexperienced users. For drawing a line the instruction '*Indicate first point*' is not quite so helpful as '*Indicate first end-point of line*'. An experienced user can find the display of prompts counter-productive, however, and so would favour the option to turn them off completely or see them only when specifically asked. Some packages give various levels of prompting and some only display an instruction when requested. Some prompts, however, have to be displayed if the software requires some typed text or numerical input for a parameter such as the radius of diameter of a circle or an angle of a line. Again, more experienced users may prefer briefer prompts such as:

Diameter (10.000)?

as opposed to:

Enter diameter of the circle (10.000):

Another enhancement to productivity which is demonstrated in these examples is the use of default values for parameters, shown in parentheses, which can be either the most common or the last value used. The user need only type in the value if it is different from the default and is useful if, for example, a large number of circles of the same diameter are to be created.

As well as prompts a package should also provide more detailed information on its functions. The user manuals which are provided with software packages are often very lengthy and specific information on how and where to use a certain function or feature of the software can be difficult to find. Many systems store abridged versions of the information from the manual with the software which can be accessed via the user interface. Many help systems of this type are *function sensitive*, that is when help is requested information is displayed about the currently selected or the user is instructed to select the menu function for which information is required. One system which uses this approach is the I-DEAS package which displays helpful information about a particular menu selection in a dedicated area on the graphics screen, which can be enlarged for easy reading and then reduced in size so as not to obscure the main design display area. Relatively few CADD systems provide this type of help, particularly those which operate on personal computers. One of the main reasons for this is that the help information has to be stored in a file or group of files on the hard disk and the size of these files can be very large and hence take up large portions of disk space and it can often be a lengthy process accessing the necessary data for display at any one time. The most common usages of help systems are during the learning period, that is when a new user is becoming familiarized with the software, and for those functions less frequently accessed by the user where a memory refresher is needed. It can be argued that such usage does not justify the disk space and programming needed to support the existence of an on-line help system but as computers become more powerful and disk drives become larger and cheaper the implementation of on-line help becomes more viable.

Thus the design of the user interface and the way it blends with the functionality of a CADD system greatly affects its efficiency and productivity and before entering into any further discussion on the efficiency of CADD systems it is worth defining the term *productivity*. At first glance it would seem that increasing productivity in the design office is producing designs or drawings more quickly and though this is largely true, it is not necessarily the complete picture. A company purchasing a CADD system may never experience a greater throughput of drawings or designs but what it may gain is an increase in complexity, functionality and quality which will put them ahead of their competitors. Being ahead of one's competitors will mean a greater share of the market and hence greater profitability. A design manager considering the purchase of a CADD system should expect the design process to be eased but not necessarily an increase in throughput in terms of physical drawings and designs.

4.2 THE DESIGN PROCESS

Graphical CADD systems are effective tools in easing the execution of the design process which, when defined simply, is the development of an idea for a new product to the launch of that product onto the market. The use of effective tools at this stage of the product development process can significantly affect both the time taken to bring the idea to the market and the performance of the product in the market place. A simplified model of the design process is illustrated in Fig. 4.8 which also shows the use of CADD and analysis systems within it. The design process is initiated by the definition and issue of a task which has arisen from a market demand or a need to respond to the launch of new products and models by the competition. The detail of the task will vary depending upon the perceived

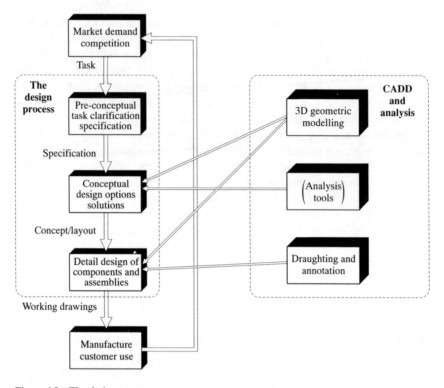

Figure 4.8   The design process

needs of potential customers and current attempts at meeting those needs either by the company or its competitors. For example, with a well-established product such as a television the task may be quite detailed specifying perhaps that it needs to replace an existing model but with enhancements. It may specify maximum size, power consumption or even design life. This could be in contrast to a less specific task statement such as 'Design a television' or 'Design a portable colour television' or even more broadly 'Design a complete modular home entertainment system'.

It is the job of the design team, therefore, to clarify the task and to eventually produce a final specification. It is this stage that provides a good opportunity to apply innovation as the design team interprets the task into a marketable and ingenious idea to meet the competition. Once the specification has been set then the conceptual and detail design process can be undertaken which will involve the use of those computer-aided engineering tools devised for the construction, modelling and analysis of components and assemblies. For maximum productivity a *concurrent*, *parallel* or *simultaneous* engineering approach should be adopted; the three terms are used synonymously to refer to the same methodology, which is discussed briefly in Chapter 1 and is the subject of more detailed treatment in Chapter 9. This approach requires that the design process, and hence the design team, involves the activity of personnel from a number of relevant departments such as product designers, process engineers, manufacturing engineers and marketing and sales personnel. This has the effect of speeding up the design process by significantly reducing the need for design changes needing to be made farther on in the product development process. Some sources, e. g. Charney (1991), estimate a ten-fold increase per stage in the cost of a design change as the product progresses through to final production. In other words if the cost of a design change made during the detailed design costs £1000 then to make a change during the design testing stage may cost £10 000 and in process planning £100 000, and so on. The benefit of concurrent engineering is that difficulties in the process planning stage, such as a component being too complex for low-cost manufacture, are very likely to be identified by the process engineer at the earliest possible time if he or she is involved from the outset of the design project. Planning and manufacturing engineers can examine designs at the earliest stages for tooling and machining purposes and any difficulties can be identified before committing them to an assembly layout. Also the use of concurrent engineering allows easy implementation of design for assembly and design for automation (DFA) techniques to be implemented with consultation with the manufacturing engineering representatives. DFA guarantees that all components are designed to a set of rules which ensure that assembly is eased particularly if automation is used. These rules and standard components (such as fasteners) which follow them can be stored in a library as part of the CADD system.

CADD packages can improve productivity at both the conceptual and detail design stages. Three-dimensional systems techniques such as *surface modellers* or *solid modellers* can be used to generate an outline of concept for a component or assembly and then modified until a final component model is completed. Assembly layouts can be devised and modified and with some systems, interference between parts can be checked and the effects of and errors from tolerance stack-up can be identified and corrected. Surface modelling, which is described in more detail later, allows the designer to create mathematical models of complex shell type components. Using this modelling technique the profile of a sculptured surface can be modified until it is both functionally and aesthetically correct and the geometry thus created used to design press or mould tools or devise CNC programs for manufacture. Solid modellers allow the creation of mathematical models of solid components which can be sectioned and analysed for mass properties such as volume, mass, surface area, and moments and products of inertia. The geometry of a solid model can also be used for manufacturing purposes and any three-dimensional geometric model can be viewed from any vantage point and thus a full working orthogonal drawing can be generated and annotated.

Many companies may not use complex geometric modelling techniques initially because of their relatively high cost. To begin with, smaller companies may wish to increase the efficiency of the design office by just automating the production of drawings as this, along with the maintenance, modification and management of a drawing office, represents one of the biggest bottlenecks in the design process. The choice of a simple draughting system, however, should always be made with the view to possible expansion to more complex geometric modelling. Many comprehensive CADD systems are modular in design and therefore allow users to begin with simple draughting and, later on, purchase modules to assist with other areas of the design process such as solid or surface modelling, stress analysis, kinematics, dynamics and manufacturing aids.

4.3 CADD FUNCTIONALITY

The basic structure of a CADD software package has already been discussed as consisting of the geometric database which can be modified and viewed by the user through the user interface. The geometric database is a mathematical model of the drawing or design and as such needs to be represented within the memory of the computer in as accurate a form as possible. One of the main benefits of a computerized draughting and design system over those of manual methods is this ability to represent the design of a component or assembly in a geometrically accurate format so that the same model can be used for other modelling, analysis and manufacturing work.

4.3.1 Geometric Accuracy

In a manual drawing a line is drawn as accurately as is possible with a pen or pencil and scale and the only reference to its real length and position would be by the inclusion of a dimension and tolerance. A manual drawing is therefore only a visual communication of a component whereas a drawing stored in a CADD system is a true geometrical model where the sizes and positions of the features are stored using real numbers; the only geometrical inaccuracies which can occur are when the drawing is plotted out, which is, effectively, a similar but more precise process to manual drawing. As an example of this consider the manual creation and issue of a drawing to a manufacture department to produce using a CNC machine program. The only references to the real size of the component that the CNC programmer has are the drawn dimensions on the sheet in front of him and so any errors in the numerical text of the dimensions will be reflected in the finished component. Now consider the use of a CADCAM system where no paper drawing is used to create the CNC program but instead the software directly uses the geometry of the CAD model as its reference for CNC program production. Provided that the model is a true representation of the desired component the ensuing CNC part program will machine the component accurately. This is because if the diameter of a circle is required to be 50 mm then it will be stored in the model as having a diameter of 50 mm as accurately as the precision of the computer will allow. Another example would be if a CADD package is able to display an orthogonal drawing of a solid model on the screen showing several views of the component. Changing a feature in any one view will automatically change the same feature in all the views. This is because each view is a 2D representation of the same 3D model and not a separate set of lines, circles and other features as is the case with a manual system of drawing creation.

4.3.2 Software Selection

There is a large variety of different CADD packages available on the market these days and the design manager is faced with the enormous problem of selecting a package to suit the demands of the company and its product range. The size of the company and the amount of investment capital available will be one of the main deciding factors but there are many other questions to be considered:

Mainframe or PC/workstation platform? A small company will not normally be able to invest in a mainframe installation unless it can be justified in terms of its use by other departments. The choice of personal computers may impose a restriction on how far the company can expand the system using its present hardware. The technological life of a PC is generally much shorter than that of more powerful systems such as minicomputers, workstations and mainframes; a PC purchased this year can be replaced by a far more powerful system and for a lower cost next year. An investment in graphics workstations such as Suns, HP Apollo, Silicon Graphics, to name but a few, would ensure a future of easier expansion in both software functionality and hardware performance.

Two dimensions or three? Lines, surfaces or solids? A large proportion of computer assistance in the design office is still restricted to pure draughting in two dimensions. A small company may find significant benefits in this but may soon find the need to expand. Most modular CADD or CAE packages have an inexpensive 2D draughting module which can be fully integrated with its geometric modelling and analysis modules. Line modelling is suitable only for limited spatial design problems—is this enough? Depending on the type of products the company produces, surface modelling, solid modelling or both may be appropriate and worth the capital outlay.

Other analysis tools needed? Does the company become involved in complex analytical design work such as stress or heat transfer analysis or the design of kinematic, dynamic or control systems? Will the ability to transfer the geometry to these modelling and analysis systems be needed?

Interaction with manufacturing needed? Will the geometry be used directly to create manufacturing data or carry out process planning? A concurrent engineering approach to product development will require the use of design geometry for the production of CNC part programs and for the design of tooling such as injection moulding dies. The kinematic analysis of some design packages may be useful for simulating processes where robots are used.

Compatibility with other systems needed? If the company carries out a lot of contract work with other companies who use CADD it does not wish to be constrained to use the same systems as those other companies. As no two CADD packages define and store models on backing store identically a procedure of conversion to and from other CADD formats will nearly always be required. There are mainly two standards that allow CADD geometry to be defined in a neutral format for conversion to models in other CADD systems. DXF or drawing exchange format has been developed by Autodesk Inc. for use with AutoCAD and many other CADD suppliers have included DXF conversion utilities in their packages. The other system is the ANSI standard IGES (or its successors PDES and STEP) and is a more comprehensive system of geometry transfer. IGES does tend, in many cases, to be unreliable because of the many ways it specifies the definition of some geometric entities.

Once these issues, which mainly cover functional aspects of CADD software selection, are clarified then in considering each CADD system that will suit the company's requirements, other questions need to be addressed regarding the implementation, use and future of the system within the design office:

How good is the maintenance and support from the suppliers? Bad maintenance and support from the software suppliers can reduce the productivity existing even prior to acquiring the CADD system thereby nullifying the many benefits that the system may offer. If the software requires a lot of maintenance and support then it is generally of poor design. Many vendors of CADD packages offer *hot-line support* facilities where a designer can phone in with a problem concerning the use of the package and speak to an expert. These problems may be of a technical nature regarding the application of the software to a specific design problem but they also may concern errors and difficulties with the actual software use. Too many of these types of request for support are time consuming and irritating.

How much, how good and how long is the training? Many software suppliers provide their own training in using their packages. Often the purchase price includes training for one or two potential users with further trainees being paid for additionally. In some circumstances the software suppliers may offer the option of an *in-house* course and send one of their trainers to the company to give instruction on the company's hardware using relevant design problems. If a commitment from the designers to study 'after hours' is sought then normal office activities are not so affected than if one or more designers are absent for a week to attend a training course at the software supplier's premises. In the latter case those attending the course should still be given the opportunity to present their own design problems. Generally speaking, software courses are expensive, being of the order of several hundred pounds per day per trainee, and this cost needs to be considered in the original investment plan for the system as the normal training budgets of engineering companies are rarely up to meeting the cost.

How easy is it to expand the system? Once a company starts down the CADD path then it rarely looks back. There will always be the need to expand both the size and capability of the system. As discussed previously a CADD system which is designed in a modular fashion will allow greater scope for expansibility.

In addition to these questions the software needs to be examined and demonstrated thoroughly so that the design manager is satisfied that it is easy to learn and use and that it will genuinely increase the productivity of his or her department and that of other engineering departments.

4.3.3 Function Availability

The ease of use of a CADD system is centred mainly around good user interface design and the performance around function availability. The two can never be separated because high functionality is useless without the ability to access it quickly and be guided carefully through its use with minimum possibility of errors. The number and range of functions in a typical CADD system are normally extensive even for the simplest draughting and line modelling systems for use on PCs. To ease the discussion and understanding of CADD system operation the functions can be said to fall into three categories:

- synthesis
- modification
- management

Synthesis type functions are concerned mainly with the creation of geometric features and drawing details. *Modification* functions include those which allow for the deletion and editing of existing geometry or detail. *Management* functions are concerned with how the drawing is presented both on the screen and eventually on paper. The three categories are explained in greater detail below as specific examples of functions are examined and can be used to categorize the functionality of complex geometric modelling systems such as surface or solid modellers as well as 2D draughting and 3D line modelling. The following discussion is restricted to draughting and line modelling and will be expanded later to include surface and solid modelling.

Geometry creation   Geometry creation is a synthesis type function. A CADD software package should have facilities to create all the necessary geometric entities in a variety of standard line types according to a known drawing standard such as BS 308. Geometric entities in a draughting system include:

- *Straight lines* for outlines, centre and hidden lines.
- *Circles* for holes and other circular features.
- *Arcs* for curved edges, fillets, centre lines.
- *Points* for reference.
- *Curves*, i. e. conic sections and fitted curves.

Functions should also be available to create regular shapes consisting of a number of these entities such as *rectangles*, *polygons* and *polylines*. In some cases these constructions will be stored in the database as separate line or arc segments and in other cases they may be treated as one entity. Some geometry creation functions are difficult to classify as pure synthesis, for example the creation of fillets, whether they be arcs or chamfers, requires some mathematical calculation to position the fillet and trim the lines which construct it. It could be considered as a mixture of a synthesis and modification type function because even though a rounded or chamfered edge is synthesized, other features are modified to accommodate it.

We have discussed the importance of a drawing or design being a geometrically accurate model of the design and in order to achieve this the entities need to be positioned precisely. There should be a number of drawing aids available in the package for doing this which include such tools as snapping to a predefined grid, locating the end points or centres of existing entities, locating the intersection of two entities or the common tangent of two or more entities. Figure 4.9 shows the display screen for a simple 2D draughting system ARDRAFT during the creation of a line segment between two points indicated on the screen using a snap tool. (ARDRAFT is a simple 2D draughting program developed for educational purposes by the author.)

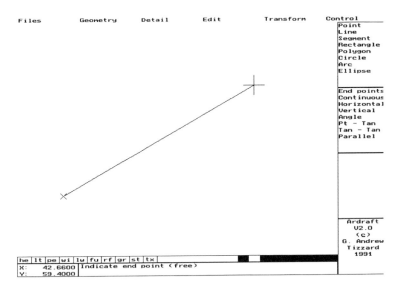

Figure 4.9 Creating a line in ARDRAFT V2.0

The history of the function selection is shown by the display of the sub-menus and is *Geometry/Segment/End points*. These are the functions selected from the main menu positioned along the top of the screen to create a line segment defined by specifying its end points. A menu showing the different ways of indicating coordinates is popped-up by pressing the middle mouse button from which the *Snap* option can be selected. The cursor will then only move to the nearest snap position as the mouse is moved and the desired end point location indicated when another mouse button is pressed. The incremental distance can be changed in both directions from the *Control* menu. The line shown in the illustration is not complete as the screen has been captured just as the user is moving the cursor to the second point. The line drawn between the first point and the cursor is referred to as a rubber band. Rubber banding is a useful facility which allows the user of a graphics package to see how the entity is to be positioned before actually doing so.

Drawing details In producing a drawing either with a pure draughting package or from a 3D design in a CADD system the software needs to be able to provide facilities for details or annotation on the drawings namely: *notes, labels, dimensions, tolerances, arrows* and *cross-hatching*. Each will use text, geometric entities or a mixture of the two. The user will need to be able to draw text of varying height, width, angle and text style or font. Dimensioning needs to be automatic so that only the feature to be dimensioned and the position of the dimension line or text needs to be specified. Some packages use associative dimensioning so that, when the size of a feature is changed, the dimension and its text automatically changes.

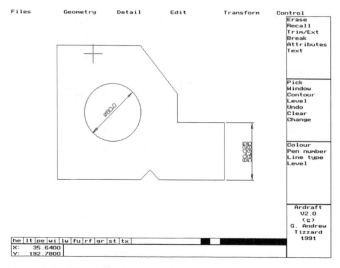

Figure 4.10   Dimensions in ARDRAFT V2.0

Figure 4.10 shows a linear vertical and diameter dimension created by ARDRAFT. The positioning tools were used to pick the end points of the dimensioned line and these points become the reference points. The position of the dimension text was indicated using the cursor and the dimension lines; arrows and text were automatically drawn. ARDRAFT does not use true associative dimensioning so if the height of the component or hole diameter were ever changed then the dimension would have to be erased and redefined.

Cross-hatching again needs to be automatic as the algorithm or programming procedure is relatively simple but gives significant productivity gains. Consider the difference in time taken for a draughtsman to painstakingly draw the sectional view in Fig. 4.11 on a drawing board and the simple procedure of using the CADD system to select the geometry and simply state the angle of the cross-hatch lines and their separation, leaving the software to do the rest. Many packages provide various cross-hatching styles for different applications.

Predefined components and features   One the main areas where CADD increases productivity is in the ability to draw on previous design experience. Companies often manufacture parts of similar geometry or use particular parts many times within their product range. Also items which are used often such as fasteners (screws, nuts, bolts, rivets) should not have to be drawn over and over again when, for example, an assembly drawing is being created. Many CADD systems provide a variety of ways to create libraries of standard parts or shapes which can be inserted into a drawing at any position, scale and rotation as part of the synthesis of a design. These library

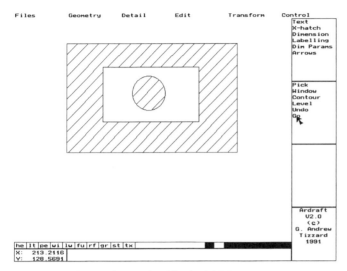

Figure 4.11 Automatic cross-hatching in CADD

elements are known by many names depending on the system and how they are created:

- *Pattern.* A group of geometric/detail entities which define a component which can be positioned, scaled and rotated (e.g. CADKEY).
- *Block.* Often used instead of pattern (e.g. AutoCAD).
- *Shape.* A set of lines which make up a known shape but may have limited geometrical accuracy (e.g. AutoCAD).
- *Symbol.* A group of entities like a pattern which may or may not have limited geometrical accuracy (e.g. DOGS).
- *Macro.* Somewhat different in concept to any of the above as the term normally refers to a sequence of function selections which create a component, detail or feature automatically. In other words it is like a program which carries out the operation procedure a user would in synthesizing a part of a design but may have points at which the user can insert his or her own variables or parameters.
- *Parametric.* A group of geometric or detail entities which are defined geometrically relative to each other or have entities or features which can be of varying size. The values of the variable will be entered by the user when prompted during the insertion of the parametric into the drawing or design. This is particularly useful for storing families of components of similar geometry but differing feature sizes, e.g. gears, fasteners, etc.

Modification The synthesis of a design has been examined as consisting of those functions which create the basic design from the designer's concept. In addition to synthesis the design can be developed further by modification which includes the erasure of entities which have been inserted by mistake or simply added for construction purposes, as well as changing the form, position, size and attitude of already designed features. If a particular complex feature appears several times in a design there should be no need to recreate the feature at every point it appears. It should be possible to copy the feature to any position, at any scale and at any rotation as many times as possible. This is illustrated in Fig. 4.12 where the arrangement of holes was defined only once and then copied once to provide two side-by-side. The two thus created were copied twice more in order to create the six arrangements as shown. Such a function is known as *transformation*. There are three types of transformation:

- *Translation*. The movement of entities from one coordinate position to another.
- *Scaling*. The changing of the physical size of each entity by a known factor relative to a known datum.
- *Rotation*. Rotating each entity by a known angle about a known origin.

With each type of transformation the entities can be either just moved or copied to the new position, size or attitude. Such facilities are very powerful in increasing productivity as the arrangement shown in Fig. 4.12 took a fraction of the time that it would have done if each arrangement was created individually. Other features which can be classified as modification are

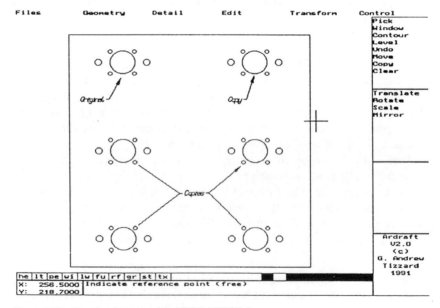

Figure 4.12 Copying features with ARDRAFT V2.0

deletion of entities, trimming entities to different sizes using other entities and the creation of fillet radii and chamfers.

Management   The management of a drawing or design is an important part of the process. Functions which can be classified as management functions include:

- *Display management.* Zooming, panning of views for ease of display and detailed work. The arrangement (in 3D) of view ports showing views of a model from different directions.
- *Entity attributes.* Colour and plotter pen allocation. Each entity will have its own display colour and possibly its own pen number for plotting purposes. Often the pen selected when plotting is derived from the display colour.
- *Line types.* Each geometric entity will have its own line type or style depending on its purpose in the drawing. Typical line styles include solid, centre lines (line of symmetry) and dashed (hidden lines).
- *Detail attributes.* Detail entities such as text and dimensions need to be specified by attributes such as text height, font, aspect ratio, tolerance size and type.
- *Groups, levels or layers.* Entities can be grouped together for easier handling in modification. Entities can be placed on different layers or levels similar in concept to overhead projection slides. Each layer can be handled separately for modification purposes or turned on or off. An example of layer usage would be to place each component of an assembly on a different layer so that the assembly process can be evaluated and demonstrated.

Most of the management functions involve the setting of modal variables. For example if the current drawing colour is set to green then all subsequently created entities will be green until the drawing colour variable is changed. Display management is perhaps the most important factor in increasing productivity during the design synthesis. The ability to zoom into some detail for creation or modification allows for greater detail and accuracy. The ability to view a 3D model from many directions gives a better understanding of the design created so far. Figure 4.13 shows the CADKEY screen set up with four viewports, three of the which show the design in the three basic planes: xy, yz and xz. The fourth viewport shows the design in isometric projection.

4.4 CADD OPERATION

As previously discussed the structure of CADD software, particularly that which uses interactive graphics, is based on the design or drawing being

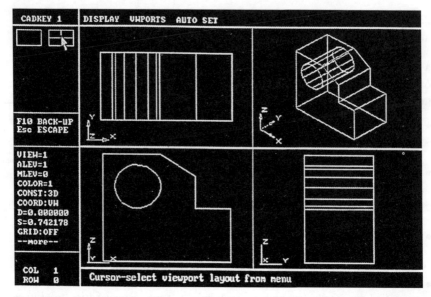

Figure 4.13   Four viewpoint display in CADKEY

represented as a geometrically accurate model. This model is made up of a number of *data structures* each of which represents a geometric or detail entity. A data structure is essentially a *record* of information containing *fields* or variables of values pertaining to the geometry of the entity. Field contents include such data as the *x*-coordinate of a point, the radius of a circle or the colour or line type of the entity. For a two-dimensional draughting package, examples of geometric entities include points, lines, circles and arcs and examples of detail entities are text, dimensions, and cross-hatching. It is this data base of entities which is added to and modified by the user during the design synthesis, modification and management via the user interface.

4.4.1 Geometric Parameters

In order to achieve the desired geometric accuracy each entity is represented in the database as a set of parameters expressed as real numbers. The number and meaning of the parameters are different for each entity type and it is the set of parameters which together define the data structure for the entity type. It is important to note that the parameters which define the geometry of an entity are expressed as real numbers, that is they have a mantissa and exponent so that the numeric range is at least -10^{-17} to 10^{17} and in many cases it is much greater than this. The minimum precision one can expect in a CADD package for a geometric parameter is equivalent to six decimal places.

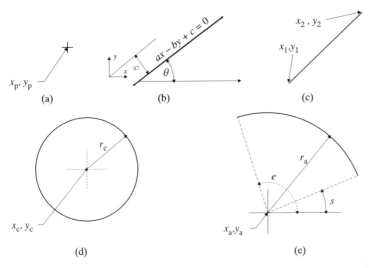

Figure 4.14 Geometric parameters for (a) point; (b) infinite line; (c) line segment; (d) circle; and (e) arc

The geometric parameters for a number of geometric and detail entities for 2D draughting are described below; some typical geometric entities are shown in Fig. 4.14. The point entity, which is quite commonly found in 2D and 3D CADD systems, is used mainly as a reference during design synthesis. The geometric parameters are the coordinates of the point x_p, y_p for a 2D package and for a three-dimensional system this definition can be expanded to three coordinates x_p, y_p, z_p. The method of representing the point will vary from system to system, for example in CADKEY it is drawn on the screen and plotted as a plus sign or ' + ', while with other packages it may be represented as an 'x' or simply as a small dot.

The straight line entity can often appear in two forms, namely the *infinite line* and the *line segment*. In fact a true mathematical definition of a line is that it is of infinite length and any line of finite length is simply a segment of that line. Many CADD packages allow both types of line to be defined and others normally only define line segments. A straight line is defined by the equation:

$$ax - by + c = 0 \qquad (4.1)$$

where

$$a = \sin \theta, \qquad b = \cos \theta, \qquad (4.2)$$

and c is the perpendicular distance from the origin (0, 0) to the line. The infinite line can therefore be defined by the parameters a, b and c. The line segment is defined by its end points which for two-dimensional systems is four parameters x_1, y_1 and x_2, y_2; for three-dimensional systems this becomes six parameters or three coordinates for each end point. A line segment can easily be converted to an infinite line by Pythagoras' theorem. The length of a line segment is evaluated from the equation:

$$l = \sqrt{(y_2 - y_1)^2 + (x_2 - x_1)^2} \qquad (4.3)$$

and

$$a = \frac{(y_2 - y_1)}{l}, \qquad b = \frac{(x_2 - x_1)}{l} \qquad (4.4)$$

and

$$c = by_1 - ax_1. \qquad (4.5)$$

The *circle* entity is defined simply by three parameters, whereas the arc entity requires five parameters. Many CADD packages do make a distinction between circles and arcs but they can be in fact defined by one data structure. An arc is defined by the coordinates of its centre point, its radius and its start and end angles measured clockwise from the horizontal axis. A circle is simply defined by its centre coordinates and its radius. However, a circle is a closed arc where the start angle is $0°$ and the end angle $360°$ (2π radians). The start and end points of an arc can be easily calculated; the start point by

$$x_s = r_a \cos s, \qquad y_s = r_a \sin s \qquad (4.6)$$

and the end point by

$$x_e = r_a \cos e, \qquad y_e = r_a \sin e. \qquad (4.7)$$

Detail entities such as text, cross-hatching and dimensions also require some geometric parameters. Cross-hatching is, in most cases, defined as a series of line segments grouped together so that they can be manipulated as an entirety. Dimensions are again a collection of entities grouped together. A typical dimension such as that shown in Fig. 4.15(a) consists of two leader

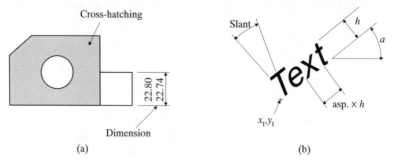

Figure 4.15 Detail entities (a) cross-hatching and dimension; and (b) text parameters

lines (line segments), a dimension line (one or two lines with arrow heads) and some text.

Text in CADD systems needs to be defined such that it can be drawn on a plotter. Therefore each character needs to be defined as a series of small line segments. The complete collection of characters specified in this way is known as a font and is normally stored as a file on disk. There is normally a range of such files to provide a range of different text styles which can be loaded into the system as required. There must be the ability to display a piece of text on a drawing at any height h and angle a and in order to show text in italic form a *slant angle* or *obliquing angle* for each character may be specified. The *aspect ratio* or *width ratio* defines the ratio of the width of each character to its height and hence specifies the physical length of the text. The coordinate position of the text may be defined as its physical centre or as the lower left corner of the first character, shown as x_t, y_t in the illustration of Fig. 4.15(b).

4.4.2 Attribute Parameters

In addition to the parameters which define the geometry of entities a CADD package must also store, for each entity, its attributes. Examples of entity attributes are:

- colour;
- line type;
- plotter pen number;
- the layer or level on which it appears.

The *colour* attribute is that in which the entity appears on the graphics screen and is stored as a field in the record for the entity as an integer representing the colour number in the palette of the graphics system. It may also refer to the *pen number* which is selected when the entity is plotted, in which case the pen number attribute is not required. Some CADD systems only use the colour number for pen selection, others give the user a choice as to whether to use colour or an alternative pen numbering system. The *line type* attribute would be an integer value representing the line type style to be used for the entity. The numeric value for each line type will then be mapped to a physical type or style in the CADD system, for example *solid, dashed, dotted, chain-dot* or *chain-dashed*. The use of *layers* or *levels* in CADD systems is common: different entities can be placed on different layers which can be optionally displayed. This is particularly useful for assembly drawings or complex designs which have many interacting parts which need not all be displayed as one drawing. The layer attribute may be just an integer value specifying the layer number or a character string storing its name.

For those readers familiar with the Pascal programming language, the parameters which define the entities are illustrated further in Fig. 4.16

```
type
    elemtype=(pttype, segment, lntype, arctype, cirtype, ellipse, texttype, hatchtype, dimtype,
                                                                                        symtype);
    textline = record
        nextptr    :       pointer;
        s          :       string;
    end;
    textptr = `textline;
    vertex = record
        xv,yv      :       real;
    end;
    oneseg = record
        x1,y1,x2,y2    :     real;
    end;
    seglist = array[1..2000] of oneseg;

    vertexlist = record
        n    :     word; {size = n*sizeof(vertex)+sizeof(word)}
        v    :     array[1..4000] of vertex;
    end;
    dimstr = string[20];
    dimdata = record
        sega,segb,segc,segd,dia:     boolean;
        x1, y1, x2, y2, v, sc   :    real; {actual dim points and size}
        xa1, ya1, xa2, ya2      :    real; {first extension line}
        xb1, yb1, xb2, yb2      :    real; {second extension line}
        xc1, yc1, xc2, yc2      :    real; {dimension line}
        xd1, yd1, xd2, yd2      :    real; {dimension line}
        xt, yt, ang             :    real; {text pos and angle}
        s1, s2                  :    dimstr; {dimension text strings}
    end;
    dimptr = `dimdata;
    hatchptr = `seglist;
    vertexptr = `vertexlist;
    filename = string[8];
    grouptype = record
        prevptr, nextptr : pointer;
        name             : string[20];
    end;
    gptr = `grouptype;
    element = record
        prevptr         : pointer;
        nextptr         : pointer;
        col, linetype   : word;
        temp            : integer;
        pen             : byte;
        group           : gptr;
        number          : integer;
        level           : byte;
        tag             : boolean;
        arr1, arr2      : real;
        case e          : elemtype of
            pttype      : (xp,yp : real);
            segment     : (x1,y1,x2,y2 : real);
            lntype      : (a,b,c : real);
            arctype     : (xa,ya,sta,enda,ra : real);
            cirtype     : (xc,yc,rc : real);
            ellipse     : (xe,ye,ste,ende,xr,yr,ang : real; res : word; vp : vertexptr);
            texttype    : (xt,yt,h,angt,aspt,slt : real; font: word; st : textptr);
            hatchtype   : (xh,yh : real; nsegs : word; hp : hatchptr);
            dimtype     : (xd,yd : real; dtol,dtyp,npl : byte; dfnt : word;
                                        dhgt,dasp,ds1,tol1,tol2 : real; dp : dimptr);
            symtype     : (xy,yy,sx,sy,angs,skew : real; sf : filename; symno : byte);
    end;
    elemptr = `element;
```

Figure 4.16   Extract from database unit of ARDRAFT 2.0

which is the entity data structure definitions for ARDRAFT V2.0. The main area of consideration here is the data structure *element* which defines all the attribute parameters for all elements or entities and the geometric parameters for each of the entities: point, line, segment, circle, arc, ellipse, text, dimension, cross-hatch and symbol. Using these parameters each entity added to the database can be accessed and used to carry out the activities of normal CADD operation. The drawing can be displayed on the graphics screen by taking each entity in turn, applying calculations for the current window settings for the display, that is the area of drawing in which the system is zoomed, and calling the standard library of graphics routines to draw lines, arcs, etc., on the screen using the colour and line-style for the entity. The geometric parameters can also be used in the various numerical methods needed throughout the creation of an engineering drawing.

4.4.3 Numerical Methods in CADD

There are many instances in the use of CADD where entities are created or edited using other entities and these tasks require the use of certain numerical methods. Examples of such tasks include trimming or extending lines and circles, creating fillet radii and chamfers and constructing lines for cross-hatching. Also facilities will exist to create circles using three existing or specified points. One example of the numerical methods to be discussed in this section, which enable such synthesis and modification to take place, is the calculation of the point of intersection of two lines. The method and algorithm can be expanded further to generate routines for evaluating the intersection of a line and a circle or a circle with another circle and the method of constructing a circle through three points. Further development and use of these numerical methods can lead to the method of generating a cross-hatch pattern of made up of angled line segments.

Intersection of two lines Figure 4.17 shows two lines of which the intersection point x, y is to be found. If the two lines are segments then

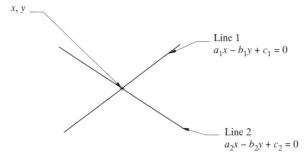

x, y

Line 1
$a_1x - b_1y + c_1 = 0$

Line 2
$a_2x - b_2y + c_2 = 0$

Figure 4.17 Intersection of two lines

the parameters a, b and c for each can be found using Eqs (4.3), (4.4) and (4.5). The following procedure is simply an implementation of elementary coordinate geometry but serves to illustrate how the geometric parameters need be accessed to carry out a common CADD procedure.

The two lines are defined by the equations:

$$a_1 x - b_1 y + c_1 = 0 \tag{4.8}$$

and

$$a_2 x - b_2 y + c_2 = 0. \tag{4.9}$$

from Eq. (4.9)

$$x = \frac{b_2 y - c_2}{a_2}; \tag{4.10}$$

substitute Eq. (4.10) for x in Eq. (4.8):

$$\frac{a_1 b_2}{a_2} y - \frac{a_1 c_2}{a_2} - b_1 y + c_1 = 0, \tag{4.11}$$

i.e.

$$a_1 b_2 y - a_1 c_2 - a_2 b_1 y + a_2 c_1 = 0;$$

therefore

$$y = \frac{a_1 c_2 - a_2 c_1}{a_1 b_2 - a_2 b_1}. \tag{4.12}$$

Substituting Eq. (4.12) for y in Eq. (4.8) gives

$$x = \frac{b_1 y - c_1}{a_1}. \tag{4.13}$$

4.5 GEOMETRICAL MODELLING

Geometrical modelling is a general term applied to three-dimensional computer-aided design techniques. There are three main types of geometrical modelling used, namely: *line* or *wireframe* modelling, *surface* modelling and *solid* modelling. Each have their own particular applications in the design of engineering components which is dependent on the ability of the method to model certain geometric structures effectively and generate the correct data for analysis. The function of computer-aided design has already been examined as the means to be able to model a component or product as a geometrically accurate mathematical model. The usefulness of the model in the design process depends on whether it is a line, surface or solid model or in fact any combination of the three. Each method has its own capabilities in allowing the designer to visualize and analyse the model but all should interface to 2D draughting so that a working engineering drawing of a 3D model can be generated.

4.5.1 Line or Wireframe Modelling

Line modelling or, as it is often called, wireframe modelling is the simplest form of geometrical representation of an object. Two-dimensional draughting is in fact a form of line modelling, the major difference being that point information is stored as three coordinate values and the definition of circles and arcs may specify a plane of orientation. As with 2D draughting, a component is stored in the computer as a series of geometric entities which simply represent the boundaries, edges or vertices of the component model. Figure 4.18 is a wireframe model of a simple component and at first glance it is not easy to determine the shape of the object as no hidden lines have been removed. A line modelling package has little or no real ability to carry out hidden line removal automatically, as to do so requires some knowledge of the form of the surfaces between the edges. Most three-dimensional packages which run on personal computers tend to be restricted to simple line modelling. It is still possible to model a component in three dimensions but the difficulty lies in the understanding of the component geometry and how it should be represented in the CAD

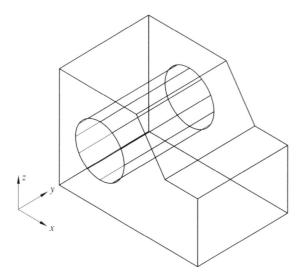

Figure 4.18   A line or wireframe model

model. A sphere for example is difficult to model because the system can only understand circles defined in any one plane.

The use of a 3D line modelling system is somewhat different from that of 2D draughting because the software is only able to present one or more two-dimensional images of the model on the graphics screen. The horizontal or x direction and the vertical or y direction on the screen may not correspond to the real world x and y directions. The component being modelled will, in many cases, have features defined in auxiliary planes other than the standard xy, xz and yz orthogonal planes and so some clearly defined and easy to use method of drawing in other planes is required. The creation of the model in Fig. 4.18 is relatively simple and can be done by creating the profile, including the hole, in the xz plane and then instructing the software to give the profile a depth. The process by which the software then creates the 3D model is to copy the profile in the y direction and join up the vertices with line segments. To create a feature, for example a hole or boss, on the sloping face presents a more complex problem. In this case a new working or reference plane with an origin at the face will need to be defined which will then be a new coordinate system for defining new features, as illustrated in Fig. 4.19.

A similar, yet alternative approach to this, is to define the reference plane as a view which will then be displayed on the screen with the xy plane coincident with the plane of the screen and the new z direction normal to the screen towards the user.

A component modelled using three-dimensional line modelling is very simple to convert to a 2D orthogonal drawing but will require some

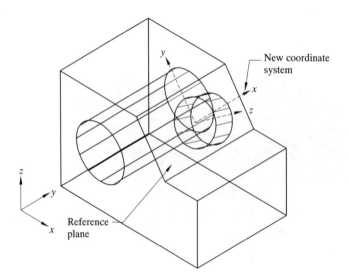

Figure 4.19 Auxiliary coordinate system for 3D modelling

processing. Normally this involves copying the component as seen from relevant points in space to produce the desired views, positioning them on the drawing sheet and removing or editing hidden lines in each view as required. The resulting views will therefore be inaccurate copies of the actual model because edges and vertices will have been removed by the hidden line removal process, but they are geometrically accurate in two dimensions and so are suitable for hard-copy presentation purposes.

4.5.2 Surface Modelling

Surface modelling defines a component with greater mathematical integrity as it models the surfaces to give more definitive spatial boundaries to the design. It is particularly useful for modelling objects which can be modelled as shells, such as car body panels, aircraft fuselages or fan blades. Figure 4.20 is an example of the kind of modelling application for which surface modelling is ideally suited. A complex surface can be very difficult to visualise without a physical model and surface modelling using a computer eases this process considerably. Before computer-aided surface modelling existed, automobile profiles had to designed by making a clay model of the car body work and by trial and error methods this model was shaped until aesthetically and functionally satisfactory. The geometry of the body panels was then determined by physical measurement of the clay. With surface modelling and the facilities which exist within a good surface modelling package, the aesthetic shape and the three-dimensional geometry are defined in one process and can be altered or sculpted interactively on the graphics screen.

The basis of a surface is the definition of a curve in two dimensions in a given plane. This can then be *swept* along another curve defined in another

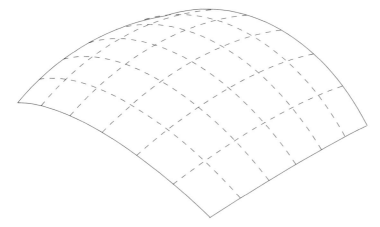

Figure 4.20   A surface modelled shell

plane. It is the definition of the sweeping and swept curves which determine the characteristics of the *surface patch*. The surface modelling software should contain curve fitting techniques such as Bezier curves, cubic splines and B-splines. The method of operation curve fitting techniques is to define a number of control points in the required plane and fit the desired curve type through the points; this is described in more detail in a number of texts, including Onwubiko (1989) and Hsu and Sinha (1992). The shape of the curve can then be accurately controlled by adjusting the positions of the control points which provides the interactive sculpting facility.

As a surface model defines adequate data on a component's surface geometry hidden lines and surfaces are readily and automatically removed as required. This gives rise to non-ambiguous visualization of the object when viewed from any direction. It is also possible to render or shade the view which is a valuable visualization tool available to a designer as it enables an almost real image to be displayed. The principle of shading is to create an imaginary light source to shine on a three-dimensional image. The amount of reflectivity from the object's surface can be adjusted for greater realism. The software calculates the amount of light reflected back to the user from different areas on the surface and each area is colour filled with varying shades accordingly.

4.5.3 Solid Modelling

Solid modelling takes the designer into areas of still greater realism than that of surface or line modelling. As well as the object's surfaces being mathematically represented the solid mass between the surfaces is also defined. There are two types of solid modelling methods used in modern CAD systems: *boundary representation* (B-Rep) and *construction solids geometry* (CSG). With the B-Rep method a shape or profile is defined and then either a solid of revolution is produced about a given axis or the shape is extruded in a given direction. The solid model thus produced is defined in the geometric database by a data structure specifying the positions of vertices and the form of surfaces. Construction solids geometry modellers provide a range of solid primitives such as spheres, cylinders, cuboids, wedges, etc., which can be defined at any size, position and orientation. The principle is used that any object can be constructed from a combination of the primitives supplied. The primitives are combined together using *Boolean operations* which enable two or more objects to be added, subtracted or intersected together and the model is defined as a list of primitives and their positions and the Boolean operations carried out between them. The example in Fig. 4.21, produced using the solid modeller in I-DEAS, can be defined by a vertical cylinder with a horizontal cylinder subtracted from it.

I-DEAS, like many other solid modelling systems such as CATIA, is not in fact a pure CSG modeller but has CSG functions for the creation of and

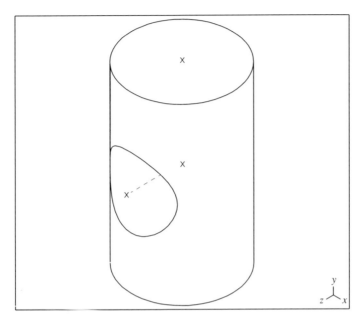

Figure 4.21   A solid model

operations on solid primitives. There are also geometry construction
facilities for creating profiles and generating models by extrusion and
revolution of those profiles as illustrated in Fig. 4.22. The solids thus
generated can then be treated as primitives so that other generated solids or

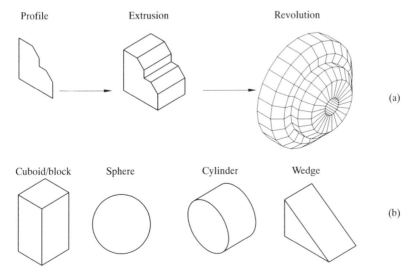

Figure 4.22   Solid modelling function: (a) B-Rep operations; and (b) common CSG primitives

primitives can be used to modify them by Boolean operations. Most modern solid modellers therefore are not generally constrained to use on one modelling method but are a hybrid of both B-Rep and CSG methods. This gives greater flexibility and the ability to define more complex objects. The use of CSG alone can limit the complexity of the model created, even though the range of primitives may be extensive and include those shown in Fig. 4.22(b) as well as torus, cone, pipe, pyramid and sections of these such as frustum, cylinder section and hemisphere.

Boolean operations which can be carried out between primitives are:

- *Addition, union, join.* Primitives are joined together to form one solid and a prerequisite for the success of this operation is that the two primitives are touching or partially intersecting one another. An application of this operation would be the addition of a projecting feature on the main body of a component; the addition of a circular boss would require the generation and the positioning of a cylinder followed by a union operation.

- *Subtraction, cut.* One primitive is subtracted from another to leave a void or hole which requires complete or partial intersection between the two solids. The subtracted primitive or solid is used as a template for the cavity desired in that which it is subtracted from. An application of subtraction would be the creation of a hole or cavity in a component. The cut operation can also be carried out by the creation of a cutting plane as opposed to another solid primitive. The solid is cut or split in two by the cutting plane and the option given to the user as to which side to keep or remove.

- *Intersection.* The two primitives or solids are intersected and the resulting solid is the common solid material between the two. The operation obviously requires complete or partial intersection between the two solids in the operation. This operation has a useful application in the creation of a solid model of complex geometry where the profiles when viewed from two or more orthogonal planes are known. Each profile can be generated in each plane and extruded to the correct depth or height and the two extrusions intersected to create the final model.

In addition to profile construction and operations, primitive creation and Boolean operations which can be classified as synthesis type functions, many solid modellers provide useful modification functions for the creation of chamfers, fillets and rounded corners. Although they are modification tools from the user's point of view, they mainly involve the creation of geometry and Boolean operations which are transparent to the user. An edge can be chamfered by the creation of an angled block or cutting plane followed by a subtraction, cut or split operation. A fillet, for an internal corner, is generated by the addition of a section created by a triangular prism from which a cylinder has been subtracted. An external edge can be rounded by chamfering to the correct size and adding a cylinder.

The main differences between pure CSG and B-Rep modelling systems, however, are in the ways in which a model is represented and stored in the geometric database and how that data is processed for graphical output. A CSG model is defined as an ordered binary tree in which the primitives are defined by their position, size and orientation and objects are represented as Boolean expressions between the primitives. Further construction of an object is stored as Boolean operations between additional primitives and an existing object or between two objects. Figure 4.23 shows a simple object modelled with a CSG system and Fig. 4.24 shows how such a model would be typically represented within the geometric database. The final object, OBJ3, is constructed from three blocks or cuboids and one cylinder and the modeller defines primitives according to how they are defined by the user.

With this pseudo-modeller, a block defined with its centre as a reference point is specified as BLCEN and one referenced by its corner as BLCNR. Therefore the block BLK1 is defined by its centre: its dimensions are 100 mm long by 80 mm wide by 70 mm high, its centre point is at the origin

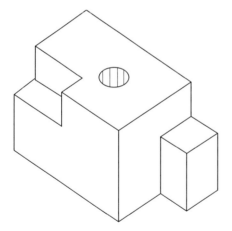

Figure 4.23 CSG modelling example

```
BLK1 = BLCEN(100,80,70,0,0,0,0,0,0)
BLK2 = BLCNR(45,30,20,-50,-40,35,0,0,0)
OBJ1 = BLK1 - BLK2
CYL1 = CYLEN(90,10,10,0,0,90,0,0)
OBJ2 = OBJ1 - CYL1
BLK3 = BLCNR(25,50,30,50,-40,35,0,0,0)
OBJ3 = OBJ2 + BLK3
```

Figure 4.24 Example of CSG model representation

(0, 0, 0) and it is not rotated about any of the three Cartesian axes. The cylinder, CYL1, is defined as being 90 mm long with a 10 mm radius, its centre point is at $x = 10$, $y = 0$, $z = 0$, and rotated about the x axis by 90 degrees.

In order to display a pure CSG model, the software must be able to evaluate the positions of all the vertices and edges of the model after evaluating the Boolean expressions which go to make it up.

The representation of a B-Rep model within the geometric database is based on the notion that a solid is bounded by a number of faces and these faces are effectively bounded surfaces. By establishing with the database the side of the surface where there is material, a solid can be defined. Such a system is far more memory intensive in the storage of a solid model than a pure CSG modeller but, because edges and vertices are more fully defined within B-Rep, the programming procedures for its presentation onto a graphics display are far simpler. The procedures for converting a CSG model into B-Rep are well established.

The majority of commercial solid modellers available nowadays use a combination of B-Rep and CSG modelling techniques and representations. Objects can be created using the sweep methods of revolutions and extrusion and the results stored as B-Rep data, but identifiable as primitives so that they can be combined with other objects and primitives to realize the final design.

EXERCISES

Assignment

Consider the drawing of a simple component, Fig 4.25.

Recreate the drawing using a simple draughting package.

Create a three-dimensional model using a line or wireframe modelling system.

Create a solid model of the component using a solid modelling system.

Discuss the major differences between the three models you have created in terms of their ease of creation and usefulness for visual and geometric analysis. Discuss the relative costs both of the software and minimum hardware requirements for each modelling method.

Questions

4.1 With the aid of a simple block diagram describe the structure of a typical CADD software package.

4.2 The functions of a CADD package can be categorized into three main areas: synthesis, modification and management. Explain the meaning of each category and give two examples of CADD function for each.

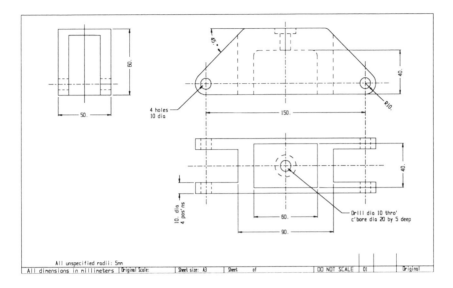

Figure 4.25   CADD assignment example

4.3 State with explanations, two computer-aided draughting functions, which you may or may not have given for (4.2) above, that can provide exceptional productivity benefits over manual methods.

4.4 State with reasons, four factors which may affect a design manager's choice of a CADD system for use in his/her department.

4.5 Figure 4.26 on page 124 shows a simple component to be modelled. Describe, by means of sketches and relevant accompanying notes, how you would generate the model using a solid modeller with which you are familiar, by:

(a) creating profiles, extrusions and intersecting (B-Rep); and

(b) using primitives and Boolean operations (CSG).

Show clearly the dimensions and orientations of the profiles and primitives.

(c) Describe any useful visual and numerical analyses which the solid modeller can carry out on the model.

REFERENCES

Charney, C. 1991, *Time to Market. Reducing Product Lead Time*. Society of Manufacturing Engineers, Dearborn, Michigan, USA.

Goss, L. D. 1990, *Fundamentals of CAD with CADKEY For Engineering Graphics*. MacMillan, New York.

Hsu, T. R. and D. K. Sinha. 1992, *Computer Aided Design: An Integrated Approach*. West, St. Paul, Minnesota, USA.

Onwubiko, C. 1989, *Foundations of Computer Aided Design*. West, St. Paul, Minnesota, USA.

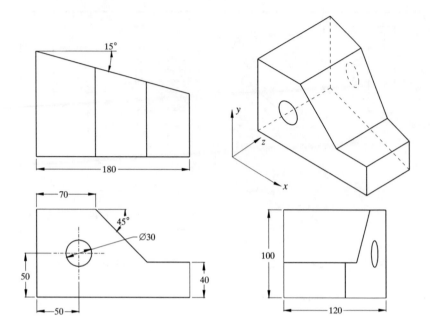

Figure 4.26 Solid modelling example

CHAPTER FIVE

NUMERICAL METHODS

In Chapter 4 we observed how a geometric model could provide spatial, visual and mass property analysis of an engineering component or product. These are just some ways in which a computer can assist with mathematical modelling and numerical analysis techniques during the planning and execution of a design. In this chapter we examine other forms of analysis tools which are available to the computer-aided engineer, namely: the *finite difference*, the *finite element* and the *boundary element* methods. In all cases the computer can be used to accurately model and analyse the behaviour of engineering components under their predicted operating conditions. No design can be said to be complete until the engineer is satisfied that the individual components and hence subassemblies and final assembly will function safely and reliably. To ensure this, many tests will need to be performed before the product is committed to manufacture and launch. Before the advent of the relatively inexpensive and powerful computing hardware and software that is commercially available today, the only way of establishing the effectiveness of a product's performance was to build a physical prototype and put it through rigorous tests. This is an expensive process and because the design process is iterative, many modifications or even reconstructions of the prototype may be required before a final satisfactory solution is produced. With numerical methods and their application by computer, the engineer can build a mathematical model of a component or assembly for analysis by the software. In this way the behaviour of the component can be predicted without the need to test a prototype. If the components to be investigated are of simple geometry, such as a bar in tension or compression or a cantilever beam with a point load, then the analysis is a straightforward strength of materials problem based on mathematically or empirically derived formulae and need not require a computer to evaluate. Real-life situations, however, are rarely so simple and even though assumptions can be made to simplify a problem such that the component can be designed to be strong enough with a suitable factor of safety applied, problems involving complex geometries, material properties or applied conditions generally require the use of numerical analysis methods. Each of the three methods discussed in this chapter can be applied to a number of situations which could include stress analysis, temperature distribution and heat transfer, fluid flow and electrostatic field analysis. For these types of engineering problems system variables such as stresses, displacements, temperature and electrical potential vary continuously throughout the body or *continuum* under consideration and so the study of the numerical methods described form part of what is known as *continuum mechanics*. The behaviour of the variables can be defined in terms of differential equations for one-dimensional problems or partial differential equations for two or three dimensions. The most popular applications for the methods for mechanical engineers are the solution stress analysis, heat transfer and fluid flow problems.

5.1 THE FINITE DIFFERENCE METHOD

The finite difference method is the most established of the three numerical analysis techniques discussed in this chapter. The method is most suited to the solution of problems which can be defined in two dimensions such as the temperature distribution in a thin plate, the velocity profile of a fluid at a cross-section of a duct, the deflection of a supported thin flat plate under a uniform pressure or the stress distribution at a cross-section of a cylinder under torsion. The solution domain is divided up horizontally and vertically into a number of *cells* as shown in Fig. 5.1 and the partial differential equations describing the behaviour of the function to be solved written in terms of difference equations. The result of this is a system of linear algebraic equations which, when solved, yields a value for the function at each interior grid point provided the boundary conditions are supplied and satisfied.

A variety of engineering problems of this nature can be modelled using Poisson's equation, that is:

$$\frac{\partial^2 \phi}{\partial x^2} + \frac{\partial^2 \phi}{\partial y^2} = f(x, y) \tag{5.1}$$

or in some cases the Laplace equation:

$$\frac{\partial^2 \phi}{\partial x^2} + \frac{\partial^2 \phi}{\partial y^2} = 0 \tag{5.2}$$

where ϕ is the function under investigation, for example temperature or deflection.

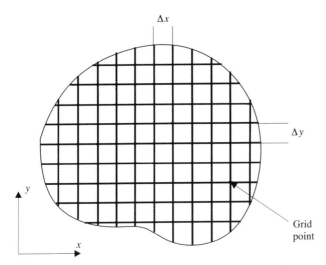

Figure 5.1 A continuum divided for finite difference analysis

5.1.2 Difference Equations

The methods for solving a problem modelled on the Laplace or Poisson equation are relatively easy to understand and program. They involve developing an approximation to the second derivative of the function (ϕ) into a difference equation. The development of this approximation can be shown for the one-dimensional case with reference to Fig. 5.2.

At the point where $x = P$:

$$\frac{\mathrm{d}\phi_P}{\mathrm{d}x} \approx \frac{\phi_i - \phi_{i-1}}{h}; \tag{5.3}$$

and for $x = Q$:

$$\frac{\mathrm{d}\phi_Q}{\mathrm{d}x} \approx \frac{\phi_{i+1} - \phi_i}{h}; \tag{5.4}$$

and so the curvature or second derivative at x_i is given by

$$\frac{\partial^2 \phi}{\mathrm{d}x} \approx \frac{1}{h} \left(\frac{\mathrm{d}\phi_Q}{\mathrm{d}x} - \frac{\mathrm{d}\phi_P}{\mathrm{d}x} \right)$$

$$= \frac{\phi_{i+1} - \phi_i - \phi_i + \phi_{i-1}}{h^2} \tag{5.5}$$

$$= \frac{\phi_{i+1} - 2\phi_i + \phi_{i-1}}{h^2}.$$

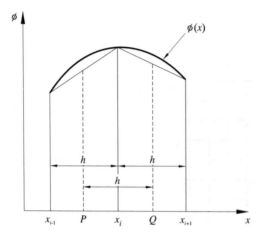

Figure 5.2 Approximation of second derivative of ϕ at x_i

For the case where the Laplace equation is solved for ϕ in two dimensions, that is for the grid depicted in Fig. 5.3, Eq. (5.5) can be applied to the partial derivatives such that for all y or j inside the grid ($j \neq 0$ or n):

$$\frac{\partial^2 \phi}{\partial x^2} \approx \frac{\phi_{i+1,j} - 2\phi_{i,j} + \phi_{i-1,j}}{h^2} \tag{5.6}$$

and similarly for all x or i:

$$\frac{\partial^2 \phi}{\partial y^2} \approx \frac{\phi_{i,j+1} - 2\phi_{i,j} + \phi_{i,j-1}}{h^2} \tag{5.7}$$

and so the Laplace equation can be expressed as the Laplacian difference equation:

$$\phi_{i+1,j} - 2\phi_{i,j}2\phi_{i-1,j} + \phi_{i,j+1} - 2\phi_{i,j} + \phi_{i,j-1} = 0$$

or $\tag{5.8}$

$$\phi_{i+1,j} + \phi_{i-1,j} + \phi_{i,j+1} + \phi_{i,j-1} - 4\phi_{i,j} = 0.$$

This relationship holds true for all interior points on the grid and so a Laplacian difference equation can be written for each, but only provided the values of ϕ are known for each grid point on the boundary. In most engineering problems which can be solved using this technique, the values for ϕ on the boundary are known or can be evaluated because the derivatives $\partial\phi/\partial x$ at $j=0$, $j=m$ or $\partial\phi/\partial y$ at $i=0$, $i=n$ are known. If the value of ϕ is known and therefore set at a grid point on the boundary then this is known as a Dirichlet boundary condition and if the derivative is known then it is referred to as a Neumann boundary condition.

In the case of a Dirichlet boundary condition the Laplacian difference equation for the grid points next to the boundary ($i=1$ or $m-1$, $j=1$ or

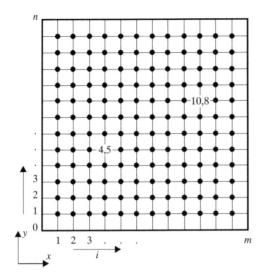

Figure 5.3   Finite difference grid

$n-1$) now contain one or two known values depending if it is a corner point or not. For a point $(1, j)$ the Laplacian difference equation becomes:

$$\phi_{2,j} + \phi_{0,j} + \phi_{1,j+1} + \phi_{1,j-1} - 4\phi_{1,j} = 0 \qquad (5.9)$$

where $\phi_{0,j}$ is the known boundary condition and for the corner point $(1,1)$ the term $\phi_{0,j-1}$ is also known. Therefore the Laplacian equations for all interior points in the grid constitutes a system of $(m-1)(n-1)$ simultaneous linear algebraic equations with as many unknowns. For example the simplest finite difference grid is that where $i = 0$ to 4 and $j = 0$ to 4, which has 3×3 or 9 interior grid points. Therefore as many simultaneous equations need to be solved to evaluate the value of the function ϕ at all points and these are shown in Eq. (5.10):

$$
\begin{aligned}
-4\phi_{1,1} + \phi_{2,1} \qquad\;\; + \phi_{1,2} &= -\phi_{0,1} - \phi_{1,0} \\
\phi_{1,1} - 4\phi_{2,1} + \phi_{3,1} \qquad\;\; + \phi_{2,2} &= -\phi_{2,0} \\
\phi_{2,1} - 4\phi_{3,1} \qquad\qquad\;\; + \phi_{3,2} &= -\phi_{4,1} - \phi_{3,0} \\
\phi_{1,1} \qquad\qquad - 4\phi_{1,2} + \phi_{2,2} \qquad\;\; + \phi_{1,3} &= -\phi_{0,2} \\
\phi_{2,1} \qquad\qquad + \phi_{1,2} - 4\phi_{2,2} + \phi_{3,2} \qquad\;\; + \phi_{2,3} &= 0 \qquad (5.10) \\
\phi_{3,1} \qquad\qquad + \phi_{2,2} - 4\phi_{3,2} \qquad\qquad\;\; + \phi_{3,3} &= -\phi_{4,2} \\
\phi_{1,2} \qquad\qquad - 4\phi_{1,3} + \phi_{2,3} &= -\phi_{0,3} - \phi_{1,4} \\
\phi_{2,2} \qquad\qquad + \phi_{1,3} - 4\phi_{2,3} + \phi_{3,3} &= -\phi_{2,4} \\
\phi_{3,2} \qquad\qquad + \phi_{2,3} - 4\phi_{3,3} &= -\phi_{3,4} - \phi_{4,3}
\end{aligned}
$$

Solution methods   Any system of simultaneous linear algebraic equations like that shown in Eq. (5.10) can be solved by means of a simple computer program which implements *Gaussian elimination* techniques. A system of n equations with n unknowns can be represented in general terms as follows:

$$a_{11}x_1 + a_{12}x_2 + a_{13}x_3 + \dots + a_{1n}x_n = c_1$$
$$a_{21}x_1 + a_{22}x_2 + a_{23}x_3 + \dots + a_{2n}x_n = c_2$$
$$a_{31}x_1 + a_{32}x_2 + a_{33}x_3 + \dots + a_{3n}x_n = c_3$$

$$\quad \cdot \qquad \cdot \qquad \cdot \qquad\qquad \cdot \qquad \cdot$$

$$\quad \cdot \qquad \cdot \qquad \cdot \qquad\qquad \cdot \qquad \cdot \qquad\qquad (5.11)$$

$$\quad \cdot \qquad \cdot \qquad \cdot \qquad\qquad \cdot \qquad \cdot$$

$$a_{n1}x_1 + a_{n2}x_2 + a_{n3}x_3 + \dots + a_{nn}x_n = c_n$$

or in matrix representation:

$$[A]\{\mathbf{x}\} = \{\mathbf{c}\} \tag{5.12}$$

where $[A]$ is the matrix of coefficients a_{ij}, $\{\mathbf{x}\}$ the vector of unknowns x_i and $\{\mathbf{c}\}$ is the vector of the constants of the right-hand side of each equation in the system c_i. Gaussian elimination works by systematically eliminating each x_i term and reducing the number of equations by 1 each time until an expression for x_n can be evaluated. The term containing x_1 can be eliminated from the second equation by multiplying the first equation by a_{21}/a_{11} and subtracting the result from the second equation so that the coefficients for the second equation become

$$a'_{21} = a_{21} - \frac{a_{21}}{a_{11}}a_{11} \qquad (= 0)$$

$$a'_{22} = a_{22} - \frac{a_{21}}{a_{11}}a_{12}$$

$$\qquad \cdot \qquad\qquad \cdot \qquad\qquad \cdot$$

$$\qquad \cdot \qquad\qquad \cdot \qquad\qquad \cdot \qquad\qquad (5.13)$$

$$\qquad \cdot \qquad\qquad \cdot \qquad\qquad \cdot$$

$$a'_{2n} = a_{2n} - \frac{a_{21}}{a_{11}}a_{1n}$$

and similarly the x_1 term for the third equation can be eliminated by multiplying the first equation by a_{31}/a_{11} and subtracting from the third and so on from the fourth to the nth, or in general:

$$a'_{ij} = a_{ij} - \frac{a_{i1}}{a_{11}}a_{ij}. \tag{5.14}$$

Eliminating the x_i term from all the equations gives

$$a_{11}x_1 + a_{12}x_2 + a_{13}x_3 + \dots + a_{1n}x_n = c_1$$
$$a'_{22}x_2 + a'_{23}x_3 + \dots + a'_{2n}x_n = c'_2$$
$$a'_{32}x_2 + a'_{33}x_3 + \dots + a'_{3n}x_n = c'_3$$

$$\qquad \cdot \qquad\qquad \cdot \qquad\qquad\qquad \cdot \qquad \cdot$$

$$\qquad \cdot \qquad\qquad \cdot \qquad\qquad\qquad \cdot \qquad \cdot \qquad\qquad (5.15)$$

$$\qquad \cdot \qquad\qquad \cdot \qquad\qquad\qquad \cdot \qquad \cdot$$

$$a'_{n2}x_2 + a'_{n3}x_3 + \dots + a'_{nn}x_n = c'_n$$

Ignoring the first equation a similar procedure can be carried out on the remaining $(n-1)$ equations to eliminate the x_2 term from them all and so on until the system becomes:

$$a_{11}x_1 + a_{12}x_2 + a_{13}x_3 + ... + a_{1n}x_n = c_1$$
$$a'_{22}x_2 + a'_{23}x_3 + ... + a'_{2n}x_n = c'_2$$
$$a''_{33}x_3 + ... + a''_{3n}x_n = c''_3$$

$$\qquad . \qquad\qquad .$$
$$\qquad . \qquad\qquad .$$
$$\qquad . \qquad\qquad .$$

(5.16)

$$a_{nn}^{(n-1)}x_n = c_n^{(n-1)}.$$

This whole procedure is termed *forward elimination* from which the variable x_n can be evaluated as

$$x_n = \frac{c_n^{(n-1)}}{a_{nn}^{(n-1)}}$$

(5.17)

and subsequently by *backward substitution* the system can be solved for all x_i using the general relationship:

$$x_i = \frac{c_i^{(i-1)} - \sum_{j=i+1}^{n} a_{ij}^{(i-1)} x_j}{a_{ii}^{(i-1)}} \qquad (i = n-1, n-2, ..., 1).$$

(5.18)

There are a number of problems which can occur when implementing Gaussian elimination in software. The first is that if any of the coefficients are zero then it is possible that division by zero may occur during forward elimination and backward substitution. The second is that of round-off errors. Computers can only store real numbers with limited precision, that is with a certain number of significant digits and a rounding error will occur if the result of an arithmetic operation requires a greater precision. Most modern programming languages specify real numbers to have a range of not less than 10^{-39} to 10^{38} with a minimum precision of 7 to 8 significant decimal digits, and so significant accuracy can be achieved.

Division by zero can be eliminated and rounding errors minimized by using a method known as *partial pivoting* during forward elimination. This ensures that the multiplication factor, that is $|a_{21}/a_{11}|$ in Eq. (5.13), is as small as possible so that the loss of any decimal precision is minimized. The process involves searching the current system of equations for the coefficient with the largest magnitude of the term to be eliminated and swapping that equation with the first. Therefore, at the start of the elimination the system of equations is searched for the largest absolute value of the coefficient for x_1

and the whole equation with this coefficient is swapped with the first equation ensuring that $|a_{11}|$ is as large as possible. The process is repeated before eliminating x_2 by searching from the second equation onwards for the coefficient of x_2 with the largest magnitude and swapping. In the case of finite difference evaluation, it can be seen from Eq. (5.10) that the coefficient with the largest magnitude is always that of the term to be eliminated as the elements of the leading diagonal of the coefficient matrix all have the value -4, whereas all the other elements have a value of 1 or zero. This means that if Gaussian elimination is to be used to solve the system of equations generated by a finite difference grid then partial pivoting will not be required.

Although Gaussian elimination is highly satisfactory for solving systems of simultaneous equations it is, as mentioned previously, prone to round-off errors. Also, large finite difference grids generate very large systems of equations; a grid of 7 by 7 internal points will generate 49 linear algebraic equations and hence a coefficient matrix of 2401 elements. Any equation in the system generated by a finite difference evaluation will only have a maximum of five non-zero coefficients which means that invoking the program procedure for Gaussian elimination on a large system involves many wasted computations and also significant amounts of wasted storage for the zero coefficients. Another approach to the solution of finite difference problems involves an iterative procedure known as Liebmann's method. The Laplacian difference equation, Eq. (5.8), can be rewritten

$$\phi_{ij} = \frac{\phi_{i+1, j} + \phi_{i-1, j} + \phi_{i, j+1} + \phi_{i, j-1}}{4}, \tag{5.19}$$

which gives an evaluation of the function at any internal point (i, j) on the grid as a function of the four points surrounding it to the north, south, east or west. If every value of $\phi_{i,j}$ for every internal point is evaluated iteratively, that is repeatedly, then these values will eventually converge to form one unique solution for the grid. The rate at which this convergence takes place can be increased by using a technique known as *over-relaxation* which involves applying a formula to each grid value, $\phi_{i,j}$, before and after each iteration, which is

$$\phi_{i,j}^{\text{new}} = \lambda \phi_{i,j}^{\text{new}} + (1 - \lambda)\phi_{i,j}^{\text{old}}, \tag{5.20}$$

where $\phi_{i,j}^{\text{new}}$ is $\phi_{i,j}$ after evaluation of (5.19) and $\phi_{i,j}^{\text{old}}$ is that before computation for any one iteration. The iteration process is continued until every value of $\phi_{i,j}^{\text{new}}$ is within a desired percentage difference of $\phi_{i,j}^{\text{old}}$, that is when

$$\left| \frac{\phi_{i,j}^{\text{new}} - \phi_{i,j}^{\text{old}}}{\phi_{i,j}^{\text{new}}} \right| \times 100 \le \epsilon \tag{5.21}$$

where ϵ is the required percentage precision.

The treatment of the finite difference method so far has concentrated on Dirichlet boundary conditions where the value for ϕ at the boundaries of the grid ($\phi_{0,j}$ or $\phi_{i,0}$) is known. In many real problems, Neumann boundary conditions (that is where the derivative of ϕ with respect to one dimension is known) are applied, and the case where this derivative is zero is referred to as a *natural boundary condition*. The first derivative of the function in the x direction at the boundary $(0, j)$ can be approximated by

$$\frac{\partial\phi}{\delta x} = \frac{\phi_{1,j} - \phi_{-1,j}}{2h} \tag{5.22}$$

or

$$\phi_{-1,j} = \phi_{1,j} - 2h\frac{\partial\phi}{\partial x},$$

and hence for the point $(0, j)$, Eq. (5.19) can be written

$$\phi_{0,j} = \frac{2\phi_{1,j} + 2h\partial\phi/\partial x + \phi_{0,j+1} + \phi_{0,j-1}}{4} \tag{5.23}$$

and this analysis can be applied similarly to any of the boundary points: $(i, 0)$, (n, j) and (i, m).

Programming   When programming a finite difference solution it is more effective both for speed and memory usage to use the Liebmann method. Gaussian elimination is fairly easy to program once the system of equations has been defined, as can be seen from the Pascal program in Fig. 5.4. In addition to this, however, the complete program must also contain procedures to build the system of equations from the finite difference grid and its boundary conditions and to present the final solution in terms of the grid.

Programming using Liebmann's method is also very simple, as shown in Fig. 5.5 on page 135. With this method the time overhead of building a system of equations from the finite difference grid is eliminated but instead the evaluation is carried out by the iterative procedure to a desired precision. The greater the desired precision then the greater the number of iterations required.

An alternative method of carrying out Liebmann's method is to use a standard spreadsheet which allows the formula defined in Eq. (5.19) to be placed in the spreadsheet's cells, each of which corresponds to a grid point as shown in Fig. 5.6 on page 135 which illustrates a 3×3 grid and the formulae for each cell. Once these formulae are defined, which is very quickly achieved using the spreadsheet *copy* function, then the solution to the finite difference grid can be obtained by continually selecting the spreadsheet *calculate* function until stable values are seen in all the cells.

```
procedure gauss(n :integer;var  a :matrix;  var  c,x :  vector;
                                          var  tfe,tbs : real;

{Gaussian elimination without partial pivoting n is number of
equations, a is matrix of coefficients, c - rhs of equations.
x is solved values.  tfe and tbs return time taken to complete
forward elimination and backward substitution respectively}

var
    i,j,l,m,p    :     integer;
    f,sum        :     real

begin
    {function timenow returns current time in
     1/100th seconds from midnight}
    tfe := timenow;
    for k := 1 to n-1 do
    begin
        for i := k+1 to n do
        begin
            f := a[i,k]/a[k,k];
            for j:=k to n do a[i,j] : =a[i,j] - f*a[k,j];
            c[i] := c[i] - f*c[k];
        end; {for i}
    end; {for k}
    tfe := timenow-tfe;
    {perform back substitution into vector x}
    tbs := timenow;
    x[n] := c[n]/a[n,n];
    for i := n-1 downto 1 do
    begin
        sum := 0;
        for j := i+1 to n do sum := sum + a[i,j]*x[j];
        x[i] := (c[i] - sum)/a[i,i];
    end;
    tbs := timenow-tbs;
end;
```

Figure 5.4 Pascal procedure for Gaussian elimination without partial pivoting

Applications A simple application which demonstrates the finite difference method is the evaluation of the temperature distribution in a thin rectangular plate which is insulated everywhere except at its edges, and these are held at constant temperatures. Figure 5.7 on page 136 shows such a plate and it can be shown that in a steady-state condition the temperature distribution across the plate can be defined by the Laplace equation:

$$\frac{\partial^2 T}{\partial x^2} + \frac{\partial^2 T}{\partial y^2} = 0 \qquad (5.24)$$

The analysis is described in more detail in Chapra and Canale (1988) which also compares the results of the finite difference method with a known

```
procedure liebmann(m : integer; orel, est : real;
                        var g : grid; var its : integer; var tl : real);
var
    bst      :    boolean;
    i,j      :    integer;
    gnew     :    grid;

begin
    tl := timenow;
    its := 0;
    repeat
        bst := true;
        for j := 1 to m-1 do
        begin
            for i := 1 to m-1 do
            begin
                gnew[i,j] := (g[i+1,j]+g[i-1,j]+g[i,j+1]+g[i,j-1])/4;
                gnew[i,j] := orel*gnew[i,j]+(1-orel)*g[i,j];
                bst := bst and
                            abs((gnew[i,j]-g[i,j])/gnew[i,j])*100<=est);
                g[i,j] := gnew[i,j];
            end;
        end;
        inc(its);
    until bst;
    tl:=timenow-tl
end;
```

Figure 5.5   Pascal procedure for Liebmann's method

	A	B	C	D	E
1		100	100	10	
2	30	(C2 + A2 + B3 + B1)/4	(D2 + B2 + C3 + C1)/4	(E2 + C2 + D3 + D1)/4	50
3	30	(C3 + A3 + B4 + B2)/4	(D3 + B3 + C4 + C2)/4	(E3 + C3 + D4 + D2)/4	50
4	30	(C4 + A4 + B5 + B3)/4	(D4 + B4 + C5 + C3)/4	(E4 + C4 + D5 + D3)/4	50
5		0	0	0	
6					

Figure 5.6   Liebmann's method using a spreadsheet

analytical solution and shows that a 7 by 7 grid yields results to an accuracy of better than 1 per cent. Comparison of the Gaussian elimination and Liebmann methods using the procedures listed in Fig. 5.4 and Fig. 5.5 shows that even though 33 iterations are required for a 7 by 7 grid using an over-relaxation value of 1.5 to achieve a precision to four decimal places, the Gaussian elimination method on the same grid takes over 10 times longer.

Another application of the finite difference method is the analysis of the deflection of a thin rectangular plate which is simply supported at its edges as depicted in Fig. 5.8 on page 136. The theory can be studied in a number of texts such as Rees (1990), the result of which states that the deflection in the z direction can be solved by the bi-harmonic partial differential equation:

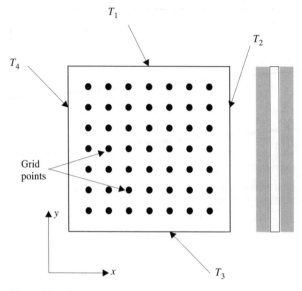

Figure 5.7   Thin rectangular plate for temperature distribution analysis

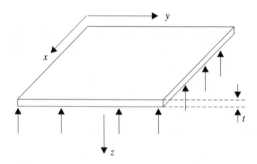

Figure 5.8   Simply supported plate example

$$\frac{\partial^4 z}{\partial x^4} + 2\frac{\partial^4 z}{\partial x^2 \partial y^2} + \frac{\partial^4 z}{\partial y^4} = \frac{p}{D} \tag{5.25}$$

The value p is the pressure applied to the top surface of the plate and D is the *flexural rigidity* defined by the equation:

$$D = \frac{Et^3}{12(1 - \nu^2)} \tag{5.26}$$

where E is Young's modulus and ν is Poisson's ratio. By defining a new variable:

$$u = \frac{\partial^2 z}{\partial x^2} + \frac{\partial^2 z}{\partial y^2} \qquad (5.27)$$

then Eq. (5.25) can be reduced to Poisson's equation:

$$\frac{\partial^2 u}{\partial x^2} + \frac{\partial^2 u}{\partial y^2} = \frac{p}{D}. \qquad (5.28)$$

The problem can therefore be solved using two finite difference grids; one for Eq. (5.27) for $u = 0$ and the other for Eq. (5.28). The spreadsheet method for this type of problem is relatively straightforward. Two grids are created similar to that shown in Fig. 5.6, where each cell inside the grid contains the formulae:

$$u_{i,j} = u_{i+1,j} + u_{i-1,j} + u_{i,j+1} + u_{i,j-1} - \frac{\Delta^2 p}{D} \qquad (5.29)$$

and

$$z_{i,j} = z_{i+1,j} + z_{i-1,j} + z_{i,j+1} + z_{i,j-1} - \Delta^2 u_{i,j},$$

where Δ is the distance between the grid points.

5.2 THE FINITE ELEMENT METHOD

The finite element method is probably the most commonly used numerical analysis technique for mechanical engineering design. Having been developed over a number of years, the method is available in a wide variety of packages, mostly for mainframe and workstation platforms but also, more recently, for personal computer systems as well. The early software systems were text based, that is the definition of the model had to be described in a text file, and the results were also presented in that format. The advent of pen plotters allowed graphical display of results to simplify their interpretation and modern computer graphics techniques afford a more interactive approach to modelling with finite elements.

Perhaps the most common use for the finite element method is that of stress analysis, though there are also many users who adopt the approach for heat transfer and electrical field analyses. Like the finite difference method the principle of operation is to divide up the continuum under analysis into a number of smaller elements of known size, geometry and physical properties—hence finite elements. The elements are bounded at the vertices and sometimes at points along the edges by *nodes* which can be considered analogous to the grid points in a finite difference model. The main advantages of the finite element method over that of the finite difference method are that more complex shapes and discontinuities, such as holes, can be more easily modelled and a far wider range of analysis scenarios can be investigated. With the finite difference method the modelling of complex geometry (curves etc.) requires specialist extensions to the mathematical handling of the model and the range of applications which can be modelled is limited. The finite element method has been the subject of many specialist texts in recent years, for example Desai and Abel (1972) and Baker and Pepper (1991).

5.2.1 Finite Element Software

There are many finite element software packages available on the open market for a range of different hardware platforms. Some systems, such as PAFEC, are stand-alone, that is they just carry out FE analysis on the data input to the system. PAFEC was, in fact, one of the first commercially available systems in the United Kingdom to gain wide acceptance in the engineering community. Although originally requiring input in the form of a text file defining the positions of the nodes and element types, it can now be considered as part of the suite of PAFEC CAE products, including PIGS, for interactively creating a PAFEC input file and graphically displaying the results of the analysis. As well as stand-alone FE solvers there are also those which were designed as an integral part of a design system. One such package is I-DEAS from SDRC, which is able to generate a finite element model directly from a solid model and graphically display the results for interpretation.

It was discussed in Chapter 1 that most CAE software systems can be described by a general model in which a database is manipulated and examined interactively by the user. Modern FE packages should also follow this general model to provide optimum productivity benefits available from interactive graphics. This general model is reproduced in Fig. 5.9 with relation to finite element modelling.

The nature of the database defining a finite element model is somewhat different to that of the CADD system described in Chapter 4 because, even though the geometry of the component or system being modelled is defined, it is implicit in the positions of the nodes which bound the finite elements themselves. In addition to the node positions, the model definition is completed with descriptions of how the nodes are restrained and loaded and the material properties and types of the elements. The boundary conditions for the system of equations which is generated and manipulated by the finite element solver are defined, for the case of stress analysis, by the restraints and forces placed on the relevant nodes. For heat transfer analysis these boundary conditions are defined by fixed temperatures and heat fluxes, respectively. In a model undergoing stress analysis, a node can be totally free to move in all six degrees of freedom, that is three linear Cartesian directions

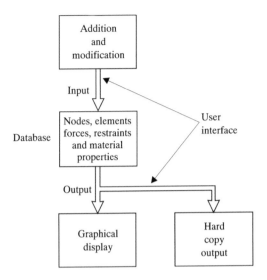

Figure 5.9 Finite element analysis software model

and rotation about the three axes, or can be restrained to move in any one or more. A force acting in any direction can also be applied to any node.

Before describing the mathematical basis for finite element modelling and analysis, we shall first examine the procedure for building a model and interpreting the results of the analysis from a user's point of view. While it is helpful to understand the mathematical approach to the method, most analysts use the software with little or no reference to it, as a more important key to the successful use of such software is to have an extensive understanding of the model being analysed. An experienced stress analyst will know that discontinuities, such as holes in the continuum, act as stress raisers and therefore require more elements in that region. He or she will also know the range of results to expect such that errors in the model can be detected rather than the erroneous results being accepted as fact. Figure 5.10 shows the operational procedure for finite element modelling. Most modern FE software systems, particularly those with interactive graphics capability in the user interface, will have the functionality to enable this procedure to be carried out with relative ease.

Before the analyst can begin to generate a finite element model of a component, the geometry must in some way exist. Early FEA systems had no interface to graphics and so geometry was defined by positioning nodes at key points in space in Cartesian or polar notation. These key points would be identified by specific features such as corners and straight or curved edges at regular intervals, and elements could then be defined with respect to the nodes. Modern systems tend to have some form of graphical preprocessing tools to assist in the positioning of nodes; nodes may be

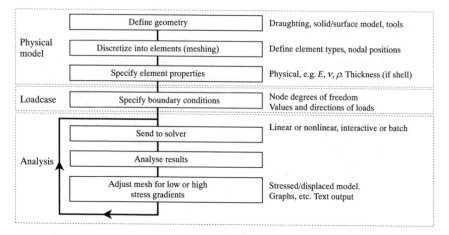

Figure 5.10   Finite element modelling and analysis procedure

positioned at the graphics cursor and simple geometry such as circles and arcs can be defined for reference. By far the most effective method of generating geometry for finite element analysis is to use that which already exists in a CADD model. This, in the simplest case, could be just two-dimensional geometric entities of a drawing or, for more sophisticated integrated systems, a solid or surface model.

As previously mentioned, the principle of finite element analysis is to divide up the continuum into a number of smaller units of which the geometry and physical properties are known. This division is often referred to as *discretization* or *meshing*. The set of elements thus defined is known as the *finite element mesh* and there are a number of ways in which meshes can be generated with relative ease. PAFEC uses a concept known as PAFBLOCKS which are defined with respect to a small number of previously positioned nodes; a PAFBLOCK may take the shape of the complete continuum or at least a large proportion of it and will generally consist of four sides or edges, any number of which may be curved. A PAFBLOCK can then be further divided into elements of the desired type and the nodes associated with those elements are automatically positioned. The finite element modeller in I-DEAS can generate a mesh automatically from a solid model or object simply by specifying parameters such as maximum element size and selecting the solid to be meshed. The algorithm which carries out the meshing automatically detects discontinuities where high stress concentrations are expected such as holes, apertures, fillets and sharp corners. Figure 5.11 shows a simple component which has been automatically meshed from which it can be noted that there is a concentration of smaller elements around the hole. The nodes are not shown but there is one at the vertices of each element as well as one at the

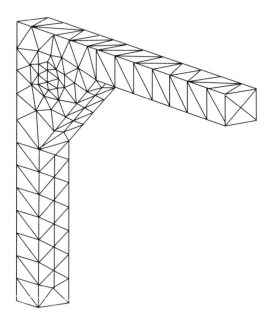

Figure 5.11   An automatically meshed finite element model

midpoint of each element edge. This particular example could have been modelled with two-dimensional elements and analysed using calculations for thick shell elements which would simplify a non-automatic meshing procedure and would take less computing time to solve. Automatic meshing facilities may not always detect such simplifications and instead create fully three-dimensional tetrahedral, hexahedral or *brick* elements which will make the final solution more complex and hence lengthy.

The geometry of the component to be modelled will generally dictate the types of elements to be used. Although curved surfaces can be modelled by straight sides or *linear* elements, a sufficient number are needed to model the curve accurately. Elements with curved sides could be used and the simplest of these are those whose edges are defined by a second-order polynomial or *quadratic* elements. The two types are shown as two-dimensional triangular and quadrilateral elements in Fig. 5.12 where it can be seen that linear elements can be defined by a node at each vertex whereas quadratic elements need an extra node on each edge to provide the three points required to define a quadratic curve.

A quadratic element will closely model a feature with a circular profile and increasing the number used in any one area will provide a close approximation to curves of other functions. The use of quadratic elements will increase the time for the software to generate a solution, first because of the greater number of nodes in the model, and second because of the increased complexity of the function which can determine, or interpolate,

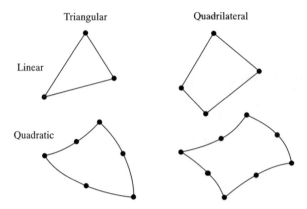

Figure 5.12 Two-dimensional element geometries

the stresses and displacements of points within the element—known as the *interpolation function*.

In stress analysis two-dimensional elements can be used for those components whose geometries are simple in the third Cartesian direction or z axis; that is if the component is an irregular plate or shell. In situations such as these, the element types can be defined as *thin shell* or *thick shell* elements and the choice depends, as their names suggest, on the thickness of the component; the method of solution is also different.

With thin components, it is helpful for the sake of simplification to assume that the stress in the z direction is zero or

$$\sigma_z = \tau_{yz} + \tau_{zx} = 0 \qquad (5.30)$$

where σ is tensile or compressive stress in any given direction and τ is the shear stress. This is known as the *plane stress* case; the use of thin shell elements will ensure that this assumption is made. For thick components, that is where the thickness is large compared with the lateral dimensions, the assumption of *plane strain* can be adopted and this assumes that the strain in the z direction is zero or

$$\epsilon_z = \gamma_{yz} + \gamma_{zx} = 0 \qquad (5.31)$$

where ϵ is the normal strain and γ is shear strain and this can be achieved when using thick shell elements.

For more complex geometries where plate or shell definitions cannot be used then there is, in three-dimensional finite element software, the capability to define fully three-dimensional elements of various geometries based mainly upon tetrahedrons and hexahedrons, both regular and arbitrary. As with two-dimensional elements the curves making up the edges of the elements can be defined by a polynomial which, for most applications, is normally quadratic for meshing nonlinear component geometries.

Having divided the continuum up into elements of appropriate geometries the physical properties of each element need to be specified. In most cases these physical properties will be identical for every element as a component under analysis will generally be of one material, but some applications will involve modelling components, assemblies or fabrications of different materials. For stress analysis these properties include Young's modulus (E) and Poisson's ratio (ν) for linear elastic analysis and in some cases it is necessary to specify the material density (ρ) so that mass and the effects of gravity on the results can be taken into account. As the geometry of each element is known, its volume and centre of mass can be evaluated and hence the volume, mass and centre of gravity of the model can also be established. It is after the geometry, element types and material properties are specified that the physical model can be said to be complete. The analysis situations can then be prepared which involves the definition of one or more *loadcases*.

A loadcase is essentially a scenario of boundary conditions on the model defining how the component is restrained and loaded. Restraints define how any area or part of the continuum is prevented from moving under any applied loads; any node may have up to six degrees of freedom, that is three linear along and three rotational about the x, y and z axes, any one or more of which may be specified as inactive.

The number of degrees of freedom that a node has depends upon the type of element to which it is attached. The nodes of a fully three-dimensional element will have all six degrees of freedom whereas thin shell elements will have only five; the rotation about the z axis being undefined. If a boundary or area of the component is clamped in reality then some or all of the degrees of freedom of the nodes at those positions will be restricted. For example, a built-in beam will have the nodes at the fixed end restricted in all degrees of freedom—that is they are *encastred* and a bar under tension will have the nodes at the clamped end restrained only in the direction of the tensile force. As part of a graphical user interface, this is simple to achieve: the user either defines a restraint and applies it to one or more nodes by selection of the screen or selects a group of nodes and defines the restraints in terms of each of their degrees of freedom. It should be made quite clear at this point that clamping the nodes of a finite element model makes the assumption that, at the points and in the degrees of freedom restrained, the model is rigidly restricted in movement. This, of course, is almost never the case and consideration should be given, when modelling any one component in isolation, to the components to which it is joined when interpreting the results.

As the way in which a component or structure is clamped is modelled by restraints, the actions of forces are modelled by applying loads to specific nodes. The forces on a body can come from a variety of sources and be defined in a variety of ways. There may be loads acting at singular points, which could be modelled as a force acting at one node, or the load may be distributed over a larger area that is divided in some way across a number of nodes. In some cases it may be appropriate to define a pressure acting on a face or surface, in which case the software will evaluate the force and its direction at each node from the value given for pressure and the area covered by the surface. In cases where large structures are being modelled the forces owing to the mass of the model under gravity may contribute significantly to the stresses in the structure. In finite element software systems the user is often given the option of specifying the direction of gravitational force and its value and having specified the density and geometry for each element, the mass and relevant forces can be evaluated.

The principle of the analysis of a finite element model, which will be seen later when the mathematical basis for the method is discussed, is to solve a set of simultaneous equations built up from the geometry and physical properties of the elements and the governing equations for the problem; for stress analysis these are defined by the relationships between stress and strain and hence forces and reactions and displacements as specified by Hooke's law. The result of a finite element analysis is therefore an evaluation of the displacements and stresses, both linear and shear, at each node in the Cartesian axis directions and from these the values and directions of the maximum and minimum principle stresses can be derived. The form of the displaced object can also be ascertained as this may have a bearing on the design of the final product of which the model is a component part or subassembly.

There is, in some software systems, a choice of solution techniques depending on the application of the model. In certain circumstances the material properties do not follow the normal laws; for example in the case of stress analysis a material will not obey Hooke's law once it is past its yield point. Certain composite materials respond differently to stress in different directions. In cases where the displacement of a particular point or area of a model is large then those elements in that region will change shape significantly, which may render their interpolation functions invalid, thus the solution of these problems depends on an iterative procedure which requires a new solution for each increment of displacement. In all cases, however, whether linear or nonlinear, small or large displacement, the interpretation of the results of the analysis has to be carried out with some care.

The actual output from a finite element analysis is the displacement of all the nodes in the model and the stresses, and their directions, acting at each of those nodes. In complex models this can lead to significant amounts of textual data which can be very tedious to examine and the successful use of these data is highly dependent on the skill and intuition of the analyst. In general an experienced stress analyst will have a sound intuitive feel as to how a component will behave under the stress set up in its operating conditions as without this a justification to build the model in the first place cannot be made. The need for any form of complex numerical analysis techniques like the finite element method is to quantify the behaviour of a design so that more informed changes can be made. Thus the analyst can examine those areas of the components suspected of causing problems but it is insufficient in itself to rely solely on experience and judgement.

Nearly all finite element systems have the ability to display the results of an analysis in graphical form. In early non-interactive systems this mainly took the form of exaggerated displaced forms and stress contour maps produced on a pen plotter. With modern interactive systems this post-processing of finite element analysis can be displayed on a computer graphics display. The displaced model can be compared with the original geometry, the stresses can be displayed by different colour bands on a shaded contour image and directions of principal stresses shown by arrows. All in all some of these features present the model and its solution looking very much like a weather map—a (shaded contour) stress display is shown in Fig. 5.13.

As emphasized previously the output of results for a finite element analysis can be very lengthy and it is the graphical display of stresses by a contour map that can assist the analyst in interpreting the results. The display will highlight those areas where the stresses are high and further investigation of the results at those areas will yield more detailed quantitive analysis. The analyst must take care to check a number of criteria in order to

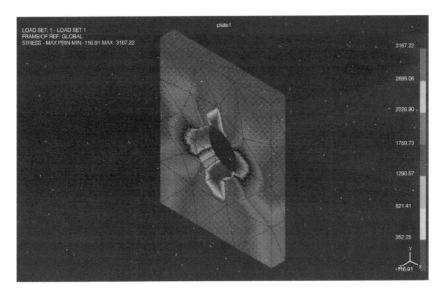

Figure 5.13 A shaded contour stress display of a finite element model

be confident that the model and the results are valid. In the first instance the correct area of the model must be investigated, which may be a laborious procedure if there are many thousands of nodes in the model. Most solvers present the stresses and displacements at each node in element order. In other words, when a node has two or three adjacent elements, as shown in Fig. 5.14 where nodes 5, 6 and 7 are common to both the elements numbered 1 and 2, the desired stress values must be checked from the node listings for all the adjacent elements. Any significant discrepancy between the values given for the same node but with respect to different elements will indicate an inaccuracy in the model. Such inaccuracies can occur if the element geometry is unsound; very acute corner angles in an element is an example of this.

Another source of inaccuracy in the results can be from an insufficient density of elements in areas of high stress concentration and gradient. An experienced analyst will know that certain geometries of continua and discontinuities, such as holes or corners, will generate areas of stress concentration and will therefore define a higher density mesh in these areas. Automatic meshing systems are also generally designed to take these problems into account. The solution may yield, however, higher stress gradients than initially thought and so in order to produce a result in which more confidence can be placed, the model may need remeshing and resolving. Some finite element modellers have such an optimization technique built into the system, an example of which is I-DEAS from SDRC. In this case the automatic meshing system takes into account the previous solution to increase the mesh density in areas of high stress concentration and decrease it in areas where the gradients are low. It may take several iterations before optimum mesh is achieved.

Mesh optimization is therefore one form of iteration that may need to take place with finite element modelling. The principal aim of this form of numerical analysis is to provide a means of modelling the performance of a design under normal and extreme working conditions. Thus if an analysis

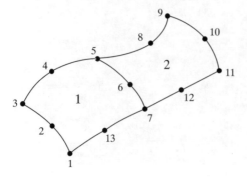

Figure 5.14 Adjacent elements and common nodes

indicates problems with a design then modification will be needed which will correct the adverse response to loads and at the same time maintain the functionality and in many cases the aesthetics of the final component or product. This will, therefore, also require remeshing the modified model and a new solution, both of which can be very time consuming.

5.2.2 Further Applications of Finite Element Analysis

We have so far seen that finite element analysis can be used to solve problems involving heat transfer and stress analysis, in particular for static situations where the applied load is constant over time. The method can also be used for dynamic and vibration analysis such as when an object will be subject to an excitation force or impact. These types of problem are still very much dependent on the application of Hooke's law which forms the basis of the governing equations in stress analysis. Systems under vibration can be subject to high stresses caused by large displacements set up by natural frequencies, and in these cases an in-depth analysis using tools like the finite element method may be the only way of identifying such problems without building physical models and putting them through expensive test procedures.

Another application of the finite element method is to assist in the design of plastic injection mould tools where both heat transfer and stress analysis solutions are used to examine the effects of cooling in the mould on the final geometry of the part. Optimization of the mould geometry can then be carried out, significantly reducing the number of expensive prototypes which need to be made. This application is essentially a computer-aided manufacturing activity and is the subject of further discussion in Chapter 6.

5.2.3 Finite Element Solution Methods

The description of the numerical methods for finite element modelling is not so easy to understand as that for the two-dimensional finite difference cases given earlier in the chapter. The main reasons for this are that finite difference problems are carried out using regular geometry discretized into regular shapes. Finite elements, on the other hand, are mostly triangular or irregular quadrilateral for two and $2\frac{1}{2}$-dimensional problems and have even more complex geometries if full three-dimensional elements are defined. One of the basic procedures in the solution of a finite element model, therefore, is to establish and evaluate how the required parameters vary throughout an element. The governing equations which are used to do this are known as *interpolation functions* and are expressions relating a parameter to the geometry of the element. For stress analysis, interpolation functions relate displacement of a point in the element to its geometry and hence contribute to the system of equations those terms needed to evaluate the displacement of all the nodes in the model. It is the stress analysis case that will be used to introduce some of the principles of the finite element method here.

Interpolation functions are approximations to the behaviour of an element and to give an example of the structure of an interpolation function, consider the triangular element shown in Fig. 5.15.

The interpolation function is based on an assumption of the components

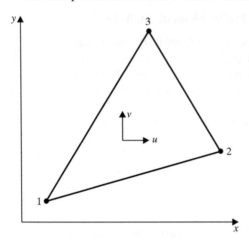

Figure 5.15 Triangular element internal displacement

of the displacement (u, v) of any point (x, y) in the element and is given by:

$$u = \alpha_1 + \alpha_2 x + \alpha_3 y$$
$$v = \alpha_4 + \alpha_5 x + \alpha_6 y. \tag{5.32}$$

For a quadratic element the interpolation function contains more terms involving x^2, y^2 and the product xy. The terms α_1 to α_6 are arbitrary constants related to the element geometry. From the functions defined by Eq. (5.32), a relationship for the displacement of each node 1, 2 and 3 can be expressed in the matrix form:

$$\begin{bmatrix} u_1 \\ u_2 \\ u_3 \\ v_1 \\ v_2 \\ v_3 \end{bmatrix} = \begin{bmatrix} 1 & x_1 & y_1 & 0 & 0 & 0 \\ 1 & x_2 & y_2 & 0 & 0 & 0 \\ 1 & x_3 & y_3 & 0 & 0 & 0 \\ 0 & 0 & 0 & 1 & x_1 & y_1 \\ 0 & 0 & 0 & 1 & x_2 & y_2 \\ 0 & 0 & 0 & 1 & x_3 & y_2 \end{bmatrix} \begin{bmatrix} \alpha_1 \\ \alpha_2 \\ \alpha_3 \\ \alpha_4 \\ \alpha_5 \\ \alpha_6 \end{bmatrix} \tag{5.33}$$

or in short:

$$\mathbf{r_g} = A\alpha. \tag{5.34}$$

The above system is the basis for generating the *stiffness matrix* for the element and eventually the whole model. As we have already seen, the boundary conditions for a finite element model which defined a loadcase are in terms of specified displacements of particular nodes and a system of applied forces. The stiffness matrix relates the reaction forces at each node with the displacements to form a system of equations which can be solved using similar methods to those used for the finite difference method. Having obtained the relationship for displacement and element geometry as shown above, the strains can be obtained by the differentiation of the displacements with respect to x and y. From the strains, the stresses can be evaluated using the governing equations for plane stress or plane strain which are in equilibrium with the nodal forces. Thus the system of equations based on the stiffness matrix is a combination of the element geometry and the laws of stress analysis.

To demonstrate this using two-dimensional elements would be beyond the scope of this book and so an introduction to this procedure is given by a demonstration of the principles using one-dimensional elements.

A one-dimensional element is modelled by a straight line and has some use in finite element stress analysis in modelling bars in tension and compression. By increasing the degrees of freedom of the end nodes, such an element can model a simple beam and form the basis for the analysis of plane trusses. A typical one-dimensional element is shown in Fig. 5.16.

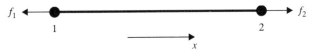

f_1 ← ● —————————————— ● → f_2

1   2

—————→

x

Figure 5.16   A one-dimensional element

The interpolation function for the element is a simple linear relationship where displacement of any point on the element is proportional to the distance x. The constant of proportionality in this case is the strain in the element owing to the applied forces. Therefore the stiffness matrix which relates the forces f_1 and f_2 to the displacements of nodes 1 and 2 (u_1 and u_2) is based on the simple application of Hooke's law:

$$f_1 = k(u_1 - u_2)$$
$$f_2 = k(u_2 - u_1) \tag{5.35}$$

where k is the stiffness of the element evaluated from the cross-sectional area (A), length (L) and Young's modulus E:

$$k = \frac{AE}{L}. \tag{5.36}$$

A simple application where one-dimensional elements can be successfully used is in a situation where a bar in tension varies in stiffness along its length, such as when the diameter changes in steps. The model for such a situation is shown in Fig. 5.17.

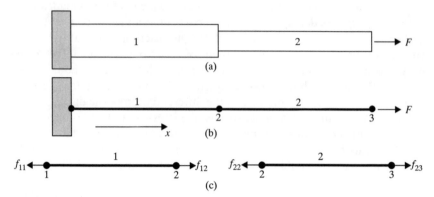

(a)

(b)

(c)

Figure 5.17 Simple one-dimensional model: (a) physical; (b) FE model; and (c) forces on individual elements

A composite bar with two sections of different diameters is in tension and each section is modelled by a single element. The first element (1) is bounded by nodes 1 and 2 and the second element (2) by nodes 2 and 3. The individual components of force at each node are designated by the element and the node so that the force on element 1 node 1 is f_{11} and that at element 2 node 3 is f_{23}.

Applying Eq. (5.35) to element 1 gives:

$$f_{11} = k_1(u_1 - u_2)$$
$$f_{12} = k_1(u_2 - u_1) \tag{5.37}$$

which in matrix form is

$$\begin{bmatrix} f_{11} \\ f_{12} \end{bmatrix} = \begin{bmatrix} k_1 & -k_1 \\ -k_1 & k_1 \end{bmatrix} \begin{bmatrix} u_1 \\ u_2 \end{bmatrix} \tag{5.38}$$

The above analysis can be similarly applied to element 2 to give

$$\begin{bmatrix} f_{22} \\ f_{23} \end{bmatrix} = \begin{bmatrix} k_2 & -k_2 \\ -k_2 & k_2 \end{bmatrix} \begin{bmatrix} u_2 \\ u_3 \end{bmatrix} \tag{5.39}$$

and for a model consisting of any number of one-dimensional elements concatenated in a straight line the same relationship will hold for each.

Having established a relationship between forces and displacements for each element individually, the complete stiffness matrix for the whole model can be derived which will generate a system of equations from which a model solution can be evaluated. This can, by summing the nodal force components for each element at each node, produce the total node force or *reaction.* For example the force at node 1 is f_{11} and at node 3 is f_{23} which is the applied force. At node 2 the total reaction is the sum of the forces at node 2 for each element, that is the sum of f_{12} and f_{22} or

$$
\begin{aligned}
F_2 &= f_{12} + f_{22} \\
&= k_1(u_2 - u_1) + k_2(u_2 - u_3) \\
&= -k_1 u_1 + (k_1 + k_2)u_2 - k_2 u_3.
\end{aligned}
\tag{5.40}
$$

Thus the system of equations relating reaction forces, **F**, to displacements, $\mathbf{u}_g$, can be generated from the individual matrix equations giving:

$$
\begin{bmatrix} F_1 \\ F_2 \\ F_3 \end{bmatrix}
=
\begin{bmatrix}
k_1 & -k_1 & 0 \\
-k_2 & (k_1 + k_2) & -k_2 \\
0 & -k_2 & k_2
\end{bmatrix}
\begin{bmatrix} u_1 \\ u_2 \\ u_3 \end{bmatrix}
\tag{5.41}
$$

or

$$
\mathbf{F} = \mathbf{K}\mathbf{u}_g
$$

where **K** is the stiffness matrix. Examination of this matrix gives an indication as to how a computer algorithm could be devised to build it from the stiffness matrices of each individual element as shown in Eqs (5.38) and (5.39). Figure 5.18 shows the matrix **K** partitioned to reveal the individual matrices which go towards its make-up.

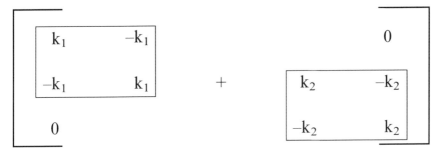

Figure 5.18 Building the stiffness matrix

5.3 THE BOUNDARY ELEMENT METHOD

The boundary element method is a relatively new technique used to solve problems of the type already discussed in this chapter and is included here to give a complete picture of continuum mechanics methods available to engineers. As the technique is so new, the number of proprietary boundary element solvers on the market is few but more and more systems are emerging. For the same reasons, the number of texts available for further

emerging. For the same reasons, the number of texts available for further study is also far less than those covering the finite difference method and the finite element method but a very comprehensive coverage of the basis and use of the boundary element method for solving engineering problems is given by Becker (1992).

Though it can be said that the finite element method is far superior to the finite difference method for solving many problems, the same cannot be said for the relationship between the boundary element method and the finite element method. The boundary element has emerged as an alternative to finite element modelling as opposed to an improvement, though there are many who would argue that the boundary element method has significant benefits over the use of finite elements.

5.3.1 The Principles of BE Modelling

The fundamental principles of boundary element modelling, as the name suggests, is that the boundary or surface of the continuum is discretized into elements rather than the volume. Therefore a problem which can be simplified with two-dimensional geometry is 'meshed' with elements around its boundaries and a three-dimensional geometric model generates a boundary element model from its surfaces. Therefore a boundary element is represented by either a curve in two dimensions or a shell in three. Figure 5.19 shows a typical simple example of a boundary element model with loads and constraints added. A boundary element used for two-dimensional problems like that shown can be linear, quadratic or of a higher order in the same way that finite elements can. The example shows the use of quadratic elements which require three nodes in order to define a quadratic curve.

Whereas the numerical analysis for finite element solvers is based on the generation of interpolation functions for each element in order to build the stiffness matrix in stress analysis problems, the boundary element method uses a concept based on *shape functions*. The fact that the element for two-

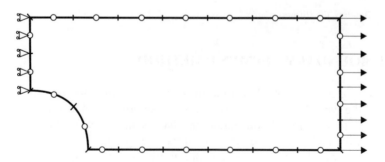

Figure 5.19   Simple boundary element model example

dimensional problems is a line or a curve gives greater resolution to the final results. Therefore one of the underlying principles behind the mathematics of the boundary element method is the fact that two-dimensional problems are reduced to a one-dimensional model and three-dimensional models are reduced to two. If the reader is led to believe that the mathematics, as well as the geometry representation, is simpler for boundary element analysis than that for the finite element method then this is far from the truth. The mathematics behind a boundary element solver is complex and incorporates techniques not used anywhere else in engineering analysis.

5.3.2 Comparison between Boundary and Finite Element Methods

One of the main differences already highlighted between the two methods is that the finite element method models the area or volume of the continuum, whereas the boundary element method uses the boundary or surface as the underlying base geometry. This does make the generation and meshing of boundary element models very much simpler in the majority of cases. The number of elements and nodes for similar models is often far less in a boundary element model which can be more economical on the use of computer memory.

The case where this is not necessarily so is if a finite element solver uses compressed forms of the stiffness matrix for storage purposes. If one were to extend the pattern observed in the generation of the finite element stiffness matrix given in the previous section, as shown by Eq. (5.41) and Fig. 5.17, to three or more elements, the resulting matrix would be symmetrical with a significant proportion of zero terms, that is it would be sparsely populated. The same is not true for the boundary element method which tends to produce asymmetric matrices which are densely populated.

One of the main problems facing a design office when considering the use of boundary element software is that there are comparatively few packages available on the market at the moment. This is beginning to change but the speed of introduction of BE solvers is hampered by the engineering community's sense of security with FE solvers. The finite element method is tried and tested with all of its problems, inaccuracies and shortfalls known and most graduate engineers have some understanding of the mathematics involved. The boundary element method needs more exposure and use in all its fields of application before confidence in its reliability as a numerical method is gained.

EXERCISES

Assignments

Use a proprietary spreadsheet package to create a finite difference grid for the problem given in the text in Fig. 5.8.

Produce 9 by 9 grids (8 grid spaces) and make your spreadsheet flexible in use so that different values of material properties and sizes can be entered into a table. Print out the final results and produce a graph of deflection versus x at the middle of the plate. Use these values:

$E = 207 \times 10^9$, $\nu = 0.27$, $t = 50$ mm, plate length $(L) = 1$ m, density $= 7750$ kg m^{-3} and applied pressure $= 0.5$ bar $(50$ kN m$^{-2})$.

What is the central deflection when the thickness of the plate is halved?

Now recreate the plate geometry using a finite element package and mesh it in similar manner to the finite difference grid, applying the same loadcase. Compare the results obtained with those from the finite difference analysis.

Questions

5.1 What are the limitations of the finite difference method? List three applications which can be solved using finite difference methods.

5.2 Given Laplace's equation:

$$\frac{\partial^2 \phi}{\partial x^2} + \frac{\partial^2 \phi}{\partial y^2} = 0$$

derive the Laplacian difference equation for ϕ with respect to a finite difference grid in two dimensions.

5.3 Describe the principles of Liebmann's method for solving a finite difference problem.

5.4 Explain the following terms in relation to the finite element method; use diagrams if it will aid your explanations:

    (i) node;
    (ii) mesh;
    (iii) load case;
    (iv) linear element;
    (v) quadratic element.

5.5 By means of a block diagram or otherwise, describe the procedure for building, solving and analysing a model using finite elements. Describe the ways in which the process is iterative.

REFERENCES

Baker, A. J. and D. W. Pepper. 1991, *Finite Elements 1-2-3*. McGraw-Hill, New York.

Becker, A. A. 1992, *The Boundary Element Method in Engineering. A Complete Course*. McGraw-Hill, London.

Chapra, S. C. and R. P. Canale. 1988, *Numerical Methods for Engineers*, 2nd edn. McGraw-Hill, New York.

Desai, C. S. and J. F. Abel. 1972, *Introduction to the Finite Element Method. A Numerical Method for Engineering Analysis*. Van Nostrand Reinhold, New York.

Rees, D. W. A. 1990, *Mechanics of Solids and Structures*. McGraw-Hill, London.

COMPUTER-AIDED MANUFACTURE

Computer-aided manufacturing is perhaps the oldest application of computing to engineering. Its beginnings can be traced back over 30 years when it was used to assist with programming NC machines and now it can be said to also include the design and simulation of plant layout, robot task design and programming, the programming and control of flexible manufacturing systems, and tool design. Some of these activities can also be categorized with computer-aided production planning and control which is the subject of Chapter 7 and some will also involve the use of simulation techniques as described in Chapter 8. Thus the majority of that which is referred to as CAM is understood to mean computer-aided part programming for CNC machines and CADCAM is the process whereby the model of a component designed on a CAD system is directly used by the CAM software for machining preparation purposes. This chapter describes the more traditionally accepted aspect of CAM such as part programming and CADCAM as well as robot task simulation and programming. It also introduces some of the generally not so well-described CAE tools for manufacturing, namely assembly modelling, mould tool design and rapid prototyping.

6.1 COMPUTER-AIDED NUMERICAL CONTROL PROGRAMMING

Numerical control machine tools were first developed in the early fifties and towards the latter part of the decade a need for some means of automating, and hence easing, the preparation of complex programs was identified. This led to the development of a higher level NC programming system to run on mainframe computers and named automatically programmed tools or APT. The advent of physically smaller and cheaper microprocessor-based computers of suitable performance enabled the development of CNC machines but, prior to this, NC machine tools were not capable of performing circular interpolation, that is they did not have the ability to machine circular profiles with a single part program instruction. Therefore if a component had a complex profile consisting of curves, a numerically controlled machine tool could only generate the shape by programming many point-to-point tool movements which required a great many calculations from the programmer. Part programming preparation systems such as APT were developed to meet this need and could calculate points on arcs and curves to a specified tolerance to simulate curve interpolation or continuous path programming. The additional functionality which came with CNC machine tools eased manual continuous path programming but there were, and are even more so today, considerable productivity benefits in using computer assistance. Manual programming of CNC machines is described in Chapter 3.

6.1.1 Part Programming Software Structure

As with all CAE systems so far described in this book, the structure of computer-aided part programming software can be described in terms of the general CAE software model introduced in Chapter 1. The CAM version of this model is shown in Fig. 6.1 and follows this general pattern in that the use of a computer-aided part programming system revolves around the creation and management of a database.

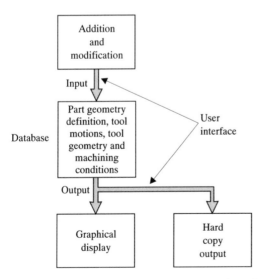

Figure 6.1 Computer-aided NC part programming software model

This database contains not only the relevant geometry of the part to be machined but also the geometric definition of the tools used for the machining as well as the speeds, feeds and movements of those tools. The definitions of the component geometry in the database represent a truly mathematical model of the features to be machined in precisely the same way as they do in a CADD system though most computer-aided part programming packages such as APT, and other modern part programming CAM applications, deal with the geometry as surfaces as this more correctly describes the requirements of the part geometry after machining. APT was the first commercially available part programming system on the market and will be described in more detail later in this chapter.

There are many part programming packages available today which vary in complexity and functionality. Some are fully three-dimensional but the continuous path machining of three-dimensional objects is for rather specialized applications. The majority of CNC machining is carried out in 2½ dimensions which means that continuous path machining takes place only in two axes whereas only linear moves are supported in the third axis. In such systems, a simple two-dimensional representation of the part can be used but the geometry actually represents surfaces. For example, a circle in the xy plane is in fact a cylindrical surface extending to infinity in both directions in z.

6.1.2 Computer-aided Part Programming Procedure

Figure 6.2 shows a flow chart describing the procedure for generating a part program for an NC or CNC machine using a CAM system. Systems developed in recent years normally have graphical user interfaces, though the procedure has changed very little in structure with the advent of computer graphics and CADCAM systems. The functionality and ease of use of older systems like APT were significantly less when compared with recent CADCAM packages. APT was originally a text-based system where geometry, tool movements and machine control were represented by an APT part program consisting of definition statements; there was nothing, or very little, in the way of interactive graphics to guide the programmer through the machining sequence. Early and even many modern graphical-based CAM systems are based upon this APT language to build up the database defining the mathematical or geometrical model. APT also provides control over the final format of the finished program which is loaded and executed at the machine tool controller.

Geometry definition and specification The first step to producing the part program is to define the geometry in the database which is stored and managed by the software. The structure and techniques of defining this geometry is very similar to that employed by computer-aided design

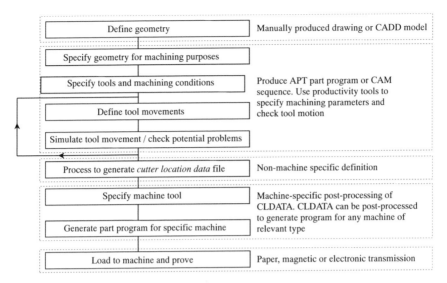

Figure 6.2 Computer-aided part program generation procedure

systems. In 2½-dimensional systems infinite lines and line segments, circles, arcs and curves are the basis of geometric construction of the component's surfaces and in three-dimensional systems these will be defined in terms of planar and curved surfaces. The similarity between geometry defined in a CADD system and that used in part programming CAM systems is so close as to make data transfer from CAD to CAM a simple one. When using a CAM system without any interface from a CADD system all the geometry required for machining the component must be generated using the functionality of the CAM package from the data supplied on a paper drawing. Most stand-alone CAM systems incorporate geometry creation functions similar to those found in CADD systems. If geometry generated by a CADD system is to be used for part programming purposes then only that part geometry relevant to machining need be specified as it is not a very common occurrence that a complete component is machined in one operation with one CNC part program.

Specify tools and machining conditions   Once the geometry is specified then the machining parameters and sequence can be built up, which involves specifying the machining conditions, such as speeds, feeds and coolant flow, defining the tools and generating tool motion around geometry. At this stage it may be necessary to know something of the particular characteristics of the machine tool which will eventually produce the part if the programmer wishes to make use of some of the special facilities provided by the numerical controller. For machining centres this may include the use of the machine tool's cutter radius compensation or inside corner cutter compensation. With these facilities, manual program creation is made simpler when machining a profile because of the need to specify only the actual shape of the profile rather than that followed by the centre of the cutter. It also means that the cutter diameter need not be rigidly specified as the actual diameter or radius is entered into the memory of the controller itself and the offset for every machining movement calculated by the controller's firmware. In preparing programs for turning centres using computer assistance, it is often necessary to define the geometry of the tool turrets, holders and tips to detect any collisions during machining and to calculate the more complex offsets presented by turning tools; this geometry may vary between machines from different vendors. One of the advantages, however, of computer-aided part programming is that a program can be prepared without specifying the precise machine tool for manufacture. In most cases it is better to allow the CAM software to calculate tool radius offsets and use any compensation provided by machining centres to allow for variations in tool diameter owing to manufacturing tolerances and regrinding.

The specification of a tool in the machining sequence will generate a tool change in the final NC code. In some systems the specification at this point will include the tool type, geometry, cutting speed and feed rate. Cutting speed may be specified in revolutions per min and feed rate in length units per minute but facilities often exist whereby spindle speed can be stated as surface speed (e.g. m min^{-1}) and feed rate as length units per revolution (e.g. mm^{-1}). An important feature of modern CAM systems is the presence of a material database where such conditions are specified for each material under ideal conditions. This database often comes relatively complete from the CAM system vendor but the data can be modified and added to in the light of individual user's experiences. Such information will also specify the type of coolant supply required, whether this be no coolant, a mist or a flood.

Define tool movements Having defined or transferred the geometry and decided on the tools and machining conditions, the programmer can then specify the cutting sequence. This takes the form of a description of the movement of the tool with reference to the part geometry which will be defined as three distinct types specifying the type of machining as shown in Table 6.1. When writing an APT program the geometry is specified as the individual lines and circles which make up a boundary or a pattern of points for hole centres. A boundary is machined in APT by specifying the tool motion along each of the geometry elements in turn and this is described more fully later on by means of a worked example. In a modern CAM system, specification of any of the geometry types described above will generate the necessary NC instructions to carry out the machining of the shape or pattern of holes. Additional facilities exist to program an arc lead-

Table 6.1 Geometry types for CAM tool movement

Geometry type	Tool movement type
Boundary	External profiles for milling or turning with area or stock clearance
Boundary	Internal profiles for pocket milling
Point	Hole centres for drilling, reaming, boring or tapping.

in and lead-out to minimize any witness at the start and end point or to roll the cutter around sharp corners.

In general the simple procedure of specifying an external boundary, which is stored as a continuous profile, is to indicate the boundary start and end points, depth for machining and any additional facilities and this will cause the post-processor to generate all the code for machining the shape. This is just one of the productivity benefits of this type of system as the time-consuming activities of calculating tangential points and arc centres are undertaken by the CAM software. An example of external profiling is shown in Fig. 6.3.

An external profile shape defined for a turned part can be used to generate a very effective productivity aid, known as *area clearance*, which allows the rough shape of a component to be very efficiently machined from the original bar stock. Having defined the geometry of the profile for the finished turned shape, the programmer can request area clearance by specifying such parameters as stock allowance for finishing and step size of material moved in each pass. The final cutter path generated is a series of feed and rapid moves as illustrated in Fig. 6.4.

Another important productivity aid which is easily accommodated with computer assistance is the ability to clear out and machine pockets from solid material. As with external profiling, the user specifies the boundary of

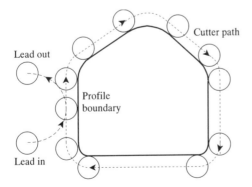

Figure 6.3 Tool path generation for external profiling

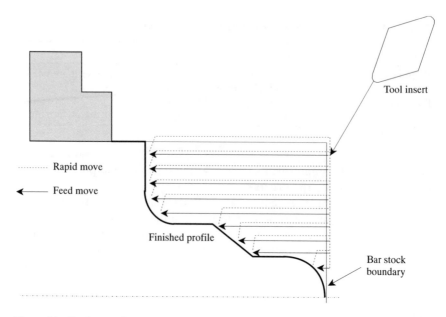

Figure 6.4 Stock area clearance cutter path

the pocket, its depth, the amount of stock for finishing and the size of the cutter, and the software automatically generates the moves to clear out the material and then finish machine the boundary and base. Figure 6.5 shows

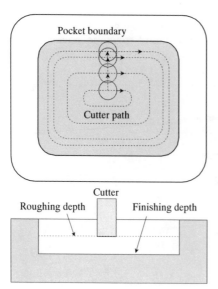

Figure 6.5 Pocket clearance cutter path

the cutter path of the moves generated by this activity. The user can also specify the minimum depth of cut that should be machined at any one time so that the clearing moves are repeated until finally the base of the pocket is machined. The illustration shows the cutter path for the pocket clearance cycle as beginning in the centre and proceeding out towards the boundary in a circular type of motion. Many CAM systems will give the option to machine pockets in a series of side-to-side movements though this does not produce as good a result as the circular route when there is a central raised boss in the pocket. In the cases of profile and pocket milling using a CAM system, the specification of the machining type also generates the rapid moves to and from the tool change position and the material.

In order to machine holes, the programmer can specify points which define the hole centres in a machining cycle. The software supplies functions to select the standard cycles such as drilling, reaming, boring or tapping before the points are indicated. These cycles generally correspond to the standard canned cycles found with most numerical control systems, which are normally activated by the G81 to G89 preparatory codes. Thus all the rapid moves to visit each hole site and the activation and cancellation of the canned cycle are automatically generated with a few simple software commands.

Simulate tool movements and check potential problems   Normally with a CAM system which has interactive graphics, each time a tool motion command is issued the actual tool path is animated on the graphics display. This tool path simulation is a valuable aid to the programmer as a means of confirming each programming step. With turning systems it shows up any collisions between the tool holders, the workpiece and the tailstock turret and for a milling environment, common errors such as incorrect tool offset selection and collisions with clamps and fixtures can be visualized and corrected. The operation of a computer-aided part programming system is such that the specification of tool movements generates a list of coordinate points visited by the cutter, along with the definition of the motion type whether it be at feed rate or rapid, linear or circular interpolation. The visual simulation is an exact representation of the description of the cutter path and so will closely resemble the actual machine movements when the program is loaded to the controller and executed.

Process to generate cutter location data file   The database of tool movements which is made up of the list described above is known as the *cutter location data file* or CLDATA file. Many CAM vendors specify their own formats for the way the CLDATA is stored but attempts have been made to standardize this; an example of this is BS 5110. The CLDATA file does not normally specify the actual machine on which the part will be produced and so there is still much flexibility of application within the constraints of the machine type. This greatly assists the production planning process as the manufacture of a batch of components need not be dependent on the availability of any one machine. If care is taken during the generation of the CLDATA file at the interactive part programming stage then any CLDATA file could be post-processed into a numerical control program for a range of different machining centres or turning centres.

Specify machine tool and generate part program It is the post-processor which specifies a particular numerical controller and the activity of post-processing is effectively a merging of the CLDATA with data which describes the controller's programming format. In many instances a post-processor for a particular CNC machine is created and supplied by the CAM system vendor but the same software used to do this is also available to the user to customize supplied post-processors or to generate new ones. Historically, two ways of generating post-processors have been developed and are in use today:

1. *Programming language approach.* Many part programming systems, in particular early versions of APT, employ this approach. A simple language allows the user to write a program which reads the CLDATA file line by line until enough information is gathered to build up a line of CNC machine programming code. Generally, CLDATA files consist of a sequential list of codes defining movement types, tools, speeds, feeds, etc., followed by a list of Cartesian coordinates visited by the tool. The program can read the information and set the values for all the necessary preparatory and miscellaneous functions and the numeric valued words and then create the line or *block* of code. This method can take a longer time to learn, is less user friendly but provides greater flexibility in the control over the final format of the CNC program. Such an approach was necessary in the early days of APT when NC machine tape syntax was far less standardized than nowadays.

2. *Machine tool definition table.* A simpler but less flexible method of generating a post-processor is to use the tools provided by the CAM vendor to create a file which describes the syntax and format of the machine program. To generate a definition table, the user answers a series of questions relating to the program format of the machine in question. The questions ask about the letters describing the preparatory and miscellaneous functions (normally G and M, respectively, but they may be different), the format of the codes, the tool change words and offset formats, the feed rate and spindle speed words and formats and the presentation of the Cartesian coordinate data. With this method a post-processor for a new machine can be built relatively quickly.

Load to machine and prove   The final program generated for the machine tool is stored in a text (ASCII) file on the computer system running the CAM package and this needs to be transferred to the machine tool controller for execution. Historically, paper tape has been used for this function; the part program is punched on to paper tape and physically carried to the machine to be read by the reader on the controller. A paper tape punch can be interfaced to the personal computer or terminal connected to a mainframe hosting the tape store via a serial or parallel port and the punching process carried out in much the same way as printing. Alternatively, some machine tool controllers use magnetic media to load part programs, these being either floppy disk, standard cassette or microcassette systems. A more effective approach which is often used in a computer-integrated manufacturing system is distributed numerical control and this has been described and discussed in Chapter 3.

Even though a tool path simulation may have been carried out, it is still essential that the program is proved on the machine tool before a batch of components is produced. The most likely anomalies to occur which may cause an inaccurate component or tool collisions will be in the post-processor machine tool definition but other sources of error are probable. These include inaccurate geometry definitions, misplaced clamps and fixture features or inaccurately defined tool geometries. There may also be a need to adjust spindle speeds and feed rate values so that optimum machining conditions are achieved.

6.1.3 Automatically Programmed Tools (APT)

APT was developed during a period covering the late fifties to the early sixties and was written in FORTRAN to cope with the need for continuous path programming and three-dimensional problems: the NC code for arcs could be generated in all planes (xy, xz, yz) and hence complex curved surfaces could be machined. It was thus a very complex software application requiring a high performance computer system on which to run. Later, simpler and more affordable subsets of APT were produced which were only $2\frac{1}{2}$ dimensional, that is they could provide continuous path machining in only one plane (xy) and only linear, point-to-point movements in the third axis (z). Examples of these subsets include 2CL (*2 C*ontinuous and 1 *L*inear) and ADAPT (*ADaptation of APT*). All of these were originally developed for operation on mainframe computers in batch or non-interactive mode and then developed to a point where there was some on-line user interaction but without graphics. The development of pen plotters allowed some tool path simulation and conformation of geometry definitions and this represented the first steps towards some user interaction with graphics. Later similar systems were generated for use on minicomputers, professional workstations and personal computers and these utilized interactive graphics of varying degrees of complexity.

Being purely text-based systems, the generation of NC part programs using APT and its derivatives was based on the creation of an APT part program to generate the geometry, specify tools and machining conditions and to define the tool movements. The basis of APT, therefore, is a complete manufacturing-oriented language, and a part program written using this language is made of four different types of statement, as shown in Table 6.2, and each is based on a clearly defined vocabulary of words. The following description of the APT language is intended to give a brief, but working, introduction; for additional treatment of the subject the reader is referred to a number of other texts such as Bedworth *et al.* (1991) and Rembold *et al.* (1993).

Table 6.2   APT part program statement and vocabulary types

Type	Function
Comments	For documentation purposes to define the various sections and describe what is happening in the program
Geometry definition statements	To define the geometry required to carry out the machining. An extensive range of vocabulary exists able to create lines, circles, points, patterns, planes and 3D surfaces relative to Cartesian space and other geometric entities
Tool motion statements	To guide the various tools around the part to be machined using the defined geometry. The vocabulary contains words to direct the cutter to specific points and guide it along boundaries
Post-processor instructions	Instructions made up of words which direct the post-processor to specify machining conditions such as spindle speed, feed rate and coolant flow and to invoke specific machining cycles

Comment statements are essential, as in all high level programming languages, to assist with subsequent reading and understanding of the program so that informed modifications can be made. A comment statement is simply a line of text commencing with the symbol '$$'.

APT geometry definitions   Geometry is defined using a range of vocabulary relating to the geometry entity types, their parameters and positioning. In general, APT words which make up its vocabulary are six characters long and so in many cases are more mnemonic than precise in their definition. The general syntax for defining APT type geometry is of the form:

NAME = **GEOMETRY_TYPE**/*position, parameters and modifiers* where *NAME* is a unique identifier for the entity and **GEOMETRY_TYPE** is any one of the specific entity types allowed. For simplicity we will confine this discussion to the $2\frac{1}{2}$-dimensional case, in which case the allowable entity types and their definition parameters are given in Table 6.3. The modifiers in a geometry definition are needed to identify one of many options as in many cases there are a number of possibilities for entities defined relative to existing geometry. For example a point defined at the intersection of a line and a circle could be at one of two possible positions and some modification to the definitions will specify which one is desired.

Table 6.3 Geometry types and definitions

Type	Definition parameters
Point	Canonical (x, y, z values) or relative to existing point, circle, intersection, etc.
Line	Through point or points, at an angle, normal or tangential to existing entities
Circle	Centre point or tangential to existing entities plus radius or diameter value
Plane	Three points, single z coordinate or angles relative to axes
Pattern	List of points on line or circle or matrix of two linear patterns

Points are used mainly for identifying the centres of holes in the machined part to be visited as part of a drilling type of operation and can also be grouped together into a *pattern* so that the machining of the complete pattern of holes can be invoked with one APT tool motion statement. Points are also used for reference purposes to provide quick and easy reference to a position in space and are stored in the geometric database as values of their Cartesian coordinates x, y, z. There are many words within the APT vocabulary to assist in the creation of geometry. A point can be simply defined by its coordinates or it can be placed relative to other geometry. Figure 6.6 shows a point defined by its coordinates as well as at an intersection of two lines. In addition to the methods shown by these examples, words exist to enable definition of a point at the intersection of a line and a circle or two circles or relative to an existing point either by specifying incremental distances or in polar notation. The principle behind providing so many options for defining all of the geometric entity types is that the programmer can pick that which matches the way in which a feature is dimensioned on the part drawing. Thus a point can be simply defined by the APT statement:

```
P1 = POINT/25,16,0
```

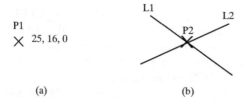

(a)   (b)

Figure 6.6 Examples of point definition in APT: (a) by coordinates and (b) intersection of two lines

or for even greater simplicity a modal z coordinate can be set which will then be applied to all subsequently defined points unless otherwise specified:

```
ZSURF/0
P1 = POINT/25,16
```

or for the case of Fig. 6.6(b):

```
P2 = POINT/INTOF,L1,L2
```

where the word INTOF specifies the modifier *intersection of* and lines L1 and L2 have previously been defined.

Lines are infinite and when used for tool motion represent a vertical surface. The *canonical* representation of a line, that is how it is stored internally in the geometric database, is either as the Cartesian position of a point through which it passes and its angle of orientation with the positive x direction, or as the coefficients of the standard equation for a line. This representation is similar to that used in a CADD package and is discussed in Chapter 4. As with points, there are many options available to the programmer to define a line in the most convenient way which generates the part geometry accurately. Two examples of line definition methods are shown in Fig. 6.7. A line can be defined through two existing points by the statement:

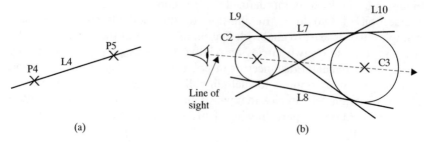

(a)   (b)

Figure 6.7 Examples of line definition in APT: (a) through two points and (b) tangential to two circles

```
L4 = LINE/P4,P5
```

or if the points are not previously defined:

```
L4 = LINE/23.5,19,76.56,52.2
```

If a line is tangential to two arcs then once the circles representing the arcs are defined the line can be specified by the use of the TANTO, RIGHT and LEFT modifiers as there are four possible lines which could result if tangency to two circles is required. From the examples in Fig. 6.7(b):

```
L7  = LINE/LEFT,TANTO,C2,LEFT,TANTO,C3
L8  = LINE/RIGHT,TANTO,C2,RIGHT,TANTO,C3
L9  = LINE/LEFT,TANTO,C2,RIGHT,TANTO,C3
L10 = LINE/RIGHT,TANTO,C2,LEFT,TANTO,C3
```

For these definitions, the programmer chooses a line of sight through the centres of the circles in order to specify which side of the circles the chosen line should pass. The other methods of line creation include through a point and at an angle or tangential to a circle and through a point and perpendicular or parallel to an existing line.

Circles are defined canonically as a centre point and a radius and when used for tool motion represent a cylindrical surface round which a cutter can pass. Figure 6.8 shows two examples of how a circle can be defined using APT.

The centre point in Fig. 6.8(a) can be explicitly stated as coordinate values or referenced to an existing point and the statement to generate the circle is:

```
C4 = CIRCLE/P7,RADIUS,15
```

For the case in Fig. 6.8(b) where a circle is defined as being tangential to two existing circles there could be eight possible alternatives and the modifier words IN, OUT, XLARGE, XSMALL, YLARGE and YSMALL can be used to identify the desired choice as shown in Table 6.4. IN and OUT

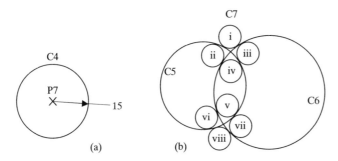

Figure 6.8 Examples of circle definition: (a) canonical and (b) tangential to two circles

specify which side of the reference circle boundaries the chosen circle is positioned and XLARGE, XSMALL, YLARGE and YSMALL indicate the relative position of the centre of the chosen circle. Other means of defining circles also require the use of these modifiers. One defined tangential to two lines can be one of up to four possibilities and the desired result is selected using the XLARGE, XSMALL, YLARGE and YSMALL modifiers and there are also up to eight possible circles tangential to both a line and a circle which will additionally require the use of the OUT and IN modifiers.

Table 6.4   APT statements for circle C7 definition in Fig. 6.8(b)

Reference	APT statement
i	C7 = CIRCLE/YLARGE,OUT,C5,OUT,C6,RADIUS,10
ii	C7 = CIRCLE/YLARGE,IN,C5,OUT,C6,RADIUS,10
iii	C7 = CIRCLE/YLARGE,OUT,C5,IN,C6,RADIUS,10
iv	C7 = CIRCLE/YLARGE,IN,C5,IN,C6,RADIUS,10
v	C7 = CIRCLE/YSMALL,IN,C5,IN,C6,RADIUS,10
vi	C7 = CIRCLE/YSMALL,IN,C5,OUT,C6,RADIUS,10
vii	C7 = CIRCLE/YSMALL,OUT,C5,IN,C6,RADIUS,10
viii	C7 = CIRCLE/YSMALL,OUT,C5,OUT,C6,RADIUS,10

A plane represents an infinite flat surface at any orientation and in a $2\frac{1}{2}$-dimensional environment, the most common definition is that of a plane parallel to the xy plane at a specified z coordinate:

```
PL1 = PLANE/ZCOORD,25
```

Tool motion statements contain words which direct the current tool to positions on the part for drilling type operations or along the geometry for contouring type operations in milling and turning. The process of contouring is governed by the principles that even $2\frac{1}{2}$-dimensional entities are treated as surfaces. The first APT statement in a contouring operation will send the cutter TO, ON or PAST a surface defined by the geometry. The modifiers TO, ON and PAST dictate how the cutter is to be positioned relative to the geometry and in real terms will determine whether the contour is an external or internal profile, with or without an applied cutter radius compensation. This first surface of the boundary, along which the cutter will travel, is known as the *drive surface* for the duration of the cutter movement along that surface. This is illustrated in Fig. 6.9 where the first drive surface of the boundary is defined by the line L1.

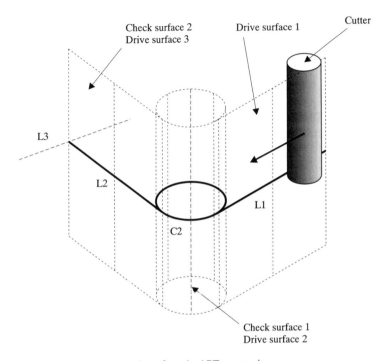

Figure 6.9 Drive and check surfaces in APT contouring

The APT statements which will perform the tool movements in Fig. 6.9 are:

```
$$'SP'IS A PREDEFINED START POINT OUTSIDE THE BOUNDARY
FROM/SP
GO/TO,L1
TLLFT,GOLFT/L1[,TANTO,C2]
GOFWD/C2[,TANTO,L2]
GOFWD/L2,ON,L3
```

The definition of a FROM point in APT allows the processor to evaluate the tool position taking into account its diameter which is stated earlier in the program. The first tool motion statement directs the cutter TO the surface and the next specifies that the next move is a left turn along L1 with the tool to the left of the surface. This latter instruction will cause the cutter to continue along L1 for ever unless its movement is checked by the next surface, namely that defined by C2. As the point of intersection between L1 and C2 is tangential then the word GOFWD (go forward) is used to redirect the cutter around C2, which is now the drive surface. If this point were not tangential then the words GORGT or GOLFT would be used. The cutter would continue to contour C2 for ever if not checked by L2 in the next motion statement. The motion continues along L2 until checked by the final check surface defined by the line L3. The program would continue with further motion statements to perform a safe retraction of the cutter and a return to the tool change position or new start point for machining another boundary. The standard format for a tool motion statement in APT can be further demonstrated by the general syntax description shown in Fig. 6.10.

Figure 6.10   General syntax for APT motion statements

As implied by the above example, the words TLON, TLLFT and TLRGT indicate the position of the cutter relative to the drive surface and are modal in use, that is they need only be stated when the relative position changes. The word GO is normally used to set the tool position for the start of the contour machining operation and direction change is specified by GOLFT and GORGT. GOFWD and GOBACK normally indicate a change of drive surface at a tangential point but can also be used to generate a change in direction through a small angle. In general, *check surfaces* and their modifiers are only stated at the end of a contouring operation and not on each line as they are normally implied by the motion statement in the next line of APT code. An example of when check surfaces are specified during a contouring operation is when there is more than one possible position where the check surface intersects the drive surface, such as when a line intersects a circle giving two possible check points.

Post-processor words   specify tool changes, tool geometry, machining conditions and operation cycles. The actions of post-processor words are only specified by the post-processor itself as the numerical control code for these actions will vary from controller to controller. Thus, even though the word, TOOLNO, is universally accepted as a means of generating a tool change, the machine instructions may vary from a simple one-line code to fetch a numbered tool from a carousel to a machine stop for a manual tool change on an older machine; in all cases it should retract the current tool safely to the tool-change position. Table 6.5 gives some examples of typical post-processor words and their parameters.

6.1.4 APT Example

The description of the APT language presented above can best be summarized by a simple example. Given the full geometry of a component to be machined, in the form of an engineering drawing, the planning

Table 6.5 Typical APT post-processor words

Word	Description	Parameters
TOOLNO	Specify tool change	Tool number
SPINDL	Spindle speed control	Speed value or gear, units, direction
FEDRAT	Feed rate control	Value, units
COOLNT	Coolant control	On or off, mist or flood
CYCLE	Specify machining cycle	Any one of drill, deep, bore, tap, c'bore, c'sink, mill
RAPID	Set up for rapid move	None—applies to next move only

engineer can label the relevant geometry so that it can be defined using APT statements. The example given in Fig. 6.11 has a complex external shape which needs to be profiled and three holes which will require machining. The ability of CNC technology to generate such shapes efficiently means that the raw material for the part can be presented to the machine fixture in the form of a rough sawn billet and the first task of the CNC programmer, in this case, is to establish how the billet is to be secured to the machine. A pre-operation for the part could be to machine the central hole in each billet so that it can be clamped to a fixture leaving the profile free from obstructions. Care must be taken here to ensure that the hole is machined in the correct position to ensure sufficient material for the machining of the part

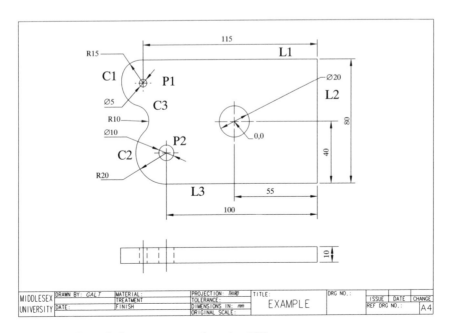

Figure 6.11 Example for part programming using APT

boundary. It is also convenient to designate the centre of the clamping hole as the origin, though this might depend on how the part is dimensioned on the drawing or how datums are specified in the proposed machine tools. Thus the machining operation for the component would be to first machine the profile and then to drill the two holes at the arc centres. This will involve accurately positioning the holes with a centre drill, drilling both holes with a 5 mm drill and finally drilling the larger hole with a 10 mm drill. Each geometry element making up the profile and the drilled holes has been labelled on the drawing and so the APT program, given in Fig. 6.12, can be produced.

In order to gain the maximum productivity benefits from a system like APT, it is better to attempt to define any geometry in a way which closely matches how the original drawing is dimensioned. To achieve this, additional reference geometry may need to be defined such as the point CP in the example; many of the component features are dimensioned from this point. The APT program demonstrates a number of different ways in which geometry can be defined; one of these being the use of the word, DELTA, to define the positions of P1 and P2 relative to the corner point CP, and the use of the words XCOORD and YCOORD to define vertical and horizontal lines, respectively.

The profiling operation uses the post-processor instruction:

```
CYCLE/MILL,-12,FTD
```

Where the word FTD means feed to depth. This will generate the necessary CNC code to position the cutter, at rapid feed, to the start position of the boundary (PAST,L2,PAST,L3 from the origin) to a safe height (2 mm) above the top of the billet defined by the statement:

```
CLEARP/2
```

and then to feed to the depth of −12 mm so that profiling can begin. The END statement instructs the post-processor to generate the necessary code to finish the machining cycle and FINI signifies the end of the APT program.

6.1.5 CADCAM Geometry Interface

The historical development of part programming systems has brought about the introduction of many stand-alone CAM systems. This began, as we have seen, with APT and later developed into systems providing interactive graphics such as GNC (graphical numerical control) and these stand-alone systems had facilities for creating the geometry for tool path generation. Alongside this development, CAD in the form of two and $2\frac{1}{2}$-dimensional draughting and three-dimensional design, also developed, and similarity between geometry creation and representation in the two systems was

```
$$ GEOMETRY DEFINITIONS
$$ CP IS BOTTOM RIGHT CORNER OF PROFILE
   ZSURF/0
CP=POINT/55,40
P1=POINT/CP,DELTA,-115,65
P2=POINT/CP,DELTA,-100,20
L1=LINE/YCOORD,40
L2=LINE/XCOORD,55
L3=LINE/YCOORD,-40
C1=CIRCLE/P1,TANTO,L1
C2=CIRCLE/P2,TANTO,L3
C3=CIRCLE/XSMALL,OUT,C1,OUT,C2,RADIUS,10
$$TOOL MOTION AND POST-PROCESSOR STATEMENTS
$$TOOL 1 IS 10 MM SLOT DRILL
TOOLNO/1
SPINDL/1800,RPM,CW
FEDRAT/120,MMPM
COOLNT/FLOOD
CUTTER/10
CYCLE/MILL,-12,FTD
CLEARP/2
FROM/0,0
GO/PAST,L3,PAST,L2
TLRGT,GOLFT/L2
GOLFT/L1
GOFWD/C1
GOFWD/C3
GOFWD/C2
GOFWD/L3,PAST,L2
$$TOOL 2 IS CENTRE DRILL
TOOLNO/2
SPINDL/2500,RPM,CW
FEDRAT/100,MMPM
COOLNT/MIST
CLEARP/2
CYCLE/DRILL,-4
GOTO/P1,P2
$$TOOL 3 IS 5 MM DRILL
TOOLNO/3
SPINDL/2200,RPM,CW
FEDRAT/100,MMPM
COOLNT/MIST
CYCLE/DRILL,-12
GOTO/P1,P2
$$ TOOL 4 IS 10 MM DRILL
TOOLNO/4
SPINDL/1800,RPM,CW
FEDRAT/100,MMPM
COOLNT/MIST
CYCLE/DRILL,-15
GOTO/P2
END
FINI
```

Figure 6.12   APT program for example in Fig. 6.11

inevitable. The development of CADCAM systems therefore made use of these similarities.

Modern integrated CADCAM systems have a unified means of defining and storing geometry across the two constituent parts but in many cases CADCAM systems have become integrated by the addition of an existing CAD system with a CAM system. Many companies will separately purchase a CAD and CAM system and rely on standard geometric data exchange standards to transfer the CAD geometry to the CAM system. These data exchange standards have developed primarily to support the need for drawings and designs to be transferred from one CAD system to another so that companies with different CAD systems could effectively work together. Two geometry data exchange standards are commonly used to transfer between CAD systems and these same standards are also often used for CADCAM interface. They are Autodesk's DXF standard and the ANSI standard IGES.

DXF or drawing exchange format was developed by Autodesk for incorporation into the popular AutoCAD system. Many other CAD vendors have adopted DXF as a standard for drawing exchange and have facilities in their systems for converting a DXF file into their own internal format and for generating a DXF representation of a drawing created on their system. Many stand-alone CAM part programming systems will also read DXF files as a basis for the geometry defining tool paths. DXF is primarily a text-based standard in which geometric entities are fully defined in a readable format, but a more compact way of storing binary versions of the format is defined. A printed version of a DXF file of even a fairly simple drawing can take up many pages as each item of data for an entity is defined on a single line and each of these data items is identified by a code on the previous line; thus the end-point coordinates defining a straight line take up eight printed lines.

IGES or Initial Graphics Exchange Standard has been developed over a number of years by a number of major US CAD vendors and supported by the US National Bureau of Standards and subsequently by the American National Standards Institute. This standard also presents a drawing or design in a text or a more compact binary form and supports a number of geometric entities including, among others, ruled surfaces, surfaces of revolution, B-splines and finite elements.

In addition to these drawing exchange standards, some CAD systems will allow the user to convert selected geometry into known CAM formats. Some systems will generate a text file containing APT definitions for specified geometry which can be used as a basis for an APT program. Another method of CADCAM interface is the conversion of specified geometry into boundaries for profiles, pockets and area clearance or point sets for drilling type operations and transferring them to the CAM system as *Kcurves*. K Curves are the medium for defining geometry for tool path generation in GNC (graphical numerical control) developed by the CAD centre, Cambridge, as a graphical stand-alone computer-aided part programming system. It is also incorporated into many integrated systems, such as I-DEAS from SDRC, as the part programming component.

6.2 ROBOT TASK PROGRAMMING AND SIMULATION

Another CADCAM procedure which is gaining considerable popularity with companies which utilize automated manufacturing techniques is the ability to model a robot and its environment and simulate the execution of its task. The major problem with robot programming has always been that a costly device is taken out of production for long periods of time while it is reprogrammed for a new task. This downtime of a robot and the lengthy procedure of teach-programming, as described in Chapter 2, is costly in terms of personnel and lost production and can seriously affect the payback period for the robot. Computer-aided robot cell design and simulation can remove this procedure from the shopfloor and greatly reduce any machine downtime. Software packages are becoming available which allow the process planning engineer to design an effective automation cell and generate the part program for the robot. A great deal of confidence about the integrity of the program is gained through the use of graphical simulation and animation techniques.

6.2.1 The Structure of Robot Part Programming Systems

A system for designing and programming robot tasks is very complex as it incorporates many different modelling techniques. The basic structure for a fully functional system is shown in Fig. 6.13 which highlights all of the various modelling processes and the contents of the database defining the model. The description of any robot in the model therefore has to incorporate not only the physical shape of the various limbs but also how they move together as a kinematic model. The method of kinematic modelling is briefly described below, but is similar in many respects to that carried out as part of the design of mechanisms which is discussed further in Chapter 8. The same is also true, in many cases, for the robot environment or cell because the parts being handled or operated upon also need to be modelled as well as any materials handling systems, such as conveyors or AGVs, which bring them to or through the cell.

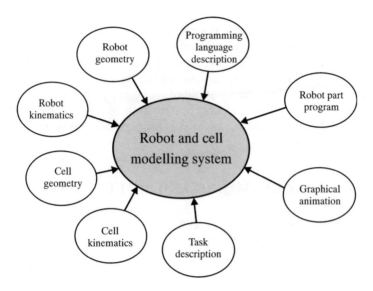

Figure 6.13   Robot modelling structure and function

6.2.2 The Geometric Model

The geometric model of the robot is normally generated from a three-dimensional CAD modelling procedure. On systems which have relatively low graphics performance, such as personal computers, the robot model is likely to be a wireframe representation of the ideal robot. The geometry defining each limb of the robot will be grouped together as an entity group, block, layer or level so that it can be transformed as part of the kinematic chain. The use of solid or surface models for the robot is reserved for higher performance computer platforms which may then give better visual animation of the robot as a hidden line or shaded image.

Generating a geometric model of a robot using solid modelling techniques, such as that seen in Fig. 6.14, is significantly easier as each separate limb of the robot is a solid object. The mass properties of each object cannot be used as part of the dynamic modelling though, unless the internal detail of the robot is also accurately modelled.

6.2.3 The Kinematic Model

As discussed in Chapter 2, a robot can normally be analysed as a kinematic chain. The base of a robot is always grounded, that is it does not move relative to the fixed environment, and from there the movement of each limb is defined relative to its parent and that movement is constrained by the type of joint coupling the two limbs. This is demonstrated in Fig. 6.15.

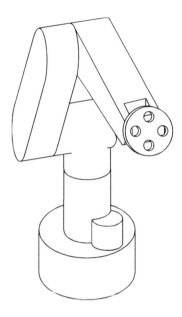

Figure 6.14   Robot geometric model

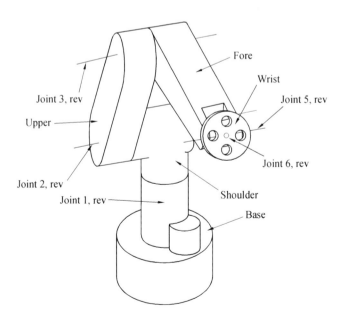

Figure 6.15   A robot kinematic chain

Each limb is defined as a separate solid object or its entities are grouped so that they can be given unique names or identifiers. In the example shown, the base part of the robot begins the kinematic chain and is grounded and the movement of the next part or limb, the shoulder, is defined relative to the base by joint 1 which is a revolute joint. From then on, the remainder of the robot constituent parts are linked to the chain by an appropriate joint which accurately models the movement type. Thus joint 2 defines the movement between the shoulder and the upper limb such that when the shoulder rotates about joint 1 then the upper limb and all others chained from that limb will rotate with it. The kinematic modeller which forms part of the robot modelling system generates the rotational transformation equations defining the movements about the joints and when these are linked together to form the chain, a complete dynamic model of the robot is defined. A basic introduction to the mathematics involved in this model is given in Chapter 2.

Robot modellers and other kinematic modellers are able to represent a range of different joint types defining different types of movements between members, parts or limbs. The two most common joint types used in robot modelling are the revolute and prismatic types as shown in Fig. 6.16. Other joint types are available and some of these are described in Chapter 8. In addition to the type of joint, the user also needs to specify any constraints on the joint such as its limits of movement and its maximum speed.

The complete model of the robot is therefore comprised of the geometric model plus the kinematic description and once fully defined in this way can be used within any environment. Most robot modelling systems are supplied with libraries of predefined models of standard industrial robots as well as other components commonly used in robot cell design.

6.2.4 Robot Task Definition

Once the robot is modelled it can then be programmed with a task which involves interactively defining points to which the robot must move and the

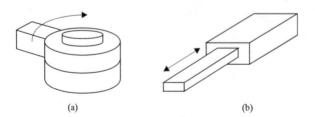

(a)   (b)

Figure 6.16 Common robot joint types: (a) revolute and (b) prismatic

path the end effector must take to safely reach those points. Once programmed, a robot task can then be animated on the graphics screen which gives a valuable visual conformation of the task definition. The task definition procedures within a robot simulation will also provide other important information to the programmer such as the ability to reach a particular point and any joints exceeding their limits of movement. The fact that the robot model has data on the speed capabilities of each joint means that the task cycle time can be evaluated and some systems will have optimization facilities to indicate shorter ways of achieving similar pick and place activities.

The positioning and orientating of the end effector in task simulation will generate the information required for the post-processor to build the robot program. Robot post-processors are designed in a similar fashion to those used in computer-aided numerical control part programming systems, in that particular information about the robot programming language format is merged with the end effector movement. Robot programming languages, however, are generally more complex and comprehensive than those used on CNC machines and so the tools for creating post-processors are less generalized.

6.3 OTHER CAM SYSTEMS

There are a number of other computer-aided tools which can be classified into the area of computer-aided manufacture. They also involve the use of design and modelling techniques and so provide a close link between design and manufacture thus aiding concurrent engineering in product development. The three CAM methodologies we shall examine briefly here are assembly modelling and simulation, injection mould tool design and rapid phototyping.

6.3.1 Assembly Modelling and Simulation

Although primarily a design function, the construction of an assembly gives a good indication of the manufacturability of a product or part of a product. Assembly modellers which form part of an integrated product design system, such as that found in I-DEAS, are very useful in modelling the assembly of many components so that a layout drawing and parts lists can be produced. Additional benefits include the ability to check for interferences between parts and, in some cases, a facility to animate the assembly or insertion of one component into another. An example of this would be to animate the insertion of a printed circuit board into a case to check if the board could be manoeuvred into position and pressed home. It is this aspect of assembly modelling which makes it a valuable manufacturing and process planning aid.

Assembly modelling also allows the integration of design and manufacturing to production planning and control. The procedure for assembly modelling requires that each component in an assembly or subassembly is modelled, normally as a solid object, and uniquely identified. The individual component models provide the basis for generating drawing layouts, geometry for analysis and manufacturing data as well as for modelling assemblies and, because of their unique identification in the database, a bill-of-materials (BOM) can be generated for each subassembly and assembly. The bill-of-materials, apart from being the basis of the parts list for an assembly or product, is a full definition of how a product is structured and is discussed in more detail in Chapter 7 in its normal context of material requirements planning or manufacturing resource planning (MRP or MRPII). An example of an assembly model with each component labelled is given in Fig. 6.17.

Another significant productivity aid of assembly modelling is the facility to access a library of predefined components which would include fasteners and other commonly used components. Again these components would be solid objects which may have full engineering drawings defining them and some suppliers of common bought-in parts often provide libraries of their product range for specific CADCAM systems.

As each component in a solid-modelling-based assembly modeller is defined as a solid object then a problem could exist where a relatively simple

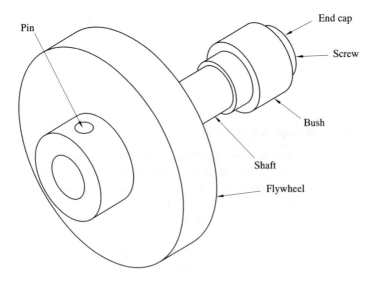

Figure 6.17 Assembly modelling example

assembly containing a large number of one particular component could generate a very large file. This is overcome in most assembly modellers using the principles of *instancing* the solid objects. The database for the assembly model contains only one copy of each component's solid model and the assembly itself is defined as a series of pointers to the component along with its position, orientation and scale. Thus an assembly with a large number of cheesehead screws of the same size, say, will contain the solid definition for only one of those screws and at each point where a screw exists in the assembly, an instance of that screw would be defined.

6.3.2 Mould Tool Design

There is a wealth of numerical methods which can assist in the designing of mould tools to achieve an optimum design of mould for high quality mouldings. Design in injection mould tools has always been an expensive process because of the need to build a prototype which may then have to undergo significant changes before a successful tool is produced. There are mould tool design systems available on the market whose main benefits are generally to reduce the development time and the number of prototype modifications for a mould tool. The productivity benefits of integrating mould tool design into a CADCAM system are that the component geometry can be used as the basis for the design of the mould which can be a relatively rapid process compared with manual methods if a library of standard tool parts is also provided. The functionality of a typical system is therefore:

1. **Initial mould design** to generate mould parts and position split lines, gates and risers.
2. **Mould fill simulation** to evaluate flow uniformity throughout the mould and fill time. The results of this analysis may generate changes to the mould design.
3. **Mould cooling** simulation is based on finite element thermal calculations to evaluate heat transfer from the plastic through the mould to the coolant. From these methods cooling time can be estimated and optimized and shrinkage and warping of the finished component analysed.

6.3.3 Rapid Prototyping

Undoubtedly, one of the most valuable aids to a designer or manufacturing engineer in visualizing a solid object is to have a physical model. We have discussed the value of geometric models generated using computer-aided design software in terms of their ability to be analysed, visualized and prepared for final manufacture, but a physical prototype of the design can be just as effective in increasing the satisfaction that the component will function correctly in the final product. It will be, more than likely, too late in the product development process to wait for the finished component only to discover that some important aspect of a component's fit or aesthetics have been overlooked. It is certainly too early to plan the complete production process for that component immediately after it has been designed. Rapid prototyping allows the generation of a physical model of a solid model within a few hours of having finished the computer model.

There are a number of different ways in which rapid prototyping can be done, namely *stereolithography, selective laser sintering* and *laminated object manufacturing*. The most common of these methods is stereolithography where the prototype is generated from a liquid polymer which is cured or solidified by ultraviolet laser light. The geometric model of the component is divided up into a number of physical slices or cross-sections and this information is formatted into a file which can be electronically transmitted to the sterolithography device. The geometry of each cross-section drives an ultraviolet laser over the surface of the polymer which solidifies to the shape; the thickness of the cross-section is governed by the position of a platform just below the surface. Once solidified, the platform lowers by the thickness of the next cross-section and the process is repeated. Depending on the size of the model, its generation may take up to several hours.

The finished prototype is therefore a close approximation, geometrically, to the designed component and can be used to assist in a range of design and manufacturing activities. The most common uses are as patterns for investment casting or as the basis for injection mould tooling. If the component is a re-design of an existing part then the prototype can be used to check fit and ease of assembly. Such forms of rapid prototyping are not yet widely available as the cost of the machinery is very high.

EXERCISES

Assignment

Depending on the facilities available, generate a wireframe or solid model of the component shown in Fig. 6.18 and transfer the geometry to a CAM system for machining the internal pocket and the holes.

Questions

6.1 By means of a diagram or otherwise, describe the process undertaken to produce NC or CNC part programs using a computer-aided part programming system. Describe two tool motion functions which are

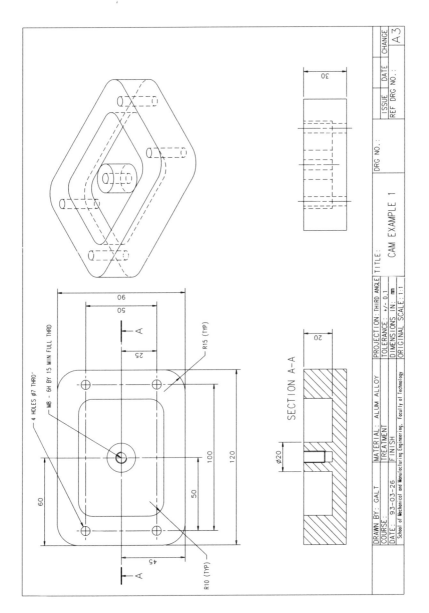

Figure 6.18 CAM assignment

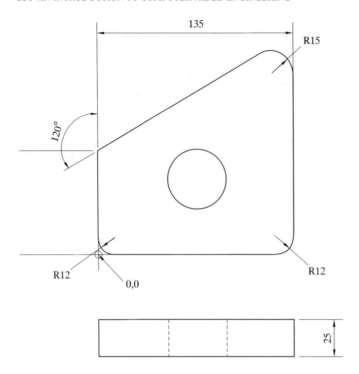

Figure 6.19 APT question

commonly available in such systems which provide exceptional productivity benefits.

6.2 Figure 6.19 shows a profile for part of a component to be machined from a rough sawn billet. The central hole is machined in the billet prior to loading to the CNC machine and this is used for clamping purposes. By sketching the profile and labelling each geometric entity write an APT program to define the geometry and machine the external profile. You need not include spindle speed and feed rate information.

6.3 From the APT code given in Fig. 6.20, sketch the tool path of tool number 1 and mark the positions of the drilled holes.

```
PARTNO/APT 2.5D SAMPLE QUESTION
$$ GEOMETRY DEFINITIONS
   ZSURF/0
P1 = POINT/0,0
P2 = POINT/P1,DELX,110
P3 = POINT/P2,DELTA,40,45
RP = POINT/67,65
C1 = CIRCLE/P1,RADIUS,15
L1 = LINE/YCOORD,-15
L2 = LINE/YCOORD,65
L3 = LINE/RP,RIGHT,TANTO,C1
L4 = LINE/XCOORD,130
L5 = LINE/XCOORD,180
L6 = LINE/YCOORD,25
C2 = CIRCLE/XLARGE,L1,YSMALL,L6,RADIUS,20
C3 = CIRCLE/XSMALL,L5,YLARGE,L6,RADIUS,10
C4 = CIRCLE/XSMALL,L5,YSMALL,L2,RADIUS,10
$$TOOL MOTION STATEMENTS - PROFILE
$$TOOL 1 IS 10 MM END MILL
TOOLNO/1
SPINDL/2000,RPM,CW
FEDRAT/150,MMPM
COOLNT/FLOOD
CUTTER/10
CYCLE/MILL,-18,FTD
FROM/0,0
GO/PAST,L1,PAST,L4
TLRGT,GOLFT.L4
GOFWD/C2
GOFWD/L6
GOFWD/C3
GOFWD/L5
GOFWD/C4
GOFWD/L2
GOFWD/L3
GOFWD/C1
GOFWD/L1,PAST,L4
$$ 4 MM DRILL
TOOLNO/2
SPINDL/2500,RPM,CW
FEDRAT/200,MMPM
COOLNT/MIST
CYCLE/MIST
CYCLE/DRILL,-15
GOTO/P1,P2,P3
END
FINI
```

Figure 6.20 APT code for tool path analysis

REFERENCES

Bedworth, D. H., M. R. Henderson and P. M. Wolfe. 1991, *Computer Integrated Design and Manufacture*. McGraw-Hill, New York.

Rembold, U., B. O. Nnaji and A. Storr. 1993, *Computer Integrated Manufacturing and Engineering*. Addison Wesley, Wokingham, UK.

SEVEN

COMPUTER-AIDED PRODUCTION PLANNING AND CONTROL

A well planned production or manufacturing process and its effective control is a mainstay of a company's financial health. The price of a product on the market is heavily dictated by the manufacturing costs, and the product's availability to the customer and its quality govern how the company fares against the competition. The majority of activities associated with the planning and control of manufacture benefit greatly from computer assistance as they involve a considerable amount of data processing and handling, which we identified in Chapter 1 as being a function more effectively carried out by computer. Production planning and control presents an extensive range of studies, some of which are beyond the scope of this introductory text and the reader is referred to a number of texts which cover the whole area in more detail, namely McMahon and Browne (1993) and Rembold *et al.* (1993). In this chapter we shall examine briefly some of the methodologies and computer-aided tools which assist in the activities of production planning and control such as process planning systems, production scheduling, material requirements and manufacturing resource planning (MRP and MRPII) and the just-in-time philosophy (JIT).

7.1 AN OVERVIEW OF PRODUCTION PLANNING AND CONTROL

The scope of production planning and control within a company is to plan manufacturing processes for the product range and to control the flow of materials, which include raw materials, components, tools and work in production (WIP), through the manufacturing plant. It is a vital aspect of an engineering enterprise because it is dependent on all areas; computer-aided production planning and control systems rely heavily on the data generated by all other areas of computer-aided engineering and can be seen as being dominant in the structure of a computer-integrated manufacturing environment, which is discussed in some detail in Chapter 9. As the name suggests the area involves two distinct, but by no means separable, types of activities: the planning of the manufacturing activities for a particular product or within the factory in general and the control of the manufacturing process.

7.1.1 Production Planning

Production planning involves a number of activities related to the preparation and modification of the manufacturing plant and the master production schedule. It includes a number of activities ranging from selecting the most appropriate processes for a component or assembly, or process planning to the design of manufacturing systems and factory layout planning.

Master production schedule   The master production schedule of a company is the statement of its expected production output over the long term. It can act as the interaction or even a contract between the management and the various departments involved in production. Its roots are in the business plan for the company which means it is a more a statement of how the company wishes or even needs to affect the market rather than how the market is actually performing.

In essence, it takes the form of a simulation which evaluates production needs from forecasts so that the manufacture of products can be scheduled through the factory facilities. In a computer-aided facility, the master production schedule is set up by the materials requirements planning or MRP system, which is discussed in more detail later.

Process planning   Planning the processes for a particular component or assembly is vital to the cost-effectiveness of a product in the marketplace. The decision as to how a component is to be manufactured may affect its function, cost and appearance and the ideal process is the one which achieves the optimum balance between all three. This is why process planning is such a vital key to the successful operation of concurrent engineering as introduced in Chapter 1 and discussed in more detail in Chapter 9. If the design of a component is completed without any reference to the process planning department then the finished item, although functionally correct, may be very costly to manufacture. Therefore the knowledge of the process planning engineer is vital in design as he or she knows the processes available in the factory and their relative costs for certain ranges of batch size. The process planning engineer can also temper a designer's desire to define tolerances too closely or to specify finer surface finishes than are necessary.

Manual process planning involves generating a set of instructions to the manufacturing plant for the production of a component or an effective order for assembly. For this activity, the memory of the process planning engineer is vital as he or she needs to be fully conversant with the capabilities and loading of particular machines, and quite often this information can be poorly documented. Computer-aided process planning tools (CAPP) fully utilize the computer's data storage and retrieval capabilities to manage a database of this information. Many such systems have been developed and are commercially available.

One type of process planning system adopts what is known as the *variant* approach which utilizes standard process plans for ranges of similar components or part families. These process plans consist of the sequence of operations for the machines and tools required for a typical family member and the process planner interacts with the database by modifying and editing the plan for a particular component. More complex CAPP packages are known as *generative*-type systems and these generally provide the means of automatically creating a process plan from the geometric description of the part, a description of the planning logic for the particular company and information relating to the availability and capabilities of machines and other resources.

7.1.2 Scheduling

An important aspect of planning the efficient manufacture of components and products within the factory is that they are scheduled so that there is optimum use of the resources available. These resources include machines, tools, personnel and materials handling equipment all of which are costly to support if they are idle for excessive amounts of time. There are a number of methods by which manufacturing jobs can be scheduled to achieve minimum machine downtime and hence maximum utilization of the resources. Many of these methods have their roots in manual systems but can be made more productive by the use of software. In a machine shop where a wide variety of components are manufactured in varying quantities and at different times, scheduling for optimum efficiency can be carried out using a number of different algorithms. In a flow line situation where components or assemblies of the same range of products are produced then it is the design of the flow line and the workstations through which a product passes during the various stages of its fabrication which is important. In this latter case, discrete event simulation, as described in Chapter 8, is a valuable tool in arranging the flow line layout so that optimum material transportation times and queue sizes can be evaluated.

In the machine shop situation in particular, but also with a flow line where the best order in which to send batches of different variants of a product needs to be decided, there are a number of algorithms which can be used. These algorithms are listed below with a short description of each—for further details on the algorithms, the reader is referred to the referenced texts.

Shortest processing time SPT methods involve ordering the jobs through the manufacturing facility or machine so that the job with the shortest processing time is placed first, the next longest second and so on. This is mainly used for scheduling jobs through one machine or facility and minimizes the mean flow time thorough the system.

Earliest due date EDD methods ensure that the jobs with the earliest due date are processed first and all subsequent jobs are scheduled in order of due date. This minimizes the possibility of a job finishing late.

Moore's algorithm This is an enhanced earliest due date method. After the jobs are sequenced in due date order, it is highly likely that, because of the processing times, there will be jobs which cannot be finished by their due date; these are known as tardy jobs. If such a job exists then the job with the largest processing time before the tardy job is removed from the sequence and positioned at the end thereby causing the tardy job to be ready by the due date. This process is continued until there are no tardy jobs in the sequence except those which have been moved thus leaving a schedule which is close to the optimum.

Johnson's algorithm. The approach represented by this method differs from those above in that it can be used to generate a schedule for jobs which need to be processed by two or more machines, manufacturing facilities or groups. It is perhaps the most well known of schedule optimization algorithms and can be readily programmed in a high level language as shown by the Pascal procedure in Fig. 7.1. Examples of where this method can be used would be if a number of batches of different cylindrical components need to first be turned on a lathe and then some or all of the surfaces ground on a grinding machine. Another example would be in manufacturing printed circuit boards of various types; first they would pass through component insertion and then through flow soldering. In both these cases the processing times for each component or assembly with each machine or cell will be different.

Johnson's algorithm minimizes the initial idle time of the second machine by forcing the jobs with the shortest processing times for the first machine near the front of the sequence. Also, in order to minimize the idle time of machine one at the end of the sequence, those jobs which have the shortest processing time on the second machine are pushed to the end of the sequence. For the Pascal procedure shown, an integer n representing the number of jobs and an array, *jobs*, of processing times for each machine is

```
type
    proctimes = array[1..2,1..20] of integer;
    schedule = array[1..20] of integer;

Procedure johnson2(n : integer; jobs : proctimes; var j2 : schedule);
{Procedure to generate a schedule of n jobs on 2 machines using
Johnson's method}
var
    s, e, m, i, j    :    integer
    minp             :    integer
    jobcopy          :    proctimes

{s indexes from the start of the schedule and e from the end.
 m alternates between the machine 1 and 2 and i & j are index
 counters
 minp retains the minimum processing time and jobcopy is a copy of
 the input jobs}

begin
    s := 1;   e := n;   m := 1
    jobcopy := jobs;
    while s <> e do
    begin
        minp := 32767;
        for i := 1 to n do
        begin
            if jobcopy[m,i] < minp then
            begin
                minp := jobcopy[m,i];
                j := i;
            end;   {if jobcopy}
        end;   {for}
        jobcopy[1,j] := 32767;
        jobcopy[2,j] := 32767;
        if m=1 then
        begin
            j2[s] := j;
            s := s + 1;
        else
            j2[e] := j;
            e := e - 1;
        end;   {if m=1}
        if m=1 then m := 2 else m := 1;
    end; {while}
end;
```

Figure 7.1 Pascal procedure for Johnson's algorithm for two machines

passed to the procedure. A one-dimensional array, *schedule*, which carries the optimized sequence is returned to the calling procedure. The algorithm works through the list of jobs and their processing times and seeks out that with the shortest time for the first machine and places this at the front of the schedule. Having done this it removes it from the job list by making the processing times very large so that they will not be picked up on subsequent scans through. It then seeks out the job with the shortest processing time for the second machine and places that job at the end of the sequence, again removing it from the list. It repeats this process of alternatively finding the shortest processing times for first and second machines and placing them towards the beginning or the end of the sequence, respectively, working towards the middle, until all jobs are sequenced.

7.1.3 Manufacturing System Design

We have already discussed the design of mechanized cells using robot modelling and simulation systems in Chapter 6. This is as much a part of computer-aided production planning as it is computer-aided manufacture and such systems represent one significant area of integration between these two areas of computer-aided engineering. Likewise, as discussed under the heading of scheduling, discrete event simulation can be used to evaluate the performance of a manufacturing system such as a flexible manufacturing system (FMS) or a flexible assembly system (FAS). The use of these systems generate optimum designs by allowing analysis of the systems modelled under varying conditions and disturbances which in turn provides a more detailed understanding of how complex manufacturing facilities operate and respond.

7.1.4 Materials and Resources Planning

A vital key to successful planning of manufacturing processes so that timely delivery of the company's products to the customer can take place is the way in which both the raw materials and components which make up that product and the utilization of resources is carried out. A materials requirement system manages the availability of the production inventory based on customer orders and is discussed in more detail later. It is generally known as materials requirements planning or MRP; later enhancements to the notion of MRP has led to MRP2/MRPII or manufacturing resource planning.

7.1.5 Production Control

No production plan can be said to be final; there are always changes to the master production schedule as customer orders and sales forecasts fluctuate. Production control therefore does not only have to ensure the correct implementation of production planning but must also provide the means to dynamically change the planning to suit such fluctuations.

A number of issues are dealt with under production control including the movement of materials and resources through the manufacturing facility, dynamic rescheduling of work in production in the event of machine or resource failure and the monitoring of quality. In a computer-aided system, the correct and timely delivery of materials can be carried out by automated materials handling devices. Failure of these systems and other process machinery is inevitable and so a key feature of successful production control, particularly in a highly mechanized environment, is a good maintenance strategy backed up by contingency plans. In some cases jobs can be rescheduled so that the failed facilities can be repaired with minimum loss of production. If the facilities are vital for a significant amount of production then measures must be taken to ensure their rapid repair. The majority of modern automated machinery is designed with this in mind.

7.1.6 Quality Monitoring

In spite of the availability of high precision machinery, no two components are produced to exactly the same size. Provided they are within the design tolerances, it can be assumed that the process is functioning correctly, but to ensure this the quality of finished components needs to be constantly monitored. Established methods of inspection can be slow, particularly if 100 per cent inspection of components is carried out. Automated inspection equipment such as coordinate measuring machines, as discussed in Chapter 3, can speed up this process and can also store and feed back the results of the inspection so that corrective action can be taken if abnormal variations occur. Statistical process control techniques exist which do continually monitor variations in the quality of finished items and can evaluate the reliability of a process.

7.2 MRP AND MRPII

In any production planning and control system it is essential that the total requirements of components which make up a product are evaluated so that the quantities for manufacture can be established in order to fulfil outstanding orders. Some of the components will be manufactured in-house whilst others are bought in and held in stores. Those which are required to be made in-house need to be done so in a timely fashion so that they can either be returned to stores for later use or immediately transported to subassembly, final assembly and delivery. Bought-in components need to be made available in sufficient time for inclusion into the products to meet promised delivery times.

Materials requirements planning or MRP was developed in the sixties in the United States to provide a computerized means of controlling the availability of materials for production. It provided the means to evaluate discrete component need from the bill-of-materials (BOM) and to provide stock inventory control. The concept of MRP developed gradually by the addition of functionality which provided support to purchasing, finance and marketing. It also encompassed the means to simulate the master production schedule so that changes in sales forecasts and shopfloor capacity could be accounted for. By the mid-seventies, the system had developed into manufacturing resource planning or MRPII.

7.2.1 MRP Operation

The operation of an MRP system is key to that of a computer-integrated manufacturing system as it utilizes data from a wide range of the computer-aided engineering facilities within a company. From design it takes information from the description of a product in terms of its components, sub-assemblies and final assembly to generate the bills-of-materials and from manufacturing, information regarding machine types, processes and processing times are input. It then operates on the principle of a multi-layer, decision-making hierarchy for the manufacturing system which is described in Chapter 9 and is also shown in Fig. 7.2. This type of hierarchy often defines a series of time horizons ranging from long term to real time. In the long term an MRP system administers the master production schedule, which maintains data on target sales, forecasts and current orders and can, by simulation, determine the future financial health of the company. It is at this point in the system that the interface to marketing, sales and finance takes place. The actual orders taken by the company can then be used to generate the medium time horizon planning.

It is at this medium-term planning stage that the actual requirements for raw materials, component manufacture and bought-in component acquisition can take place. This procedure provides a plan of the manufacturing needs in order to meet customer orders though does not take into account the actual capacity of the company's manufacturing facilities. In other

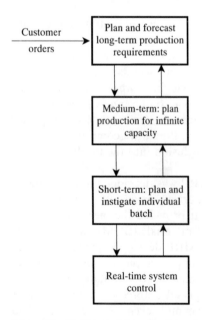

Figure 7.2 Multi-layer hierarchical description of MRP activity

words it assumes an infinite capacity to the workshops and assembly areas; no meaningful scheduling can take place but it does provide a statement of capacity requirements over the period in question. In specifying the requirements for bought-in components, it also provides the means to check stock levels of those components so that their timely ordering can take place taking into account suppliers' lead and delivery times.

The short-term planning horizon generates shopfloor scheduling on a week-by-week or even a day-by-day basis, considering single batches of components or assemblies. It is here that actual machine and resource capacities are taken into account and it is here that computer-aided procedures for scheduling are used. In any multi-layer system of this type, there is always the need to provide feedback to the higher levels which generate the information needed to make important decisions regarding the future of the company. For example, a continual inability to successfully schedule the workload through the manufacturing resources is an indication of the need to invest in more machinery or other resources. On the other hand, a significant amount of under-utilization presents the need for investment in marketing or a reorganization of the company's working practices.

At the system level, which represents the shortest time horizon, real-time control of the manufacturing activities takes place. Such real-time control is carried out by the machinery and personnel on the shopfloor but the vital link to the MRP system is the feedback from the processes regarding their actual times, reliability and consistency of quality. The feedback to the next layer up in the system may generate dynamic rescheduling of the manufacturing jobs, and when fed further up the system will cause the correction of data held in the system regarding actual capacity and capability.

7.2.2 MRP System Structure

In order to gain an understanding of the structure of MRP software let us examine a typical system. MRP software is essentially a database management system. In previous chapters we have considered databases as collections of information describing a model such as a drawing, a design, a structural definition of a component, or a system to be simulated. On the whole, these databases have contained information about the geometric composition of the model and the main way in which this information is presented and managed by the user is in graphical form. The database at the heart of an MRP system, however, is held in text form and even though some of the data can be considered as a model of the manufacturing system, it is, for the most part, an electronic filing cabinet. The database management system for MRP presents the user with a series of functions for accessing, distributing and manipulating that data and hence provides the user interface to the system, the means of outputting the information to relevant parties and an electronic calculator.

Before we go into some detail of the structure of MRP software, we need to first establish an understanding of the terminology used in databases and database management. A database can be defined as a collection of one or more data files relating to a particular application and the database management system is the software used to access and manipulate that data. Each file in a database is constructed from a series of *records*, one per item; and each record is made up of a number of *fields* which contain the attributes describing the record entry. This is illustrated in Fig. 7.3. For the example of a geometric database in a typical draughting system as discussed in Chapter 4, there is generally one file per drawing and each drawing contains a record for each geometric and detail entity, such as a line, circle, dimension or drawing note. The fields which make up these records are the numerical values of the geometric descriptions regarding position and form as well as the other parameters which describe the presentation of the entity in terms of its colour, line type and thickness.

The database controlled and managed by an MRP system consists of many files including *part master file* which gives descriptions of all the parts used by the company, the *bill-of-materials file* which lists all products and the sub-assemblies and components used in those products and other data files such as the *vendor file* which has suppliers' names, addresses, contacts and phone numbers. This latter file is used in purchasing control activities for assisted generation of orders for bought-in parts and materials. As an

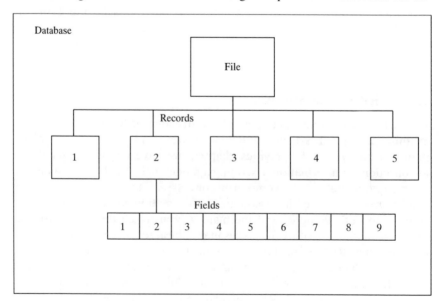

Figure 7.3 Standard database structure

example of file structure within an MRP system, each record of the part master file contains relevant data for one part or component. Each record is divided into fields as shown in Table 7.1.

Table 7.1   Fields in the *part master* file

Field identifier	Description
PART_ID	Character field giving the part number of the item
DESCN	The description of the part
U_PRICE	The purchase or manufacturing cost of the part per unit of measure
SOURCE	A single character (M or P) denoting if the item is manufactured in-house or purchased
UOM	Unit of measure—i.e. EA for single items, KG for weight, etc.

Figure 7.4 shows the main menu of a typical MRP system which lists the functionality commonly found in such software.

The bill-of-materials for a particular product is a structured list or tree of all the components which go to make it up. The generation of a BOM is originated during the design process as the main assembly is decomposed into subassemblies and then further still into individual components and raw materials. This generation of the BOM is the main interface between design, manufacture and production planning and is a standard function of most assembly modellers as described in Chapter 6. The bill-of-materials can be typically shown as a hierarchally arranged tree as shown in Fig. 7.5, where each subassembly and discrete component of a product is shown on different levels thereby displaying the composition of the complete product.

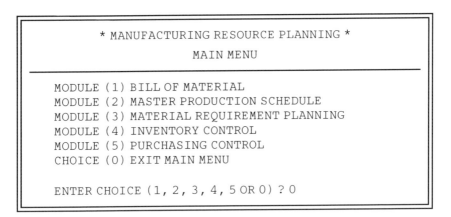

Figure 7.4   Typical MRPII software main menu

Level

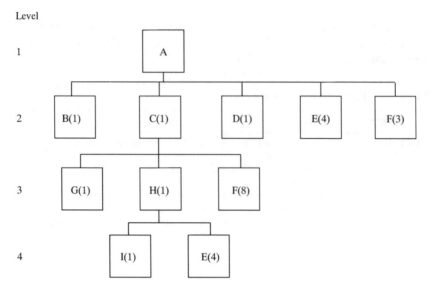

Figure 7.5 Bill-of-material explosion

In this example the product A is made up of subassemblies and components B, C, D, E and F; the numbers of each of the parts required for the main assembly are shown in brackets. The product A is known as the *parent* of these parts and, consequently, the parts themselves are known as the *children* of product A. The part C is constructed from parts G, H and F, the latter being a commonly used component such as a fastener. The example is a relatively simple one and so it must be appreciated that a more complex product may decompose into a greater number of levels and parts. There are significant benefits to such a representation in addition to those gained for the purposes of production planning; the presentation of the product in this form can feed back valuable information to design such as the need for greater variety control in order to simplify a company's range of products. The principles of variety control are also discussed in Chapter 9.

The functionality available in the BOM section of the software enables the user to examine and edit the part master file and the BOM for the whole product range. Parts can be added to the part master file so that new BOMs can be added. Manual addition of a BOM for a new product involves entering its identity number and the parts and levels which make it up, though in a fully integrated system this will be directly linked to a computer-aided design system as previously discussed.

The BOMs of all the products are stored in the BOM file which is structured so as to present, for each part, its parent, level, part id., description, the quantity required and unit of measure. The type of information that a multi-level explosion can yield assists greatly in the planning and costing of a product. Figure 7.6 shows the result of a multi-level explosion for a simple printed circuit board.

```
            ** MODULE (1) -- BILL OF MATERIAL **

               * MULTI LEVEL EXPLOSION *

                              EFF              UNIT  TOTAL
PARENT      LV PART ID   DESCRIPTION DATE   PER UOM PRICE PRICE MLT S

000324-001 1 100114-001 FIXED VALUE 17/04/92 1  EA  0.5   0.5   0.0 P
000324-001 1 100144-002 24 PINS INT 17/04/92 2  EA  1.2   2.4   0.0 P
000324-001 1 100147-001 22 PINS INT 17/04/92 1  EA  2.3   2.3   0.0 P
000324-001 1 100147-002 CLOCK CHIP  17/04/92 3  EA  2.4   7.2   0.0 P




Press any key to continue...
```

Figure 7.6   Example of multi-level explosion of BOM

The master production schedule function of the software enables the input of customer orders so that an infinite capacity plan can be generated. The user can enter an order number, product identification and required due date from which the production plan can be evaluated within the materials requirements planning section. Figure 7.7 shows an example of the material requirements planning for an order of 250 printed circuit boards, 110 of which already exist in stock. The plan recommends action to purchase sufficient components not covered by stock in sufficient time for them to be used in the production of the remainder of the order by the required date. Capacity planning will reveal whether a production schedule can deliver to the customer on time.

In order to generate the net material requirement plan, the software had to access the *inventory control file* which keeps a running record of items in stock. The inventory control part of the software enables this file to be kept up to date allowing issues to be made from stock and new items to be added to the stock record as they arrive at goods inwards or are manufactured. The complete status of the inventory can be examined or queries relating to one particular part can be addressed. The system also maintains a complete

```
* NET MATERIAL REQUIREMENT PLANNING *

ORDER NO. : 14567        QTY REQUIRED  : 250  DATE OF PLAN  : 13/09/93
MODEL NO. : 000324-001   QTY AVAILABLE : 110  DATE REQUIRED : 25/09/93
-----------------------------------------------------------------------
L              QUANTITY  QUANTITY  QUANTITY  DATE
V PART ID      REQUIRED  ON HAND   ON ORDER  ARRIVE ACTION RECOMMENDED

1 100114-001   140       10        0         / /  PUR 130 PCS BY 20/09/93
1 100144-002   280       10        0         / /  PUR 270 PCS BY 21/09/93
1 100147-001   140       10        0         / /  PUR 130 PCS BY 21/09/93
1 100147-002   420       10        0         / /  PUR 410 PCS BY 19/09/93




Press any key to continue...
```

Figure 7.7 Example net material requirement plan

history of transactions to the inventory so that receipts and issues can be traced for accounting and auditing purposes .

The inventory of bought-in parts is serviced by and also provides information for *purchasing control* which allows the issue of purchase orders of required components and raw materials. In addition to this function, this area of the software allows maintenance of the file of vendors for all bought-in items thus the generation of the physical orders sent to the suppliers is greatly assisted. The ultimate in automation for this activity would be to link order generation to electronic mail so that it becomes paperless; orders are electronically transmitted directly to the supplier over the public telephone network and received and actioned by the supplier's MRP system.

7.3 THE JUST-IN-TIME PRINCIPLE

In this chapter, we have concentrated on the need, and some of the methodologies, for realizing customer orders into production in an efficient way using computer-aided tools. This has been largely based on the traditional approach to manufacture where, although initiated and steered by customer demand, the work in progress is pushed through the manufacturing process by the availability of components and resources. That is to say, customer's requirements are realized by the generation and acquisition of stock and that stock is assembled into the final products. The holding of stock awaiting use in production within a warehouse or stores has many problems including meeting the cost of storage and handling and the amount of time required to transport it from the stores to the assembly sites. It also restricts the company in its ability to react quickly to changes in specific customer needs and the requirements of the market in general. Changes in the design of a product resulting from meeting market demand may render significant amounts of stock redundant and the temptation would be to continue production with an outdated product with poor results in sales.

If, on the other hand, the needs of the customers immediately initiated the manufacture of the components required only by those needs, and the components immediately transported to assembly areas without intermediate storage, then the costs of storage and the problems of holding and dealing with outmoded stock are eliminated. This strategy of *make to order* is one of the main principles of the just-in-time (JIT) philosophy.

7.3.1 The Aims of JIT

The roots of the just-in-time philosophy can be traced back to Japanese manufacturers in the early 1960s and it has taken some time for western manufacturers to begin to adopt the approach in order to remain competitive in a worldwide market. The philosophy is not just concerned with the elimination of stock but the principle of the elimination of waste in any form. This means stripping out of the manufacturing processes any activity or item which does not contribute to the added value of the product. This principle is envisaged in what many commentators, such as Waldner (1992), refer to as the *five zeros attitude*, namely

- zero stock
- zero lead time
- zero defects
- zero breakdowns
- zero paperwork.

Of course none of these goals can be achieved in practice, but it is the aiming towards these situations which embodies the whole concept of just-in-time production.

The just-in-time philosophy negates the traditional idea that a sizeable warehouse or stores full to the brim with components ready for the possibility that they may be used in manufacture is an asset. A just-in-time system does not boast of such an area but instead relies upon the timely delivery of bought-in raw materials and parts by the supplier at the moment they are needed for production to begin. In this way, the transportation time from stores to the manufacturing areas is pushed out onto the roads. There can be significant problems associated with this approach as it relies upon a very close cooperation between the company and its suppliers, and in some cases between the different suppliers.

Thus the whole stock or inventory for a JIT company is in the work in progress (WIP) and the principle of zero stock must also be reflected in how much of this there is. The amount of WIP can be reduced by the shortening of inter-operational transportation times which, in turn, will reduce the amount of buffering between process areas. This means ensuring that there are sufficient machines or resources available to balance processing times with waiting times to produce optimum machine utilisation. In practice this means reorganizing a workshop of randomly arranged machines into a flow line.

The principle of shortening lead times means that production is less reliant on forecasts over a long period of time and more upon customer demands and changes in the performance of the market. Lengthy lead times make the only economic form of manufacture to be in large batches and hence a need to store products in the hope of more customer orders. The just-in-time approach to manufacture is need driven, that is to say it is the individual customer orders which initiate the production of a batch of products no matter how small or how large. This gives greater customer satisfaction because upon the receipt of an order, its start and processing times can be accurately assessed thereby providing the customer with an accurate delivery time. An effective just-in-time implementation can handle batch sizes as small as one and in order to do this there must be a radical approach to the design of the products such as the use of design for manufacture, design for assembly and strict variety control within a concurrent engineering environment. These principles are described in some detail in Chapter 9.

The simplification of production planning procedures and the holistic approach to product design and its manufacture which is inherent in the concurrent engineering approach to just-in-time production means that reliable manufacturing processes are established and standardized. A greater understanding of the abilities of the processes to produce results with consistent quality is achieved thereby reducing defects to an absolute minimum. The notion that it is inevitable that a number of components will be manufactured with defects is unacceptable in a just-in-time system and constant monitoring of quality through statistical process control techniques ensures this.

The simplification of the manufacturing process by automation and the reduction of complexity in the production planning activity means that more effort can be expended on the maintenance of the resources. A systematic preventative maintenance programme of all equipment involved in the manufacturing facility reduces breakdowns. Such a programme and strategy only accepts the use of equipment which is reliable and easy to repair. Much of the activity and space not taken up by the handling of a stock inventory can be given over to the storage of necessary spare parts for equipment and the personnel specifically involved with maintenance.

stem

the operation of a just-in-time production system is
. This type of operation is often referred to as a pull
n as opposed to a push type. Traditional push type
on on a basis of forecasts and expected customer
time horizon whereas the just-in-time approach
customer needs when he or she needs it. This
principle requires that each process in manufacturing or assembly, such as a
machine group or workstation, only replaces that which has been removed
from it and only fetches the components it needs to accomplish its
manufacturing programme from the workstation preceding it. Thus each
workstation in a flow-line is a consumer of the products of that preceding it
upstream and a producer for that succeeding it downstream.

The Japanese word kanban means 'card' or 'sign' and it is by the use of
cards or kanbans that continuous flow of production within this type of
just-in-time system is regulated. Depending upon the type of parts or
products concerned, a kanban accompanies a single item, batch or container
from one workstation to the next. When those same items are passed on
further, the kanban is replaced by a different one and the original returned
to the previous workstation. Thus, there is a continual dialogue of kanbans
between any two adjacent workstations: forwards with the required items
for processing and backwards as a request for replenishment. The driving
force for such a system is therefore the point of delivery to the customer and
as he or she consumes the final products, they are replaced from final
assembly with the effect that there is a chain reaction back via goods
inwards to the suppliers themselves. This can be further explained by
examining Fig. 7.8.

Consumption begins at the furthest point upstream which ripples through
the system such that process $i+2$ requests and receives a quantity of items
from process $i+1$. Having supplied items, process $i+1$ must replenish its
stock from process i, and so on. Taking the interaction between stations or
processes i and $i-1$ as an example, quantities of items are supplied to
process i with a kanban stating the item number, name, process and
quantity. As soon as process i has used these items, it returns the kanban to

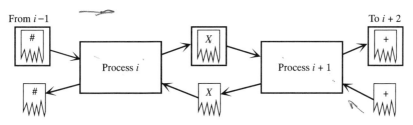

Figure 7.8 Kanban system operation

process $i-1$ where it is placed in a *first-in-first-out* (FIFO) queue known as the *kanban table*. The cyclic activity of process i, and indeed every process, is to take up the kanbans from the table and produce the items stated on it, using input from the previous processes.

EXERCISES

Assignment

By reference to textbooks and relevant journals and magazines, write a *User's Survey of Computer-aided Process Planning Systems*. State whether the systems are variant or generative and include and comment on any critical evaluation and review of the packages.

Questions

7.1 Consider the list of jobs for two machines given in Table 7.2. Using Johnson's method evaluate the optimum schedule for those jobs.

Table 7.2   Joblist for Johnson scheduling exercise

Job processing times	1	2	3	4	5	6	7	8
Machine 1	25	10	6	20	17	30	28	8
Machine 2	13	15	10	8	22	35	16	19

7.2 Using the optimum schedule derived in question 7.1 and by calculating the start time for each job through both machines, calculate the total time that jobs are waiting for machine 2.

7.3 Define the terms *record* and *field* in relation to data file structure. What constitutes a record in an *inventory control file* of an MRP system and what fields would you expect it to contain.

7.4 List the *five zeros* aimed for in a just-in-time system and explain by what methods their achievement is attempted.

7.5 By means of diagrams or otherwise, explain the operation of the *kanban system*.

REFERENCES

McMahon, C. and J. Browne. 1993, *CADCAM. From Principles to Practice*. Addison Wesley, Wokingham, UK.

Rembold, U., B. O. Nnaji and A. Storr. 1993, *Computer Integrated Manufacturing and Engineering*. Addison Wesley, Wokingham, UK.

Waldner, J.-B. 1992, *CIM. Principles of Computer Integrated Manufacture*. Wiley, Chichester.

EIGHT

SYSTEM SIMULATION

Simulation is one of the most effective design and planning tools applicable to a wide range of engineering activities. We have already seen in Chapter 6 that graphical simulation of tool path and robot movement can greatly improve productivity in the generation of manufacturing data. In product design, simulation can be used to visualize the movements of mechanisms so that collisions, excessive speeds and forces which may cause problems can be identified early on in the design process. Numerical integration techniques can be used to simulate systems whose parameters vary continuously in time, such as servo-motor speed and position control systems as used on CNC machine tools or the response of a vehicle suspension system under certain road conditions. This form of simulation is known generally as *continuous simulation* and is quite distinct from *discrete event simulation* which is widely used to assist in the design and evaluation of manufacturing systems. This chapter introduces some concepts, operation and applications of continuous and discrete event simulation as well as discussing aspects of simulation and animation of mechanisms.

8.1 CATEGORIZATION OF SIMULATION

As discussed above, simulation falls into two main categories: continuous and discrete event. The two methods are distinct in that the former is concerned with the analysis of a system's behaviour with time in response to a desired input. This behaviour varies continuously in time and so the modelling method involves some form of numerical integration in order to present a solution to the analyst. Discrete event simulation involves examining the state of a system at discrete points in time and carrying out statistical analysis of those states throughout the whole simulation run. A brief summary of the two methods is given in Table 8.1.

Table 8.1   Summary of systems simulation methods

	Continuous	Discrete Event
Mathematical modelling techniques	Numerical integration, e.g. Euler, Runge–Kutta, solution of ordinary and partial differential equations; use of transfer functions, Laplace transforms and state space representation	Stochastic modelling: queuing theory, Monte Carlo methods
Some examples	Design of instrumentation; vibrations and spring–mass systems (car suspension, accelerometers); servo-systems; kinematics	Behavioural analysis of computer systems, manufacturing systems, business models and games, ecology and environment
Typical system elements and variables	System parameters and characteristics, e.g. mass/inertia, viscous friction, stiffness, degrees of freedom, system input, simulation time and step length	Entities, resources, activity times, queue sizes and capacities, disturbances (e.g. machine failure rates) and simulation time
Some results of analysis	System response to disturbances and normal demand, e.g. step input and frequency response	Work in progress, throughput time, resource requirements and utilization, queue densities and response to disturbances

The similarity of the two methods is that they are both *dynamic* modelling systems. That is they model behaviour over a period of time and one of the main advantages of using a computer to carry out the modelling is that the whole evaluation process is accelerated. As an indication to this acceleration, many seconds of continuous simulation can be performed in a few milliseconds and minutes, hours, days, months or even years can be modelled in a similarly small amount of time using discrete event methods.

The next two sections of this chapter describe, by means of simple examples, the basis of modelling using the two methods. Continuous simulation is explained using a simple servo-motor positional control which highlights methods of numerical integration over time of an ordinary differential equation. Other forms of continuous systems analysis can include partial differential equations like those used for finite difference analysis explained in Chapter 5 which was confined to steady-state analysis using elliptical equations. The analysis of the examples given there could be extended to show variation of the system parameter over time (e.g. the temperature distribution in a flat plate) using parabolic equations. Discrete event simulation is explained using a simple manufacturing example; two approaches to evaluating, building and executing the model are shown.

Simulation, in some form or other, spans all areas of computer-aided engineering. It is a design tool for instrumentation and control systems and those parts of a product which are made up of kinematic systems. As a design tool it forms part of the range of software used for modelling and analysis, both in product and process design and evaluation. The whole area of simulation not only contains the methodologies described in this chapter but also those defined in Chapter 6, as tool path and task simulation for CNC machines and robots is an important productivity tool in computer-aided manufacturing. The modelling and analysis of manufacturing systems can be described as a CAM function but it more accurately falls within the remit of production planning and control. The design and evaluation of a proposed manufacturing flow line using discrete event simulation provides valuable information on the efficiency and operation of the system and may help in deciding which processes may be more appropriate at any stage of manufacture and how they can best be controlled.

8.2 CONTINUOUS SIMULATION

The principles of continuous simulation can be explained by a simple example like the closed-loop control system shown in Fig. 8.1 which features often in products. The example shows a simple positioning control which forms the basis of many systems, for example a CNC machine tool axis. The same basic model can be used to evaluate and design a servo-motor required to rotate at a constant speed such as the drive motor for an audio cassette player.

The desired rotational position of the motor is input to the control system as a voltage and the actual position is measured by a potentiometer across

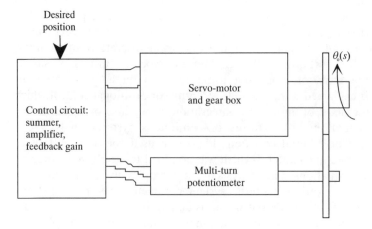

Figure 8.1 Continuous simulation example: servo-motor positional control

which a fixed voltage is placed; the wiper of the potentiometer will give a voltage proportional to position. Generally, control systems which require simulation techniques to assist in their design are more complex than this but the principles are the same.

In the above example the speed of the motor is proportional to the applied voltage for any given load. By knowing the characteristics of the motor, this speed, and hence the angular position at any one point in time, can be calculated. Thus the simulation of the system involves the integration of the angular position of the motor shaft with respect to time, as will be seen later. Such a simulation can be carried out by programming these relationships using a high level language such as FORTRAN or Pascal. Alternatively, a specifically designed software package such as ACSL (advanced continuous simulation language) or Ctrl-C can be used. Control engineers use these standard high level languages or control application languages to generate a mathematical model of a control system such that a numerical integration can be carried out. The structure of control and continuous simulation software packages is similar to the other software systems described in this book and is shown in Fig. 8.2. In this case the database describing the system to be simulated is made up of the equations which form the basis of the mathematical model and the criteria for running the model and analysing the results.

The control engineer adds to this data base when building the mathematical model and will subsequently modify system parameters or add further controlling elements to the system in order to arrive at an optimum design.

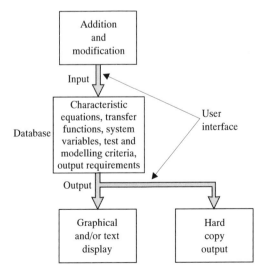

Figure 8.2 Continuous simulation software structure

8.2.1 Introduction to Control Theory

To illustrate the operation of a continuous simulation let us examine the example of the servo-motor positional control system. A DC servo-motor has particular electrical and dynamic characteristics which can be seen from Fig. 8.3.

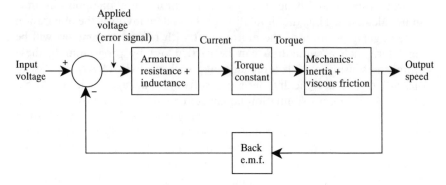

Figure 8.3 Block diagram of a typical DC servo-motor

The typical DC servo-motor consists of a permanent magnet and an armature which has electrical resistance and inductance. When a voltage is applied to the armature it passes a current which is directly proportional to the electrical resistance plus an amount which is proportional to the inductance and the rate of change of applied voltage. The current produces a magnetic field which, when interacting with the permanent magnet, generates a torque which causes the motor to rotate. This torque is proportional to the current through the armature. The acceleration of rotation of the motor is resisted by the inertia of the rotor and the speed by any viscous friction in the bearings. The resisting torque is equal to the inertia multiplied by the angular acceleration, or rate of change of speed, plus the viscous friction multiplied by the speed. The rotation of the rotor also causes a back e.m.f. (electromotive force) which has the net effect of reducing the applied voltage by subtracting a voltage proportional to the speed. In mathematical terms, if the voltage across the armature after back e.m.f. is considered is V_a, then the current through the armature is given by

$$I = \frac{V_a}{R + L\dfrac{dV_a}{dt}}. \tag{8.1}$$

The torque T is proportional to the current in the armature by a factor K_T, and the relationship between torque, speed and acceleration is given by

$$T = J\frac{d\omega}{dt} + f\omega \tag{8.2}$$

where ω is the angular speed of the motor, J is the rotor inertia and f is the viscous friction. In steady-state, that is the motor is rotating at constant speed, the current required to drive the motor provides sufficient torque to overcome the viscous friction.

Control engineers prefer to express the relationship of the output of a system to its input as a *transfer function* in *Laplace transform* notation. Laplace transforms allow integral and differential problems to be solved by expressing the governing equations in a more easily manipulated form. The theory of Laplace transforms is too lengthy to deal with in detail here but can be studied using a variety of engineering mathematics texts, for example Spencer *et al.* (1977). For the purposes of this example differential and integral function can be expressed as in Fig. 8.4.

Thus the block diagram of Fig. 8.3 can be represented using transfer functions for each of the electrical and mechanical characteristics as shown in Fig. 8.5.

Function	Transform
kx	k
$k\frac{dx}{dt}$	ks
$k\frac{d^2x}{dt^2}$	ks^2
$k\int_0^t x\,dt$	$\frac{k}{s}$

Figure 8.4 Table of Laplace transforms

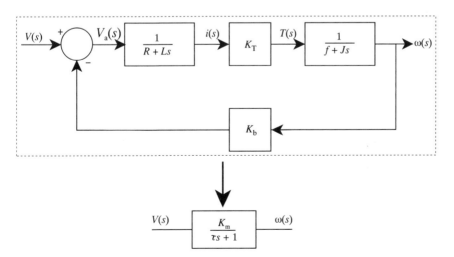

Figure 8.5 Transfer function block diagram of servo-motor

In Laplace transform notation the relationship of motor speed (ω) to the voltage V_a is given by the relationship

$$\frac{\omega}{V_a} = \frac{K_T}{(Ls + R)(Js + f)}, \tag{8.3}$$

but for many high performance servos the inductance (L) is negligible compared with R and so Eq. (8.3) reduces to

$$\frac{\omega}{V_a} = \frac{K_T}{RJs + Rf}. \tag{8.4}$$

The back e.m.f. affects the armature voltage such that

$$V_a = V - K_b\omega \tag{8.5}$$

and so combining Eqs. (8.4) and (8.5) gives the transfer function for the servo-motor as

$$\begin{aligned}
\frac{\omega}{V} &= \frac{K_T}{RJs + Rf + K_T K_b} \\
&= \frac{K_T/(Rf + K_T K_b)}{(RJ/(Rf + K_T K_b))s + 1} \\
&= \frac{K_m}{\tau s + 1}.
\end{aligned} \tag{8.6}$$

The transfer function is expressed in this way because the coefficient τ is referred to as the *time constant* and is equal to the time taken for the motor to reach 63.2 per cent of its final speed when a voltage is immediately applied and held across the motor contacts (step input). K_m is known as the *motor gain*. Thus by knowing the transfer function for a DC servo-motor the positional control system can be designed and simulated. The basis for the positional control system is the transfer function describing the rotational position (θ) of the motor under an applied voltage and because position is the integral over time of velocity the this transfer function can be expressed as shown in the block diagram of Fig. 8.6.

In order to control the position of the motor according to a desired input, a control circuit like that illustrated in Fig. 8.1 is required which can be represented in block diagram form as shown in Fig. 8.7.

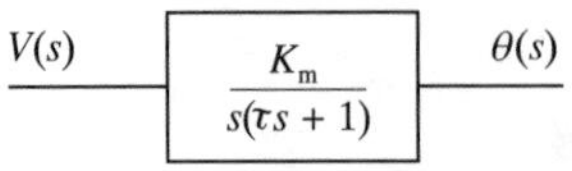

$V(s)$ $\boxed{\dfrac{K_m}{s(\tau s + 1)}}$ $\theta(s)$

Figure 8.6 Transfer function for motor position

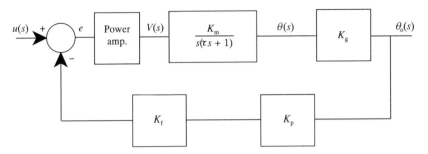

Figure 8.7 Positional feedback control system

Assuming the power amplifier has unity voltage gain the transfer function relating motor position (θ_o) with the *error signal* (e) is

$$\frac{\theta_o}{e} = \frac{K_m K_g}{\tau s^2 + s},$$ (8.7)

which yields the differential equation

$$\tau \frac{d^2\theta_o}{dt^2} + \frac{d\theta_o}{dt} = K_m K_g e$$ (8.8)

or

$$\tau \ddot{\theta}_o + \dot{\theta}_o = K_m K_g e,$$

which gives a relationship for the acceleration of the motor shaft

$$\ddot{\theta}_o = \frac{1}{\tau}(K_m K_g e - \dot{\theta}_o).$$ (8.9)

The error signal (e) is given by

$$e = u - K_p K_f \theta_o.$$ (8.10)

8.2.2 Numerical Integration

The above system can be modelled using numerical integration methods which involve predicting a value for the output (in this case angular motor position) over a small period of time (δt). The simplest way of achieving this is to use Euler's method; the principles of this are illustrated in Fig. 8.8.

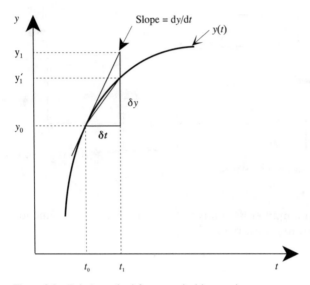

Figure 8.8 Euler's method for numerical integration

Consider a function y which varies with time t, as the rotational position of the motor does in our example. The actual position after a small period of time δt is given by the simple relationship:

$$y_1 = y_0 + \delta y$$

$$= y_0 + \frac{\delta y}{\delta t}\delta t, \tag{8.11}$$

and as δt tends to 0, or in other words, if a sufficiently small value for δt is taken, a new value for y can be evaluated as

$$y_1' = y_0 + \frac{dy}{dt}\delta t \tag{8.12}$$

and therefore the positional control system can be modelled using the equations

$$\theta_{o_i} = \theta_{o_{i-1}} + \delta t \dot{\theta}_{o_{i-1}} \tag{8.13}$$

and

$$\dot{\theta}_{o_i} = \dot{\theta}_{o_{i-1}} + \delta t \ddot{\theta}_{o_{i-1}}. \tag{8.14}$$

Combining Eq. (8.14) with Eq. (8.9) gives

$$\dot{\theta}_{o_i} = \dot{\theta}_{o_{i-1}} + \frac{\delta t}{\tau}(K_m K_g e - \dot{\theta}_{o_{i-1}}). \tag{8.15}$$

Thus the numerical integration can be programmed as the initial angular position and velocity are known at $t = 0$ and the input u is known. In this simple example we wish to analyse how the system responds when a desired input is immediately applied to the control system input. This type of actuation is known as a step input and for test purposes a unit step input can be applied, the Laplace transform of which is simply a constant value of 1, which gives rise to a relationship for the error signal e:

$$e = 1 - K_p K_f \theta_o. \tag{8.16}$$

The program for this simulation therefore is a loop in which t is incremented by δt; Eqs (8.13), (8.15) and (8.16) are evaluated for each value of t. Such a program is shown in Fig. 8.9 as a Pascal procedure, to which all the parameters of the system can be passed so that angular position and speed can be printed out for all time t.

From examination of the types of calculation required in this application it can be seen that it lends itself well to being carried out on a spreadsheet. Four columns can be defined for each of the variables for time, angular position, error signal and angular speed. Each row will hold the values for these variables at each t after the addition of δt. Having defined the spreadsheet in this way, the cell formulae corresponding to Eqs (8.13), (8.15) and (8.16), a graph can be plotted showing how the angular position (or velocity) varies with time after the application of a step input. Figure 8.10 shows a graph, generated by a spreadsheet package, of how angular position varies with a unit step input for unit feedback gain, $K_f = 1$. The major problem with using a spreadsheet to carry out numerical integration using

```
Procedure Euler_step_input(tau, km, kg,
                           kf, kp, et, dt, u : real);
{et is end time for simulation, dt is step length
angular position: p, speed: pdot
step input, u = 1}
begin
  t:=0; p:=0; pdot:=0;
  writeln('time        posn        speed');
  do while t<et
  begin
    t  := t+dt;
    p  := p+dt*pdot;
    e  := 1-kf*kp*p;
    pdot := pdot+(dt/tau)*(km*kg*e-pdot);
    writeln(t:10:3,p:10:3,pdot:10:3);
  end;
end;
```

Figure 8.9 Pascal procedure for Euler numerical integration for step input

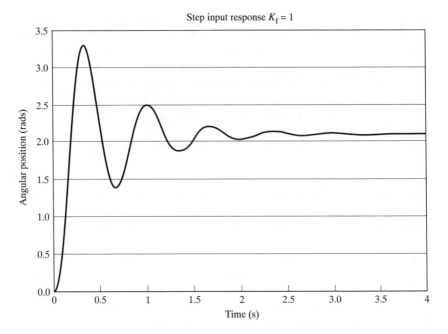

Figure 8.10   Euler step response with $K_f = 1$ and $\delta t = 0.005$

Euler's method is that a very large number of rows are required in order to calculate the variables at each time step length. The above example was simulated for 4 s using a time step length δt of 0.005 s or some 800 rows. Using a high level program like that shown in Fig. 8.9 means that a smaller number of key points in the simulation can be selected for output by using an additional loop. If greater accuracy is required then a smaller time step length must be used, as can be seen with reference to Fig. 8.8, as reducing δt will also reduce the error between y_1 and y'_1.

8.2.3 Continuous Simulation Software

As well as utilizing such tools as high level languages and spreadsheets the control engineer may find that many more facilities to carry out a complete systems simulation exist in proprietary control simulation software. Examples of the systems include ACSL (advanced control simulation language) and Ctrl-C. With such languages the system can be represented as a transfer function in Laplace transform notation and then simulated using matrix methods in *state space*. An explanation of state space notation is too lengthy for inclusion here but can be studied using a number of texts, such as Joseph *et al.* (1990).

By combining Eqs (8.7) and (8.10) a transfer function for the closed-loop system can be written

$$\frac{\theta_o}{u} = \frac{K_m K_g}{\tau s^2 + s + K_f K_p K_m K_g} \qquad (8.17)$$

and this will give rise to the Ctrl-C procedure shown in Fig. 8.11.

```
echo = 0;
.. DC servo positional control
erase
tau = input('enter motor time constant (s):');
km = input('enter motor constant (rads/vs):');
kg = input('enter gear ratio:');
vp = input('enter voltage across pot (v):');
nt = input('enter number of turns:');
kp = vp/2/pi/nt;
kf = input('enter feedback constant:');
n = [0 0 km*kg];
q = [tau 1 kf*kp*km*kg];
[a,b,c,d] = tf2ss(n,q);
t = 0:0.01:5;
y=step(a,b,c,d,1,t);
plot(t,y);
title('step input 1v');
xlabel('time (secs)');
ylabel('angular position (rads)');
pause;
w = logspace(-1,3);
[mag,p] = bode(a,b,c,d,1,w);
erase
window('211')
plot(w,mag,'logx')
title('magnitude response')
xlabel('rads/s'), ylabel('magnitude')
window('212')
plot(w,p,'logx')
title('phase response')
xlabel('rads/s'), ylabel('degs')
```

Figure 8.11 Ctrl-C procedure for positional servo simulation

The operation of this procedure is essentially divided into three distinct parts: input system parameters, calculate system equations and carry out the numerical integration and then plot out the desired results. The transfer function defined by Eq. (8.17) is defined in the procedure by the two statements:

```
n = [0 0 km*kg]
q = [tau 1 kf*kp*km*kg].
```

Each term in the square brackets represents coefficients of the Laplace transform operator (s) in descending order. This representation of the transfer function is translated into a form which can be utilised by the simulation tools in Ctrl-C, that is in state space notation by the statement:

```
[a,b,c,d] = tf2ss(n,q)
```

and a step input can be applied to the control system for simulation purposes. Some typical results from the Ctrl-C simulation are shown in Fig. 8.12 and Fig. 8.13, the step input response in the time domain and a frequency response (bode plot), respectively.

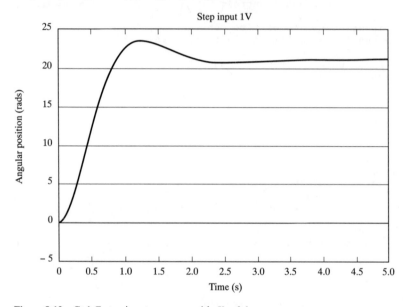

Figure 8.12   Ctrl-C step input response with $K_f = 0.1$

The user of specific control simulation software does not have to consider time step size as, quite often, these systems employ *adaptive step size control* with more sophisticated numerical integration techniques such as Runge–Kutta. The principles of these techniques are described in a number of different references, for example Chapra and Canale (1988).

8.3 DISCRETE EVENT SIMULATION

The design and verification of a manufacturing system such as a flow line require the use of discrete event simulation and an example of a small, well-bounded part of a flow line is used as an example in this section. In such a system the designer or process engineer is concerned with the state of the system at particular points in time and a statistical analysis of those states over the duration of the simulation. In discrete event simulation, an event is

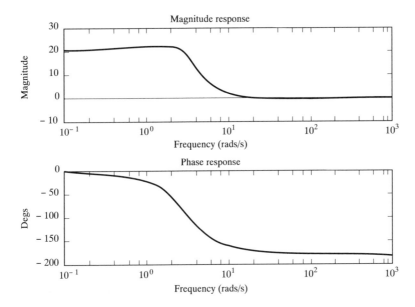

Figure 8.13 Bode plot for servo-system

defined as the start or conclusion of an *activity* such as, for example, the arrival of a product at a workstation or the conclusion of a machining or assembly operation. What happens during the activity is of little consideration to the simulation except that its duration be known, and in some cases the reliability of the machinery if a more complex analysis is required. Discrete event simulation is discussed in many texts including Poole and Szymankiewicz (1977).

8.3.1 Monte Carlo Sampling Methods

Very few situations in real life occur without a random element controlling how they behave. A human operator carrying out an assembly operation will never be consistent in how long he or she takes to finish nor will a machine break down at exactly regular intervals. Any simulation which does not take this unpredictable random element into account is termed *deterministic* simulation and will not be a very accurate model of the system under consideration. Discrete event simulation will nearly always model the randomness of real life and hence be a *stochastic* model. Even an operation carried out by a robot, which for the majority of time will be of the same duration each time, is subject to random disturbances which can be approximated and built in to the model. We have already discussed one of these disturbances as being a machine malfunction which can be modelled as an event taking place according to a predicted pattern of failure based on the robot's MTBF (mean time between failures). Its repair time can also be modelled using similar statistics based on the MTTR (mean time to repair).

The variation of time intervals between events can therefore be modelled as close to real life as possible if the pattern of variation is known or approximated; this may be defined as a standard known statistical distribution. The distribution may be mathematically derived such as normal, exponential, Erlang, triangular, rectangular, Poisson, to name but a few, or it may be based on a survey of actual observations made under similar conditions to those modelled in the simulation which may in fact turn out to follow a standard distribution. Some of these distributions are shown in Fig. 8.14; the horizontal axis represents the sample value, time for example, and the vertical axis represents the probability of the sample occurring. The exponential distribution is useful for modelling certain random events. The time interval between customers arriving at a bank or shop is most likely to be exponentially distributed, whereas a normal distribution is used to model situations where the variation is known to be symmetrical about the mean. It is possible that the variation of process time duration can be approximated using the normal distribution. In cases where the nature of a distribution is not known but the minimum, maximum and mode can be estimated then the triangular distribution may

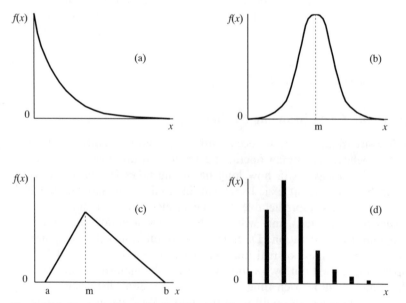

Figure 8.14 Some statistical distributions: (a) exponential; (b) normal; (c) triangular; and (d) Poisson

be the most likely choice for a simulation. The Poisson distribution is discrete in nature: that is it can only be represented in a bar chart form. It is closely linked to the exponential distribution in that if the time between events is exponentially distributed then the number of events falling within a fixed period of time has the Poisson distribution. An example where the Poisson distribution may be used is to model the size of a batch of work arriving at a manufacturing facility if it is known that the size varies randomly.

The method used to simulate variations of activity durations such that they follow a desired distribution is known as Monte Carlo simulation. This is because the way in which a random sample is taken is similar to pulling a winning number from a prize draw or spinning a roulette wheel and it was the security code name given to the mathematical technique in the early development work on the atomic bomb; it is also sometimes referred to as the *top hat* method. To illustrate how this is done, let us assume that we wish to model an assembler carrying out an assembly operation. If the model is of a proposed process then an assumption can be made that the process duration varies according to a normal distribution with an estimated mean and standard deviation. This may not be a completely valid assumption but may give us some useful results with which to work. An alternative would be to actually measure the time taken over many operations of a real-life situation similar to that proposed. If, after each operation is finished, the time taken is written on a slip of paper and put into a top hat, then a reconstruction of the situation can be done by successively drawing a slip of paper from the hat and using the time written on it as the duration of the actvity in the model.

This method would have been used in the days when simulation was carried out by hand and 'played' like a board game. As this form of simulation is generally carried out by computer these days a numerical method equivalent to the top hat approach is required and Fig. 8.15 illustrates the method for sampling from a normal distribution. The normal distribution is a known mathematical function calculated as frequency versus the time duration as shown in Fig. 8.15(b). This is known as the *probability density function* (p.d.f.). To take a random sample from this distribution the *cumulative density function* (c.d.f.) is derived. This is a relationship for the area under or the integral of the p.d.f., presented as a fraction of the whole area, versus the time duration. If a random number between 0 and 1 is generated the time duration can be evaluated from the c.d.f. by interpolating from the graph. If the random number generator is truly rectangular then the result of many samples carried out in this fashion should be a normal distribution of the same mean and standard deviation of that simulated.

The algorithm for sampling in this way involves evaluating the integral of the probability density function for the normal distribution. Given that the

Most high level languages incorporate random number generators which are fairly effective in generating a rectangular distribution between 0 and 1. Another more effective method of approximating normal distribution sampling is attributed to Box and Muller where a sample x can be evaluated using three random numbers in the relationship

$$x = m \pm \sigma \sqrt{2 \log_e \frac{1}{r_1} \sin \frac{\pi}{2} r_2} \qquad (8.21)$$

where r_1 and r_2 are separate random numbers and the decision to add or subtract is derived from a third random number.

Sampling from the exponential distribution is easier because the function defining it is known and easily integrated. The function for the exponential distribution is

$$f(x) = \frac{1}{m} e^{-x/m} \qquad \text{for } x > 0; \quad \text{otherwise } 0, \qquad (8.22)$$

where m is the mean. Integrating by parts yields a formula for sampling a value x as simply

$$x = m \log_e r. \qquad (8.23)$$

Thus the random element in a stochastic simulation can easily be approximated using any one of these methods and most packages which carry out discrete event simulation will have such functions built in to the system. Having evaluated how durations and intervals can be modelled let us now examine methods of constructing a discrete event simulation model.

8.3.2 Activity Life Cycles

Discrete event simulation involves the modelling of activities which occur in a system and the queues in which a product may have to wait prior to the commencement of the activity. For example, in the case of a flow line, a queue of products will almost certainly be formed at the entrance to a workstation or area where a manufacturing activity or process is to be carried out. The size of this queue is one of the characteristics which can be derived and optimized using discrete event simulation. One of the benefits of simulating a manufacturing system in this way is that the optimum sizes of queues or buffers can be readily determined without ever having to build the system only to find out that changes are required once production has started. Over-estimating the size of a buffer can result in the use of excessive factory space; under-estimation results in an inefficient production line. The basic principles of discrete event simulation can be demonstrated by a simple example:

Finished products arrive at regular intervals to an inspection area where they wait in a queue for an inspector to become available. They are checked and marked as either correct or faulty and then passed on for further processing: packing, rework or disposal.

For the purpose of this simple example the sorting into the three categories is outside the scope of the model, thus it can be a general example where the inspection can be any process such as a machining or assembly operation. The queues (Q) and activities (A) that any product is involved in can be listed as shown in Fig. 8.17. It can be seen from this list that the model has well-defined boundaries. What happens prior to the product entering the inspection area and what happens after it has left is not under consideration. The simulation of a large flow line can therefore be modelled piecemeal and then the various sections can be joined together for completion. Therefore, for the purposes of this example, the product has a cycle where it enters from the outside world, is inspected and returns to the outside world. During the cycle the product alternates between waiting in a queue or being involved in an activity. This is termed the *activity life cycle* of the product. The inspector also has an activity life cycle defined as shown in Fig. 8.18.

Product

In previous process (outside world)	QUEUE
Enters inspection area	ACTIVITY
Awaits inspection	QUEUE
Under inspection	ACTIVITY
In next process (outside world)	QUEUE

Figure 8.17 Activity life cyle for a product

Inspector

Waiting for product (idle)	QUEUE
Inspecting	ACTIVITY

Figure 8.18 Activity life cycle for the inspector

The life cycle for this example simply shows that the inspector is either idle and waiting for a product to enter the work area or he or she has taken the next product from the input queue and is carrying out the inspection. This accounts for both the cases when there are one or more products queuing or if there are no products queuing because they have not left the previous process. The activity life cycle can be expanded to incorporate the inspector taking a break from normal work which would have a similar description to a machine failing. In this case another activity cycle would be defined to model the repair. In simulation terminology a product, or any object which is processed by a system, is called an *entity* and the inspector, or any operator, machine, tool, cashier, is called a *resource*.

Activity life cycles form the basis of simulation using HOCUS (hand or computer universal simulator). As the name suggests the method can be used for simulating systems by hand without the use of a digital computer, which although in many cases can be long and laborious, has been in widespread use for many years. It is also available as a software package for a variety of mainframes, professional workstations and personal computers. In order to carry out the simulation by hand and to give a more easily understood representation of the model the activity life cycles can be shown diagrammatically as in Fig. 8.19.

In diagrammatic form, activities are depicted as boxes, and queues as circles, and when drawn in this way the lives of the product and the inspector are cyclic. Having examined the life cycles of both the product and the inspector, the simulation model of the system can now be completed as it can be seen that each of the two cycles share one common activity in which the product is being inspected and the inspector is carrying out his or her job function. Therefore both the activities *under inspection* and *inspect* can be defined by one common activity *inspect* as shown in Fig. 8.20.

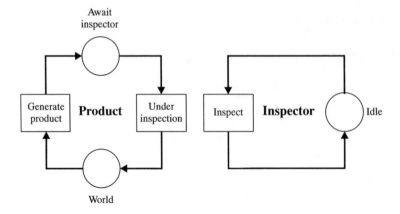

Figure 8.19   Activity life cycles for the inspection example

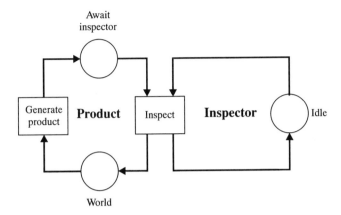

Figure 8.20   Common activity life cycles

By using tokens to represent the products and the inspector, the simulation can now be 'played' in a manner very similar to that of a board game. A suitable number of products can be placed in the queue *world* and can then be generated by evaluating and noting down the time when the next is due. This evaluation can be suitably sampled from, say, an exponential distribution and hence the time of the next event for that product can be defined. At that time, a token representing the product is placed in the *await inspection* queue. Similarly one or more tokens can be placed in the inspectors' *idle* queue; the number of tokens will define the number of inspectors assigned to the work area. One of the tests that can be made using the model would be to determine how many inspectors are needed to ensure an efficient throughput of work and allow sufficient time for breaks and other incidents.

If an inspector is available, that is if there is a spare token in the *idle* queue, then at that time a duration can be assigned to the inspection process by a sampling method. The time thus determined, which will specify when this activity ends, will define another discrete event. In other words the rule for commencing an activity such as *inspect* is that *if there is a token in all queues which feed an activity then that activity can commence*. It does so by sampling a time for its duration, adding this value to the current time (t_{now}), and adding this activity conclusion time to a list of events. A discrete event simulator operates therefore by keeping a list of events in chronological order with a description of what happens at that event. For example, an event at time t may be described as the conclusion of the activity *inspect* or *generate product*. At the conclusion of an activity the relevant tokens are placed in associated queues which in the case of the inspection being completed means that the inspector returns to the *idle* queue and the product returns to the *world* queue.

8.3.3 Analysis of Discrete Event Simulation Systems

The benefits of using a computer for discrete event simulation have already been discussed in terms of determining the optimum buffer sizes on a production line. Other information can also be readily investigated such as the utilization of machines and operators. One example already discussed is that the simulation reveals that one inspector could be considerably overworked in which case additional inspectors can easily be modelled to find out how many are needed for efficient operation.

In addition to applying the rules of commencing and finishing activities and maintaining an event list, most discrete event simulators provide facilities to evaluate and report on key statistical analysis of the states of queues, activities, resources and entities throughout the simulation run. Also, it is often possible to tag an entity as it enters a particular queue with a unique identifier and associate it with the time the entry occurred so that as it leaves or passes a defined point the time duration can be evaluated and tallied. In the inspection example above, each entity can be tagged as it enters the work area queue and the time that it was in the system tallied as it returns to the *world*. The final report therefore details the mean, variance, minimum and maximum time that the entities or products were in the system (the queue and the work area) as well as a count of how many products were inspected. This is a valuable analysis in determining the mean throughput time and hence that element of the cost of manufacture of the product.

Other important results which provide valuable insight into the performance of a system under simulation are the statistical analysis of queue sizes and operator or machine utilization. This information generally includes mean, variance, minimum, maximum and final values of entities residing in the queues and percentage of time a resource was in use with reference to the whole simulation run. For queue sizes this is done by recording the state of the queue, that is its size or length, and the time at which the change occurred and hence the time duration for which the queue remained a constant size. If the ith change in queue size s_i remains for a period of time Δt_i, then the mean queue size is defined as

$$\bar{s} = \frac{\sum s_i \Delta t_i}{\sum t_i}. \tag{8.24}$$

The mean activity duration can also be calculated in a similar way and this will give the proportion of the total simulation time that a machine, operator or other resource was active. If the ith time a resource was active was for a duration of t_i throughout a whole simulation run lasting time T, then the mean utilization for the resource can be determined, for each resource, by the relationship

$$\bar{u} = \frac{\sum t_i}{T}. \tag{8.25}$$

8.3.4 Sequential Modelling

Activity life cycle modelling is a useful approach to constructing discrete event models as it allows the analyst to consider the model as a set of individual elements each with their own patterns of behaviour and yet which interact together at specific common activities. Another way of viewing a system to be modelled is as a flow diagram beginning with the physical start of the system and finishing with the physical end. One such software system which is in widespread use and employs this type of approach is SIMAN. It can be used for both discrete event and continuous simulation and is a development from previously available languages such as GPSS, SLAM, GASP and Q-GERT. Versions available for personal computers can be interfaced to a graphics display package so that a mimic diagram of the system under simulation can be drawn on a graphics screen and animated. This gives the user the added advantage of being able to visualize the model as well as retrieving the statistical data from the simulation.

The graphic animation package for SIMAN is called CINEMA which provides functions to draw the system layout and define queues, work areas and entities on the graphics screen. The drawing functions are similar to those found in a simple computer-aided draughting package and also provides a number of predefined symbols for entities, queues and resources. With the CINEMA system is a version of SIMAN, CSIMAN, which can interact with the graphical model to present an animated version of the simulation. Most modern simulation packages supply this type of facility as the popular understanding of simulation is that it provides a pictorial model, generally in the form of an animation. This can be a valuable form of visual analysis of the simulation and can help the modeller to verify that it closely represents the real system. The graphical display of the model of a proposed system can also help to sell it to a customer or management but the aesthetics of the visual presentation must not be considered in isolation from the numerical output, which provides concrete analysis of the performance of the whole model rather than a snapshot of any one point in time. A graphical animation can, however, slow down the execution time of a model and even though faster than real time, such an analysis may be inappropriate for a complete simulation of a complex and lengthy model. The speed and quality of an animation largely depends on the graphics system in the computer and so for best results a reasonable investment in hardware is necessary.

The main principle of construction of sequential models is that only the lives of entities are considered and resources are obtained or *seized* from a pool. Rather than being considered as being drawn from and returning to the world outside the model, entities are created at the leading boundary and disposed of at the end. SIMAN uses a structured block diagram approach to the definition of models which involves joining together well-defined functional blocks in a flow chart manner. A summary of some of the more common SIMAN blocks is given in Fig. 8.21.

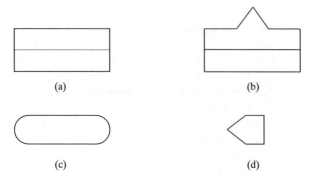

Figure 8.21   Examples of SIMAN blocks and symbols: (a) *operation;* (b) *hold;* (c) *queue* and (d) *mark*

The *operation* block is used to define a number of different functions like CREATE for creating entities, ASSIGN for giving values to entity attributes or other system variables, DELAY for defining process durations and RELEASE for freeing up resources seized for an activity. The upper portion of the operation block contains the name of the specific function and the lower portion shows the *operand* or value or assignment for the operation. For example an operand of EX(1,1) in a CREATE block specifies that an entity is created at intervals defined by exponential distribution number 1. The *hold* block defines those functions in a simulation which will hold up the flow of entities through the model. A typical and important example is the SEIZE function which specifies the physical position in the model where a resource is to be used if available. If no resources of the type indicated in the lower portion of the block are free then the entity must wait in a queue until one is. A *hold* block is therefore always preceded by a *queue* block. A *queue* block can define a queue of infinite or fixed maximum capacity and each one in the model is given a unique identifier, that is a number or a name. Contingencies for when the maximum queue capacity is exceeded can be specified. The *mark* symbol denotes where an entity is marked or tagged so that its process through the model can be monitored and, in particular, its time in the system can be tallied. A number acting as a unique identifier is placed in the *mark* symbol so that it can be referenced by the SIMAN model definition

These blocks act upon and manipulate the various *elements* within the SIMAN model: *entities, attributes, variables* and *resources.* Variables define the characteristics and state of the system during simulation such as the number of entities in a queue or the status of a machine and are therefore global to the model. As previously defined, entities are objects which engage in the activities of the system, for example workpieces, products or customers. Attributes are local variables assigned to entities and define their characteristics such as job identification or due date and resources define those units which are not moved through the model but stay fixed such as machines, operators and tools. The inspection example modelled using SIMAN is illustrated in Fig. 8.22.

In the example given, the first block *creates* entities, at intervals sampled from an exponential (EX) distribution, and these are then placed into a *queue* designated number 1. The entities wait in the queue until an *inspector* becomes available, at which time it is *seized* and a delay begins. The *delay* duration is the simulation of the time taken to carry out the inspection operation. In this case this it is assumed to follow a normal distribution (RN). After the delay the inspector is released. The SIMAN language is far too extensive to give any more detailed coverage here but the reader is referred to a number of publications on the system (Pegden 1986, Pegden *et al.* 1990). In simple terms the SIMAN block diagram is created by writing a text file in the SIMAN language; this is known as the *model frame*. Once the analyst is satisfied that the description in the model frame is an adequate representation of the real system then it need not be subsequently changed. This is because the user writes, in addition to the model frame, a second text file which defines the parameters and variables for the model. This

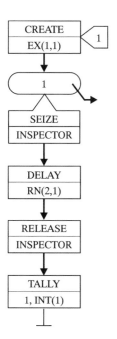

Figure 8.22 SIMAN block diagram for the inspection example

experimental frame can be changed as required to take into account the user's test specifications, for example changing the number of inspectors or the mean time duration of entity arrivals or the inspection process. The user will then run the simulation on the model using the experimental data which will produce output in the desired format. The format and type of output information can be controlled by the programmer using such blocks as TALLY and COUNT which gather information such as the number of entities generated, information relating to queue sizes and utilization of resources. This data can be passed to the output processor to produce meaningful results in the form of tables or histograms. The model frame for the inspection example is given in Fig. 8.23 and the experimental frame in Fig. 8.24.

```
      BEGIN;
10    CREATE:EX(1,1):MARK(1);    CREATE ARRIVING ENTITIES
20    QUEUE,1;                   QUEUE FOR INSPECTION
30    SEIZE:INSPECTOR;           SEIZE AN AVAILABLE INSPECTOR
40    DELAY:UN(2,1);             DELAY BY INSPECTION TIME
50    RELEASE:INSPECTOR          RELEASE THE INSPECTOR
60    TALLY:1,INT(1):DISPOSE;    TALLY TIME ENTITY IN SYSTEM
      END;                       AND THEN DISPOSE OF ENTITY
```

Figure 8.23 Model frame for inspection example

The blocks defining the model sequence are described using a strongly specified syntax and it can be seen that there is a one-to-one correlation between a block and its one-line definition in the model frame.

```
      BEGIN;
10    PROJECT, SIMPLE EXAMPLE,TIZZARD,4,7,93
20    DISCRETE,20,1,1;
30    PARAMETERS:1,25:2,30,10;
40    RESOURCES:1,INSPECTOR,1;
50    TALLIES:1,TIME IN SYSTEM;
60    DSTAT:1,NQ(1),QUEUE:2,NR(1),INSPECTOR UTIL
70    REPLICATE,1,0,1000
      END;
```

Figure 8.24 Experimental frame for inspection example

The experimental frame is constructed from a number of *elements* which define the model parameters, such as inter-arrival times, delay times or numbers of resources, how the model is executed, such as numbers of entities allowed in the system, the run length and the type of data required in the final report, such as tallies and statistical data. In the above example the entities arrive with a mean of 25 s and the inspection time has a mean of 30 s and a standard deviation of 10 s. The first execution will test the system with one inspector in the work area. Only 20 entities are allowed in the system at any one time, as specified by the first parameter of the DISCRETE element, and this limits the work in progress in a manufacturing simulation. The REPLICATE element specifies that one simulation run is to be carried out starting at time 0 and finishing at time 1000 s. The TALLIES element defines names for the TALLY blocks in the model frame and the DSTAT element request statistical analysis on queue sizes and resource utilization. NQ(1) specifies data for queue number 1 and NR(1) data for resource number 1, which is the inspector. The summary report from the simulation will list the results of the analysis: for the time in system, the average, variation, minimum, maximum and number of observations are stated and for the queue size and inspector utilization similar results are generated except that instead of number of observations, a final value is given.

8.4 KINEMATICS MODELLING AND SIMULATION

Another design tool which is proving to be valuable to engineers and which involves simulation principles is that of kinematics modelling. A number of CAD software systems incorporate kinematics simulation, either as an implicit part of the package or as an optional extra. The principle of operation is, in many respects, similar to that of robot task definition and simulation except that, instead of post-processing movements into a robot controller programme, the output can be presented in a number of ways helpful in determining the suitability of a design of a mechanism.

8.4.1 Modelling Procedure

Building a computer model of a mechanism involves specifying CAD geometry, which may be groups of line geometry, surfaces or, more commonly, solid objects as *rigid bodies* or *links* and then defining the types of movement which occur between the rigid bodies. This movement type definition is described by specifying the degrees of freedom between any two rigid bodies as a *joint*, of which there are many types. A general procedure for modelling a mechanism design is shown in Fig. 8.25.

In some systems motion can be further constrained or defined by the use of *gears*, *couplers* and *spring-dampers*, thus enabling a complete mechanism assembly model to be displayed as a working graphical animation. Kinematic modellers provide a number of predefined joint types, some of which are illustrated in Fig. 8.26, which represent common types of movement relationships between rigid bodies in real mechanisms.

The revolute and slider or prismatic joints have only one degree of freedom being either rotational about the axis of the joint or linear along the axis respectively. A ball joint defines three degrees of freedom being rotational about all three Cartesian axes; another similar joint not shown is

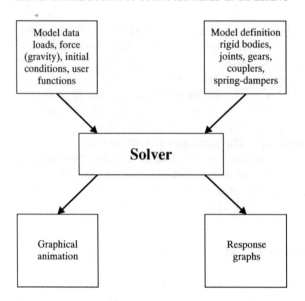

Figure 8.25 Procedure for mechanism design using kinematics modelling and simulation

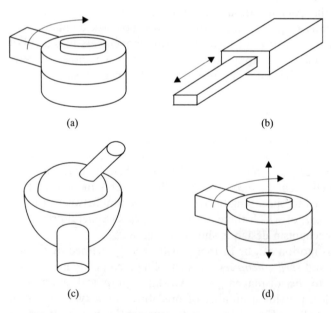

Figure 8.26 Some kinematic joint types: (a) revolute; (b) slider or prismatic; (c) ball; and (d) cylindrical

the universal joint defining two rotational degrees of freedom and is equivalent to two revolute joints at right angles to each other. The cylindrical type of joint is equivalent to a revolute joint and a prismatic joint where the joint axes are collinear. There are facilities in most kinematic modellers to define other joints where the degrees of freedom are specified by the user.

Once the physical model has been fully defined the designer can then apply the necessary inputs to carry out the simulation of the proposed real-life mechanism. These *loads* are defined to reflect as closely as possible the expected environment of the finished system; forces can be applied and a direction and value for gravitational acceleration given, an initial standard motion can be specified or a more complex user-defined function can be specified which may represent a force or motion varying over time. An example of the use of this type of input could be to model and evaluate the response and behaviour of a whole vehicle suspension to achieve an optimum design; in this case the user-defined function can represent the motion imposed on the wheels of any type of terrain.

The loads and initial conditions when applied to the model can then be solved. The method of solution is too complex to describe in any great detail here but, in general, it is based upon the application of transformations of points on the rigid bodies at a joint. These transformations numerically describe how a point on the rigid body responds to the motion defined by the constraints of a joint. For example a revolute joint will constrain the motion of a rigid body to be rotational about the axis of a joint and the motion of any point on the rotating body is defined by a rotational transformation similar to that used to rotate entities about a fixed point in a CADD package. There are a number of software packages specifically designed to offer this kind of solution in addition to those which are integral to a CAD system. Integrated CAE systems such as CATIA and I-DEAS have their own internal solvers and I-DEAS can also interface to other stand-alone solvers, for example ADAMS.

In most cases the results from the solution can be presented in two forms. Animation using the graphics display facilities of the CAD system can be a powerful tool in helping to visualize a proposed design and its behaviour and can also provide an impressive presentation for selling a design to management or customers. This, however, does not provide quantifiable results on motions and forces at key points in the mechanism. A fast-moving mechanism may have components undergoing accelerations of high magnitude and which may be generating large out-of-balance forces. A kinematics modelling system enables the user to plot position, velocity or acceleration of any point on a mechanism, relative to another, with respect to time. As the solution produces results with respect to time then kinematics modelling is a form of continuous simulation.

EXERCISES

Assignments

1. Using a proprietary control system simulation software tool (e.g. ACSL, Ctrl-C, MATLAB) or by writing a program in a high level language, create a model for the positional servo-control system described in the chapter. Use a gear box ratio of 30:1 and a 10-turn potentiometer with 30 V applied. Assume the open-loop time constant τ for the system is 0.3 s. Produce plots of response to a step input for a range of feedback attenuation constants. What attenuation is required to produce a response with no overshoot? Investigate any compensation techniques which could be incorporated into the system which would improve the step response time (settling time) with no overshoot.

2. Figure 8.27 shows a plan view of a work cell where two assemblers receive an encased electronic assembly onto which a lid is to be placed and secured with screws. There is one screwdriver which the assemblers share. Each assembler takes a case from the conveyor when it arrives and then locates the lid and the screws in position. He/she then waits for the screwdriver to become available, takes the screwdriver, tightens the screws and then places the finished item on the output conveyor.

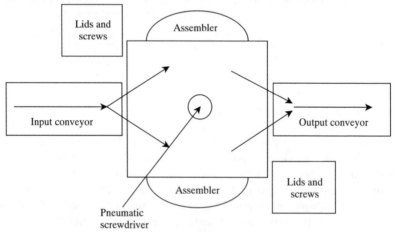

Figure 8.27   Discrete event simulation assignment

For the above situation:

(a) Draw an activity life cycle diagram each for the assembler, case and screwdriver.
(b) Join the activity life cycle diagrams into one model definition.
(c) Define the system in terms of a sequential model using a SIMAN block diagram definition or similar.

(d) Model the system using a discrete event simulation package using the following experimental data: an inter-arrival time for the boxes exponentially distributed with an average of 45 s; a time to position the lid and prepare the screws normally distributed with a mean of 30 s, standard deviation 8 s; a time to fasten all the screws using the screwdriver of mean 24 s and standard deviation of 4 s.

(e) How quickly does the input queue build up? Increase the number of assemblers to three or four and evaluate the product throughput and the assembler and screwdriver utilization. Increase the number of screwdrivers to two and compare with previous results.

(f) Add modifications to the model to include the assemblers taking a 5 min break every hour staggered to suit the number of assemblers (i.e. with two assemblers one takes a break every 30 min or 1800 s). How critical is the system to this type of disturbance?

Questions

8.1 Describe the essential differences between a *continuous* simulation model and a *discrete* event model in terms of how and when the state of a system is evaluated at any one point in time. Hence define the term discrete event.

8.2 State whether the following can be modelled using continuous or discrete event simulation:

(a) The flow rate of water through a sluice gate from a tank sourced by a varying supply.

(b) The response of the rotation of a radar transmitter to sudden wind gusts.

(c) The number of lorries required to remove earth from a construction sight to a dumping ground a known distance away.

(d) The forces on the joints of a robot lifting a load.

(e) The number of personnel required to effectively operate a switchboard

(f) The number of automated guide vehicles required to deliver material to a manufacturing process.

8.3 For each continuous simulation example identified in question 8.2 above state the input and output variables of the transfer function (you need not define the transfer function itself) which describes the system and define the type(s) of input and result(s) which would provide the necessary data to aid the system design.

8.4 For each discrete event simulation example identified in question 8.2 state the entities, resources, activities and any other variables which may be associated with the entities. For any one example describe or draw the activity life cycle diagrams for the entities and resources.

REFERENCES

Chapra, S. C. and R. P. Canale. 1988, *Numerical Methods for Engineers*, 2nd edn. McGraw-Hill, New York.

Di Stefano, J. J. III, A. R. Stubberud and I. J. Williams. 1990, *Schaum's Outline of Theory and Problems of Feedback and Control Systems*, 2nd edn. McGraw-Hill, New York.

Pegden, C. D. 1986, *Introduction to SIMAN*. Systems Modeling Corporation, Pennsylvania, USA.

Pegden, C. D., R. E. Shannon and R. P. Sadowski. 1991, *Introduction to Simulation Using SIMAN*. McGraw-Hill. New York.

Poole, T. G. and T. Z. Szymankiewicz. 1977, *Using Simulation to Solve Problems*. McGraw-Hill, London.

Spencer, A. J. M., *et al.* 1977, *Engineering Mathematics*, Vol. 1. Van Nostrand Reinhold, Wokingham.

CHAPTER

NINE

COMPUTER-INTEGRATED MANUFACTURE

In the preceding chapters a number of computer-aided engineering tools have been examined and an attempt has been made to ensure that they have not been segregated during the discussion. This is important for many reasons. In Chapter 1 we discussed that the early development of some computer-aided engineering tools was carried out in isolation even though there is a great deal of commonality in the structure and functionality between the various software systems. Modern systems are designed with the integration of the various engineering activities of the product development process in mind; there is far less doubling of effort in designing the various modules which make up an integrated computer-aided engineering system and this presents a far more efficient range of productivity tools. In this chapter we examine the principle of integrating computer-aided engineering tools into the whole product development process, that is computer-integrated manufacture or CIM. A simple definition of computer-integrated manufacture is the integration, or bringing together, of all computer-assisted functions of a manufacturing facility and the data generated by those activities into one common database in order that all such activities can be coordinated by one central computing resource. This computing resource need not be one large mainframe computer but, as will be explained later, may be a distributed system of computing devices arranged in a hierarchy. Further study of the subject of computer-integrated manufacture can be carried out with reference to Waldner (1992), Scheer (1988) and Rembold *et al.* (1993).

9.1 THE NEED FOR INTEGRATION

As there is an ever growing need to increase productivity through the use of computer-aided engineering functions, so also is there the need to ensure that different computer-assisted functions within a factory can intercommunicate. Any computer-aided engineering function is essentially an electronic equivalent of its manual counterpart and, instead of just producing human-readable output, such as an engineering drawing on paper, the main product is an electronic representation of a drawing, design, part program or production schedule in the form of a file or database. The idea of integrating all computer-aided functions is that all the data describing a product and its manufacture can be readily accessed in electronic form and used by those departments requiring them without the need to generate hard copy on paper unless absolutely necessary. This notion of the paperless environment is an ideal never quite achieved in reality, but it is something to which many suppliers and users of computing applications have aspired for some years.

There are obvious benefits to this and these include a reduction in cost of stationery and the means of transporting it as well as better communications within the factory. The typical manufacturing plant requires a significant amount of information flow which will be examined later and because this communication normally requires the use of paper, there are implicit environmental benefits arising from its reduction. The reduction in the use of paper, however, is very small compared with the savings that can be made from improved productivity in a properly installed and maintained system. An obvious disadvantage is that the whole of the factory's activities become reliant on the operation of one complex computing resource which is costly to purchase and maintain and which must be kept in strict working order. The level to which computer-integrated manufacture is implemented, therefore, is quite often restricted to the size of the company. A small company may be hard pressed to integrate its computing activities as the cost may not be justifiable and a company of any size may need to move gradually towards total integration in order to keep pace with the changes that such technology imposes. In whatever degree computer-integrated manufacture exists in a company, it is becoming more widely accepted that the ideal strategy for product development, which greatly eases its implementation, is the practice of concurrent engineering.

9.1.1 Concurrent Engineering

Concurrent engineering has already been introduced in Chapter 1 as being an effective way of reducing cost and cumulative error during product development. Any company considering implementing computer-integrated manufacture must evaluate its working practices, as no longer can departments and their work be isolated as in the 'over the wall engineering' approach illustrated in Fig. 1.3 and again in Fig. 9.1.

Quite often, the traditional approach to launching a product has been that each department has its own responsibility and when the task

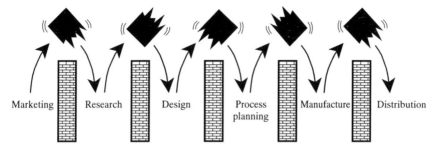

Marketing   Research   Design   Process planning   Manufacture   Distribution

Figure 9.1   Over the wall engineering

designated to that department is complete, the results are thrown 'over the wall' to the next department. The next department will then complete its task, quite often with lengthy feedback to the previous department in an attempt to iron out difficulties. This communication involves a flow of information between departments which is quite considerable, and if each department is isolated in the manner described above, this information can lead to unnecessary paperwork and use of time. If computer-aided engineering facilities are used in any of these departments and the data thus generated is passed in paper form then the productivity gained in the use of the computer can be lost during the interdepartmental communication.

To illustrate the problems that normal information flow within a company generates, let us consider Fig. 9.2, which shows a model of a typical engineering company and the paths of communications between departments. This is by no means a complete picture, but even as an indication it shows that the communication paths are many and complex involving each department or area sending out the products of its labours and receiving feedback. If an 'over the wall' type of approach is in operation then the response time between data going out and valuable feedback being received can be lengthy, which may result in significant and unnecessary costs being incurred.

This can be illustrated further by examining the type of data which is communicated and the nature of the feedback, which is summarized in Fig. 9.3. This again is a somewhat simplified view but it serves to typify the immense administrative difficulties in taking a product from customer specification to delivery. If this information can be generated in electronic form on a computer database which is accessible to all departments, then there is the potential for an increase in productivity.

Customers normally require immediate feedback on the cost of a product and while in most cases this is already calculated, the cost of customized products will need estimating, which immediately sets a budget for their design and development. Problems encountered in the process planning stage may require significant design changes and hence increase the delivery

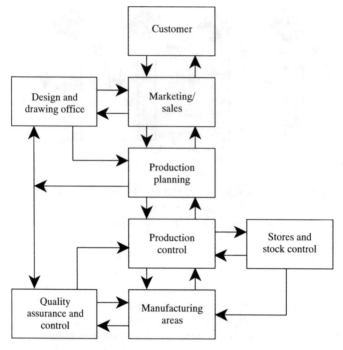

Figure 9.2 Interdepartmental communication

Between	and	Forward	Back
Customer	Marketing/Sales	Requirements	Delivery time and cost
Marketing/Sales	Design office	Customer requirements	Feasibility, design cost
Marketing/Sales	Production planning	Customer requirements	Planning, tooling costs
Design office	Production planning	Design data	Difficulties
Production planning	Production control	Machine requirements	Problems, difficulties
Production planning	Quality control	Machine requirements	Process inconsistencies
Production control	Quality control	Schedules	Inspection statistics
Production control	Manufacturing shops	Planning data, schedules	Machine availability
Production control	Stock control	Material requirements	Stock levels
Stock control	Manufacturing shops	Materials & components	Work in progress
Manufacturing shops	Quality control	Parts for inspection	Reject data and reworks

Figure 9.3 Typical information flow between departments and areas

time to the customer resulting in the company's profit being partly or completely eroded. A concurrent engineering approach ensures that process planning engineers are involved at the early design stage to ensure that the manufacture of components, subassemblies and assemblies is easily accommodated within the costs specified. It also ensures that those personnel closest to the customer or market also contribute to the design and that production control and quality assurance aspects also play an important role.

In a concurrent engineering situation, a product design project team will consist of a number of members from the various departments or areas concerned who will be involved from very early on in the process and will continue to be involved once the product is launched onto the market. The expertise of each team member will be applied in a parallel fashion to the product development as shown in Fig. 9.4. The main aim of concurrent engineering is to develop a product idea, identified from a market need or a customer's specific requirements, to the finished item with the maximum efficiency. This means reducing the lead time so that it is launched quickly thus minimizing the design and manufacturing costs. We have seen that the main problems associated with an 'over the wall' approach are that difficulties in manufacture which require some form of design change can incur considerable cost penalties. These penalties become even more unacceptable if it is discovered that the product does not perform in the marketplace because it does not meet customer requirements.

Concurrent engineering gives rise to new approaches to product development and enhances the effectiveness of existing productivity tools and these include design for the market, design for manufacture (DFM) and design for assembly.

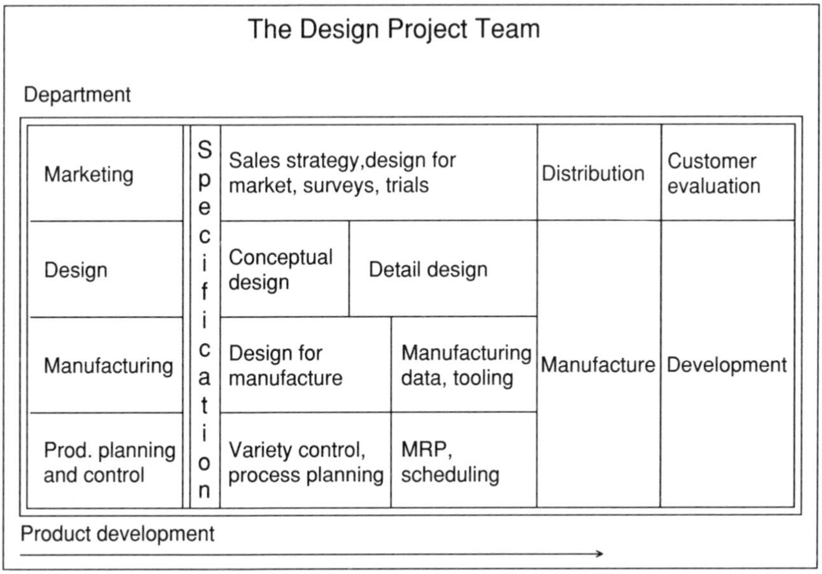

The Design Project Team

Department

Marketing	S p e	Sales strategy,design for market, surveys, trials		Distribution	Customer evaluation
Design	c i f	Conceptual design	Detail design		
Manufacturing	i c a t	Design for manufacture	Manufacturing data, tooling	Manufacture	Development
Prod. planning and control	i o n	Variety control, process planning	MRP, scheduling		

Product development

$\longrightarrow$

Figure 9.4 Parallel product development or concurrent engineering

9.1.2 Design for the Market

It is vital that those responsible for the marketing of the product are involved very early on in the design process and continue to be involved throughout the evolution of the design and manufacture. Even when an effective concurrent engineering strategy is used it still takes time to develop a product and it is not uncommon for market demand and customer's requirements to change substantially during this period. Marketing personnel are key, therefore, in the development of the initial product specification and then continue to contribute to the product development by the application of design for the market techniques.

One of the main reasons why the inclusion of design for the market principles is important to successful operation of concurrent engineering is because it also involves the design and manufacturing engineers with marketing issues. In the worst-case scenario of 'over the wall' engineering, the designer sees his or her responsibility as only meeting the company's requirements with the design; even worse still it may be only the design manager's requirements that are met! With a contribution from marketing throughout, the project team members are encouraged to think about customer requirements both at the conceptual and the detail design stages. This means that design engineers are thinking about product appearance, size, weight and ease of use and manufacturing engineers are influencing the cost to the customer. In other words, the customer has a better chance of getting what he or she wants, which is not necessarily the product itself but its function—people do not want televisions but visual entertainment systems, they do not want lawn mowers but a means to cut the grass. Design for the market also involves the customer in design decisions: physical models or impressions of the design proposals for a product are used to survey the target population who can then give their opinions on how the final product should appear.

9.1.3 Design for Manufacture

Involvement of the manufacturing and production planning and control departments provides a valuable contribution to the manufacturability of a design. Design for manufacture is the application of certain rules to the design of components that ensure cost-effective manufacture. These rules or guidelines may seem, at first sight, to be common sense but they have been sadly neglected in the past, particularly as the communication between design and manufacturing has been traditionally limited, but an increased emphasis is being placed on efficient manufacture nowadays. It has been identified that what makes a product easy or difficult to manufacture is the way it is designed rather than the way in which it is realized by a sequence of processes. The principal guidelines for design for manufacture are discussed briefly below and it is interesting to note how many of them involve simplification rather than elaboration of the design.

Standardization This is an aspect of *variety control* which is also discussed below as being a crucial factor for a design for assembly strategy. No company is so diverse in its product range that it cannot carry out some degree of standardization of component parts. Significant design time can be wasted on 'reinventing the wheel'. If a product has a function which can be fulfilled by a component already in another product then it might be possible to use the same component or a simple modification of it. An example of this may be the door mirrors in a range of cars from the small hatchback to the large executive saloon; if the same mirror is aesthetically and functionally acceptable on all or even some of the models, then why go to the expense of designing a new one. Another form of standardization which can be very effective is to have *part-finished* standard components each of which needs only a small amount of additional processing to make it into a number of variations of parts for the product range. Standardization not only reduces design time but also process setting time as it increases batch sizes and reduces the size and hence maintenance of the stock inventory.

Suitability for part function Quite often a particular component is manufactured in a certain way because a particular process is there rather than it being the most appropriate. A component may be more cheaply produced by forming, that is by impact extrusion or drawing, rather than by machining, and still be functional. The important issue is that the component functions effectively and safely and has the correct appearance, if on view. Fine surface finishes should only be specified if absolutely necessary thereby imposing fewer constraints on the choice and speed of process. The same is true for design dimensions and their tolerance and precision. The designer should always be ready to question whether general or even some specific tolerances cannot be relaxed to ease manufacturing.

Suitability for manufacturing process In a concurrent engineering situation, it is more likely that the process planning of the component affects the design rather than the design influencing the process used for its manufacture. Therefore a component's geometry and appearance and the way it is to be manufactured are arrived at more or less simultaneously. This is brought about by an application of design for manufacture rules regarding component geometry which eases the development of the process. The problem with forming processes, for example drawing and impact extrusion, is that it is often difficult to extract the finished component from the die or punch; this could easily be remedied by providing a taper. Such processes should only be adopted if the shape of the die is to be simple, that is rectangular or circular—the designer must question whether a component's geometry can be simplified even further to ease tool manufacture. Moulded components should present no excessively sharp corners, constant material thickness where possible and be designed so that extraction from the mould is quick. Components to be machined should take into account the characteristics of the machine tool. The quantity of machining should be controlled and casting or moulding should be considered as a possible pre-process to machining—some casting techniques may well produce the component to the required tolerances without the need for additional machining. The use of standard raw material stock dimensions and tolerances for some features will also reduce the amount of material removal required and relaxing surface finish requirements will reduce the need for a finishing cut.

All these considerations require a constant dialogue between the design and process planning procedures and in a computer-integrated manufacturing environment there will ideally be an associativity between CAD and CAM. This implies perhaps more than the CADCAM interface described in Chapter 6. The geometric model of the design can be used for the CAM process, that is a solid model can be used to generate tool path geometry or be used as a pattern for mould tool design but problems encountered at these stages may result in changes to component geometry which will automatically be registered in the original solid model.

9.1.4 Design for Assembly

In addition to the above criteria there is also the need to consider how components are fitted together to form a subassembly or assembly. Much of these considerations will affect component design as well as that of the overall product. Here are some of the more important guidelines.

Variety control   This, as described earlier, involves minimizing the range of parts for a company's product range as well as reducing the number of different parts within any one product. In assembly layouts it means standardizing on one type of component if it, or its function, appears many times in the assembly. An example of this is the specification of fasteners— all fastening requirements in a product may be carried out with very few or even only one type of fastener, for example a cheesehead screw of the same thread size and length. This reduces complexity of assembly as it presents the operator or robot with less variety of components, simplifies the bill-of-materials and hence its processing so reducing activities within the stores. Variety control also involves reducing the product range itself, where appropriate, and this can be carried out with confidence if there is an active design for the market strategy in place where customers' views are taken into consideration.

Reduction of parts   Although seemingly an aspect of variety control, the need to reduce the number of parts, as well as the variety, is more to do with avoiding unnecessary assembly operations. From the design point of view it normally entails assessing whether two or more existing parts, similar or otherwise, can be replaced by one single part thereby reducing pick and place type operations. An example of this type of activity is illustrated in Fig. 9.5 where two cast or machined brackets are replaced by one simple forming or extrusion which may even be available from stock as raw material.

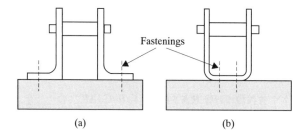

(a)   (b)

Figure 9.5   Part reduction by simplification: (a) two brackets and (b) equivalent with one U-tube

Design for automated assembly   Many of the principles which can be applied to an assembly and which make it easier to put together by automated process (for example a robot pick and place operation) can also be effective for manual assembly. Here are some of the important issues:

1. *Insertion direction and geometry.* Insertion of components from the side requires more complex programming and specialized equipment. Most standard pick and place devices (SCARA or Cartesian robots) can only effect vertical insertion. Even in manual assembly, the effects of gravity and the workbench are more effective in assisting insertion than clamps and vices. As regards the geometry of mating parts, rectangular sections require an additional orientation operation before insertion whereas circular shapes do not. An appropriate choice of tolerances, materials and surface finish can also optimize the ease of insertion of a component with its function.

2. *Layered or sandwich construction.* Orientating a partly built product at various stages throughout its assembly can be an unnecessary and costly task. This is particularly true for large and bulky items. Adopting a layered or sandwich type construction means that for the majority or even all of the construction of a product it can remain in one orientation. A television, for example, can be almost entirely constructed face-down and only turned on its base for final test, inspection and packing.

3. *Tangle-free components.* Springs and other components prone to tangling can be modified to partially or even totally eliminates the problem. If, for example, with coiled springs, end hooks are replaced by rings then intertwining cannot take place. This will ease the orientation and presentation of such components to the assembly process and in a manual situation the operator is not spending a large proportion of time untangling small items.

4. *Easy fastening.* An evaluation of the fastening together of components may also yield benefits. The fixing of screws is not an easily automated process and so *snap-together* types of fastenings for cases might be a consideration. The downside of this, however, is that such fastenings are difficult to undo for maintenance and quite often result in the case being rendered useless.

9.2 IMPLEMENTATION AND OPERATION OF CIM

To implement a fully integrated manufacturing system in an established company can be a lengthy process: many ideas and practices have to change and the changeover periods can present loss of production. With a good business plan, these problems can be eased. To give a clearer idea of how computer-integrated manufacture is implemented and operated let us return to the definition given in the introduction of this chapter, that is:

The integration, or bringing together, of all computer-assisted functions of a manufacturing facility and the data generated by those activities into one common database in order that all such activities can be coordinated by one central computing resource.

In this introduction to computer-integrated manufacture we shall briefly examine its implementation as a *bringing together* of automated or computer-assisted systems and the operation of CIM as an overall coordinating activity.

9.2.1 Islands of Automation

It has already been indicated that the degree of computer-integrated manufacture that a company can implement depends largely on its size and resources. It has been observed in the past that companies beginning to take on computer-aided engineering activities have probably done so in a piecemeal fashion. Such companies find themselves in the situation where different departments invest in new technology largely in isolation from each other as illustrated in Fig. 9.6. For example the design and development department may purchase a CADD system, production or process planning a CAM system, production control an MRP system and

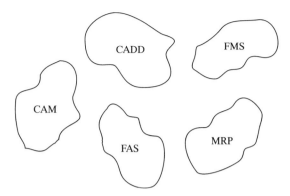

Figure 9.6 Islands of automation

the manufacturing shops CNC machines, robots and flexible manufacturing or assembly systems (FMS or FAS). This gives rise to a number of automated areas where communication between them is still done manually. These areas of technology are termed islands of automation. The first step towards integrating these islands of automation is to integrate the activities or functions carried out in those areas. This, as we have seen, is the importance of concurrent engineering. Much of the software and hardware used in the design and planning areas may need to be re-evaluated. For example, the separate CAD and CAM systems may need to be replaced by a more suitable integrated CADCAM system or the CAD system extended so that is can be used by and supply data to the MRP system (stock inventory for materials and bills-of-materials from assembly models).

The primary aim of implementing computer-integrated manufacture in a factory is to provide an electronic link between islands of automation and the design and manufacturing areas. This electronic link is normally in the form of a local area network (LAN) which is a single physical communications medium onto which all computers in the factory can connect and with which they can intercommunicate. Local area networks are discussed more fully in Chapter 10.

9.2.2 The Integrated Manufacturing Database

The coordinating activity of a computer-integrated manufacturing system lies in the creation and management of the data generated by the computer-aided functions in what were originally islands of automation. This data, instead of being generated, maintained locally and transmitted when required, is stored in the integrated manufacturing database. All data concerned with the design, planning, control and monitoring of the product development process is therefore accessible to all departments requiring its use. The structure of the database and the type of information accessed by each department is illustrated in Fig. 9.7.

An electronic database is a collection of computer files on mass storage medium (hard disk, tape, CD ROM) which are related to a particular activity. The manufacturing database is the whole collection of files generated from the development of a product, its manufacture and sales. Each department involved in the product development can gain access to relevant files in order to carry out its specific task. We have already seen a classic example of this type of work in Chapter 6 with the integration of CAD and CAM. The CADCAM system is a vital part of computer-integrated manufacture as it allows a rapid progression from the generation of a component's geometry to the CNC part program. Any problems in machining the component which are due to unsuitable geometry will be picked up very early on; modifications can be discussed between the designer and the process planning engineer to generate a fully functional component which is cost-effective to manufacture.

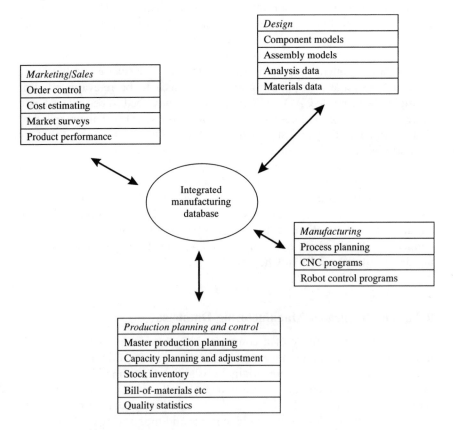

Figure 9.7 The integrated manufacturing database

The manufacturing database is therefore the hub of concurrent engineering activity as the members of the project team have a single point of access to the information concerning their common goal. Another example of this would be if the external case of a product were to be scrutinized by marketing personnel to evaluate its aesthetics for the chosen target population. The marketing expert would be able to access the case's geometric model using the CAD system and annotate it with suggestions for design modifications which could be the focus point for team discussion. With a well-designed CAD system the implementation of these design modifications is carried out quickly and easily ready for the generation of finite element models, CNC part programs, mould tools and assembly models. From the assembly modelling activity would come the parts lists and bills-of-materials (BOM) for the manufacturing requirements planning ready for when the product goes into production. With all processes planned and customer orders established then production scheduling can be carried out.

9.2.3 Integrating Engineering Software

There are a few software products on the market which are complete CADCAM integrated packages. The main feature of such products is that they can be built up from a range of software modules which share the same database and user interface. The software modules include many of the items already discussed such as simple 2 or $2\frac{1}{2}$-dimensional drawing, solid or surface modelling or both, finite element or boundary element analysis, kinematic modelling, assembly modelling, CNC part programming and robot modelling and programming. A truly integrated engineering package will be designed so that there can be some form of associativity between the work carried out on a product within modules. For example, a modification to a solid model of a component would automatically register in the assembly model and the component drawing. It should be a simple matter to redefine any tool paths and mould tools to fit the modified geometry.

Not all computer-aided engineering software is integrated in this way, however. As discussed in Chapter 6, many companies will specify and purchase CAD and CAM software separately, and the integration of the two will be part of the activity of linking islands of automation. We briefly examined some of the standard systems for exchanging data between different CADD systems and between CAD and CAM, and in many cases these standards will be used to integrate computer-aided engineering software from different vendors. One of the standards described in Chapter 6 is IGES or Initial Graphics Exchange Specification which is largely limited to transferring drawing or component geometry. Another standard is emerging from the development of IGES which is a more complete method of presenting data relating to a product and this is called STEP or Standard for Exchange of Product Data. A small section of this chapter is devoted to further description of these standards.

IGES   The first developments on IGES began as early as 1979 when the need for a standard means of transferring geometric data from one CADD product to another was identified. The standard has progressed to the release of version 5 in 1990 and is now a widely accepted means of CAE geometric model integration. The means of transferring geometric data using IGES is to convert the geometric model in the source CADD system to an *IGES file* which can be either a text or a binary file though text files are more commonly used as they are human-readable. The IGES file of the CADD model is then used as input to the IGES translator of the destination system, which may be a CAD or a CAM system, for conversion to the internal geometric database format of that system. This procedure is summarized in Fig. 9.8.

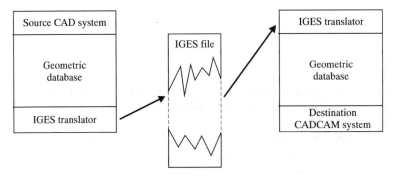

Figure 9.8   CADCAD or CADCAM interface using IGES

In an IGES file each geometric entity is defined using a unified standard. Therefore each point, line, circle, arc, curve, dimension, drawing note and many other entity types is clearly identified by its type, presentation and geometric data. The file is divided into five or six sections:

1. *The flag section* is optional and used only in special circumstances.
2. *The start section* provides a human-readable header to the file and normally contains an identifying title.
3. *The global section* identifies important features of the file which may assist the destination translator in interpreting the information contained in the rest of the file. The source system which generated the file is identified here along with the version of IGES used, the name of the source geometric database, the base units and information about the way in which *records* are separated or delimited.

4. *The directory entry section* has one record for each entity in the transferred model. This may take up several lines of text containing such details as the entity type and certain attribute parameters such as line type, thickness, colour and level or layer. The geometric parameters are not defined at this point but in the parameter data section, a pointer to the relevant geometric data is included in each directory entry for an entity.
5. *The parameter data section* contains the geometric data (position, orientation, etc.) for each entity listed in the directory entry section.
6. *The terminate section* identifies the end of the file and gives summary statistics on the length of each section.

STEP   Standard for Exchange of Product Data is an emerging standard set to replace IGES. It is an ISO standard though it has been built on the development of IGES and the American extension to it, that is PDES or Product Data Exchange Specification. The STEP specification is a drawing together and unifying of the existing standards and developments in this area. STEP goes further with the representation of a product than IGES does. IGES has been concerned largely with the transfer of geometric data and many sections of the CADD community still have not fully accepted IGES as a proper standard for graphics exchange. In many ways it is ambiguous and verbose and the translation to and from IGES complicated. STEP, on the other hand, defines the exchange of more than just graphical or topological data. A product or application can be represented by a STEP model and so its scope spans the whole of computer-aided engineering. Drawings, solid and surface models, finite element models are just some of the applications that can be defined and transferred with STEP and the methods of specifying geometric entities more akin to the way in which CAD systems structure their internal databases as described in Chapter 4.

9.3 HIERARCHICAL AND DISTRIBUTED CONTROL

The definition for computer-integrated manufacture that we have so far used has implied the existence of a single computer or computing resource. The need for the integrated manufacturing database supports this implication as there would need to be some form of contiguous mass storage to host it. The maintenance and reliability implications of such an arrangement would hardly be satisfactory as there would be too much reliance on a single complex resource to support all of a company's activities. Most integrated manufacturing systems therefore avoid the use of over-complex hosts and instead have a form of distributed control arranged as a hierarchy.

9.3.1 Types of Hierarchy

Hierarchies exist naturally in a whole range of different applications other than manufacturing industry and as such give a sound basis for any organizational structure. A hierarchy can be defined as a vertical arrangement of subsystems on different levels where a subsystem on one level influences the function of those on a lower level and responds to the influence of those on a higher level. Even though an automated manufacturing system can be described as a hierarchy of different computers or control elements, it is insufficient to do this as such a description only deals with the physical layout. There are three types of hierarchy which, between them, can be used to give a more complete description of a system: stratified, multi-layer and multi-echelon.

A **stratified hierarchy** consists of a number of levels each of gives a description of a system from a different viewpoint and perspective. The stratified description of a manufacturing system may consist of three layers as shown in Fig. 9.9. At the lowest level a manufacturing system is viewed as something which takes raw materials as input and generates finished products at the output. At the highest level it is an economic commodity providing the livelihood of a company and its employees.

Each level in a stratified hierarchy is often referred to as a *level of abstraction* or a *level of description* and while it may provide a useful model of a system, it gives no definitive explanation of structure or physical layout.

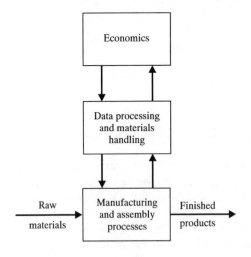

Figure 9.9 Stratified description of a manufacturing system

Multi-layer hierarchies are also known as *hierarchies of decisions* and are used to break down the procedural aspects of a system into a number of smaller subproblems. This has particular uses in describing computer-integrated manufacturing systems as the production schedules can quite often be effectively planned and described using this system. In this case each level or layer of the hierarchy defines a specific time horizon as depicted in Fig. 9.10. Each layer in this example refers to a different *time horizon* and the model describes not only the scope of each layer but also the interaction between layers. The influence of a level on the one below is to supply sufficient information for that layer to function within its time horizon. An individual process can only be concerned with a component or assembly on a one-to-one basis, but a problem occurring at that level will have an effect on the layer above. For example if the machinery malfunctions then not only will the current work be affected but also the batch schedule. This may have an effect, but a smaller one, on a plan with a longer time horizon. The main issue is that the decision-making ability at each layer is constrained only to that time horizon.

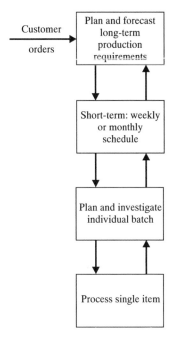

Figure 9.10 Multi-layer description of production shedule

The multi-echelon hierarchy describes the physical layout or topology of a system and is, in manufacturing terms, the description of how computing and control equipment is distributed around a plant. In such a system, a main computer may have control or feed data to a number of smaller computers and each of those may successively have a similar influence on a number of other pieces of equipment. This is illustrated in Fig. 9.11 and gives a more traditional view of distributed control in a manufacturing system where the lower levels interact directly with the manufacturing process and the more organizational control is carried out at a higher level or *echelon*. There is not necessarily a relationship between the different types of hierarchy described here but the stronger similarities in manufacturing are between the multi-layer and multi-echelon descriptions. Though there is not necessarily a one-to-one relationship between a layer in the former description and an echelon in the latter it can be said the higher levels of decision making and longer time horizon planning and control is carried out by the computers on the higher echelons.

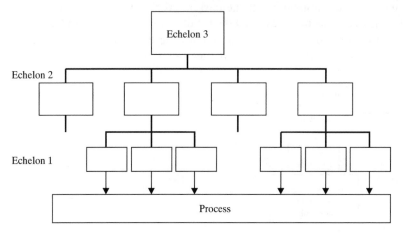

Figure 9.11 Multi-echelon organizational hierarchy

The distributed control pyramid A computer-integrated manufacturing system is likely to be defined in terms of a multi-echelon hierarchy as the basis for most systems, as discussed earlier in this chapter, is a linking of existing islands of automation. Those islands will be at various levels in the system depending on functionality and proximity to the actual manufacturing processes: CNC machines connected into the system will form part of a distributed numerical control subsystem which will be at a lower level. The production planning and scheduling facilities, CAD and computer-aided part programming systems will be incorporated into higher levels. A basic model for hierarchical, distributed control for a manufacturing system is shown as a pyramid in Fig. 9.12.

The plant level defines the computing system which carries out overall control and planning of the computer integrated manufacturing system. It must therefore have sufficient processing and storage capabilities to take on

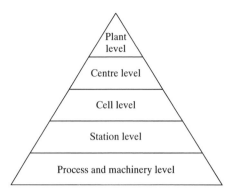

Figure 9.12   The distributed control pyramid

this role as it may host the bulk of integrated manufacturing database. For a large installation, it may be a mainframe computer but this depends on the amount of computer-aided engineering and business applications that are executed by the system. Many of these activities, however, are more likely to occur at lower levels where the hardware is more geared to coping with the needs of particular applications. Highly functional CADCAM or integrated engineering software may be more effectively implemented on professional workstations with the relevant graphics and numerical processing power situated locally in the engineering design and planning offices.

The centre level   has control over a number of cells in the manufacturing areas which form part of a flexible manufacturing system (FMS) or flexible assembly system (FAS). A flexible manufacturing system is a strategic planning and arrangement of manufacturing processes designed to provide the necessary casting, forming, machining and finishing of the components used in a company's range of products. Likewise, a flexible assembly system provides a range of work areas or stations to carry out all the assembly operations for the product range. Each process or work area is designed so that the operations or processes carried out are easily adaptable for changes to the components or assemblies as a result of development as well as the variations which occur among families of those parts and assemblies. The centre level carries out the medium to long-term planning and scheduling of work carried out in those areas and so will normally be a minicomputer, workstation or a personal computer of high specification depending on the size of the company. A group of graphics workstations, personal computers of suitable performance or graphics terminals connected to a mainframe computer executing CADD, CAM or integrated design and manufacturing software may form part of the centre level.

The cell level mostly has control of a number of functionally dedicated controllers in assembly or manufacturing shop. Short time horizon planning and scheduling for a group of CNC machines, robots or programmable logic controllers and the system for transporting work in progress and raw materials between them will be carried out by the computers at this level. The type of computer suitable for this function would be based on a personal computer or micro-controller such as a Programmable Logic Controller.

The station level groups all functionally dedicated computer controlled machines used for the processes. This range of equipment includes robots for work transfer and assembly operations, CNC machines for material removal , PLCs for controlling transport systems such as conveyors and automated guided vehicles for work and materials transport.

The process and machinery level contains no computer intelligence but consists of the robots, machine tools, driving mechanisms and sensors as distinct from the computers which control them.

The important functional properties of distributed control is that the work resulting from the production schedule is shared equally amongst the different computers at the various levels so that each has a well-defined scope and time horizon within which to work. This has many productivity benefits one of which is related to the maintenance of the equipment and the integrity of product output in the event of a failure. A malfunction at a higher level in the hierarchy will not have an immediate effect on the operation of the lower levels as each level has predetermined goals and need not have an interactive communication with the higher level in order to carry out those goals. It is more probable that equipment higher up in the hierarchy will require more frequent maintenance because of its greater complexity. The complexity of the computers and equipment becomes less the lower down the hierarchy they are and even though the failure of a robot or a CNC machine tool may hold up production in a flow line its mean time to repair (MTTR) is shorter and therefore less critical.

EXERCISES

Assignments

Carry out a literature search for reports, journal or conference papers on the implementation of computer-integrated manufacturing systems in two or more manufacturing companies. Write a report on your findings explaining the background of each case and the structure of system. Compare the experiences of the companies, drawing out, if possible, the problems they expected and those they actually met.

Using the cases studied above or others, if necessary, draw a plan of the distributed control system they used and relate it to the distributed control pyramid discussed in the chapter.

Questions

9.1 Define the term *computer integrated manufacture*.

9.2 What is *concurrent engineering*? Describe the alternative and hence discuss why concurrent engineering is essential and effective in the operation of a computer-integrated manufacturing environment.

9.3 What is *distributed control*? Describe a typical hierarchal model for distributed control specifying the type of hardware and function of each level. Why is distributed control easier to maintain than a centralized computer planning and control system?

REFERENCES

Rembold, U. B. O., Nnaji and A. Storr. 1993, *Computer Integrated Manufacturing and Engineering*. Addison Wesley, Wokingham, UK.

Scheer, A.-W. 1988, *Computer Integrated Manufacture, Computer Steered Industry*. Springer-Verlag, Berlin.

Waldner, J.-B. 1992, *Principles of Computer Integrated Manufacture*. Wiley, Chichester.

TEN

FACTORY COMMUNICATIONS

In this book, the different areas and tools for computer-aided engineering have been discussed and concluded with their integration in the preceding chapter. The final conclusion though is how the various parts of a factory operating computer-integrated manufacture communicate. Factory communications is an extensive subject in itself and this chapter presents some of the more important aspects which the mechanical or manufacturing engineer should understand if they are to be closely involved with computer integration. There are a number of texts which describe computer communications in more detail and the reader is referred to some of these for more in-depth study, namely Barnet and Maynard-Smith (1988), Tanenbaum (1989) and Dwyer and Ioannou (1987).

10.1 THE FUNDAMENTALS OF DATA COMMUNICATION

Before studying how computers communicate in a manufacturing environment it is important that we understand some of the fundamentals of the operation and problems of communicating computer data. The reader will no doubt be aware that the transmission of data from one computer system to another is not just restricted to manufacturing industry; a large proportion of the world's business and commerce is now dependent on data communications. In all computer systems there is the need to communicate data in binary form and the simplest form of this is from a computer to a peripheral device such as a printer. In this case the data to be printed is sent to the printer character by character along a cable system, each character being represented by a byte of information normally in ASCII code. There are two main ways in which this simple one-to-one communication is carried out. In many cases communication between many pieces of equipment needs to take place, and that is either by *parallel* or *serial* communication.

10.1.1 Parallel Communication

This is the most common form of data transmission from a computer to a hard copy device such as a printer. The most widespread standard used for parallel, one-to-one data transmission is the *Centronics* parallel interface which is available on most personal computer systems and printers. The principle of parallel communication is that a byte of data is transmitted along eight wires simultaneously, 1 wire for each bit of data. In addition to the 8 wires, a number of *handshaking* lines are required to carry out *flow control*. Flow control is the process in data communication where the rate of information sent to a device is controlled so that it does not swamp or overload the receiving device. When a computer is sending data to a parallel printer, it generally transmits each byte of data much faster than the printer can reproduce it onto the paper. To help overcome this, the printer has a small internal memory or buffer, where it temporarily stores the incoming characters until they can be printed and for small documents this is sufficient to ensure that no data is lost. For larger amounts of data, as soon as the printer's buffer is full, the remaining incoming characters can be lost. To avoid this there are additional communication wires between the printer and the computer which inform the computer to stop sending data if the printer's buffer is full and to also indicate when the printer has caught up again and that more data can be sent.

Another example of parallel communication is the IEEE-488 general purpose *bus* which is used to connect computing devices and instrumentation together in a laboratory environment. It allows the parallel communication of 8-bit data along its length so that any device on the bus can communicate with any other as shown in Fig. 10.1. A bus, in communications terms, can be described as a length of transmission medium, such as wire or collection of wires, onto which devices are connected. These devices can then transmit data onto the bus which will be 'seen' by all the other devices. If the data is properly tagged or labelled then all devices know which has sent the data and for whom it is intended. In order to restrict noise interference and excessive signal degradation, the devices on the IEEE-488 bus can be no more than 2 m apart and the bus no

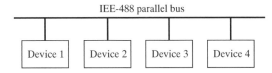

Figure 10.1 IEEE-488 parallel bus

more than 20 m in total length. The IEEE-488 bus is discussed more fully by Brey (1984).

10.1.2 Serial Communication

The main problems associated with parallel communication are that the length of cabling is restricted and the cabling itself can be costly to purchase and install. Serial communication potentially reduces the amount of cores in a cable, and even though the serial connection standard RS-232 specifies up to 25 pins on the connectors, the simplest form of serial communication can take place with just three wires: a send, a return and a common ground. The principle of serial communication is that a byte of data is sent along one wire (with a common ground) bit-by-bit consecutively and the rate at which bits of data are sent is known as the *baud rate*. This is not necessarily the rate at which all bits are transmitted because in all cases of serial communication, the data is sent in a *frame* so that the start and end of the data are clearly identified. In the RS-232 standards a frame of data has one *start bit*, seven or eight bits of data (one of which may be a *parity bit*) and 1 or 2 stop bits as illustrated in Fig. 10.2.

The standard defines logic '1' as being a line voltage of less than −3 V and greater than −25 V and logic '0' as being greater than 3 V and less than 25 V. This range allows for attenuation or lessening of the signal along the cable and makes both logic 1 and 0 distinct from the case where there is no signal at all or where there is electrical noise or other currents flowing on the line.

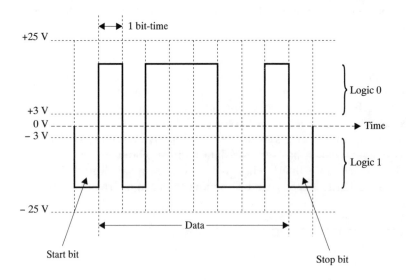

Figure 10.2   RS-232 serial transmission frame (1 start, 8 data, no parity, 1 stop).

The most recent version of the standard, RS-232-C, can transmit at a rate of up to 20 000 bits per second (20 kbps) and has a length limit of up to 15 m. A newer standard has been developed to supersede RS-232 and this is designated RS-449. It incorporates two electrical standards: RS-423-A which is similar to RS-232-C and RS-422-A which uses a *balanced line* for transmission. A signal is sent over a balanced line with two wires, one carrying the opposite polarity of the signal, so that induced noised is significantly reduced by cancellation. An RS-422-A cable can transmit at rates of up to 2 Mbps over 60 m.

10.1.3 Transmission Media

Data can be transmitted over a wide range of different media. Over relatively short land distances copper cables and optical fibres are most commonly used though some digital, as well as analogue, transmission is also carried out using radio waves. For international communication, satellites are in common use today. Fibre optics are becoming the standard means of land-line communication for long distances—more and more of the UK's telephone network is becoming fibre optic based. In buildings, such as factories using local area networks for manufacturing communications, the use of copper cable is predominant though there are some proprietary local area networks which are fibre optic based.

Copper cable comes mainly in two forms: the twisted pair or co-axial cable. Because of its characteristics, twisted pair cable is generally used for short distances such as when an RS-449 type of interface is used. Two relatively thin wires are twisted tightly together which causes any interference in one to largely cancel out that in the other. The alternative to this would be two wires lying side-by-side and not twisted and a long cable of this arrangment may act like an antenna. Co-axial cable consists of a stiff copper core which is surrounded by a relatively thick insulating medium and this is further surrounded by a copper screen in the form of a weaved mesh; the whole cable is coated by insulation. The outer screen shields the inner core from many types of interference and the insulation between the screen and the inner core helps minimize the *impedance* of the cable. Co-axial cable is commonly used in many applications—the aerial lead for your television is co-axial—and is the basis of many local area network systems. In fact, the co-axial cable used for cable television has a much higher bandwidth than that used for simple local area networks; this is *broadband* co-axial cable. Some local area networks specify the use of broadband cable so that it can be used simultaneously for other services.

The problems with copper cables of all types is that they generally consist of a number of wires or conductors in close proximity to each other. As none of these conductors is perfect, a length of cable of the magnitude used by computer networks has a significant electrical resistance. The proximity of two conductors in the same cable also gives rise to *capacitance* and significant lengths of coiled wire may also have *inductance*, though the latter is normally negligible. The resistance and the capacitance together contribute towards the impedance of a cable which is, in simple terms, its resistance to alternating currents. In fact, a significant length of twisted pair or co-axial cable forms what is known as a *low-pass filter*. A low-pass filter conducts lower frequencies of alternating current well but at higher frequencies less current flows. This is what mainly places the length restrictions on serial and parallel communications cables. The signals described by Figure 10.2 for serial transmission have a square waveform which can be mathematically defined as a summation of many different frequencies or harmonics of a sine wave. The impedance of the cable attenuates the higher frequency harmonics of the original signal which causes noticeable distortion and the longer the cable the more of this effect is generated. The pure electrical resistance of the cable also reduces the overall amplitude of the signal. What remains of a signal after its propagation along a length of copper cable is a reduced and distorted form of the original something like that shown in Fig. 10.3.

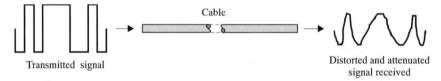

Cable

Transmitted signal

Distorted and attenuated
signal received

Figure 10.3   Distortion and attenuation of serial communication in a copper medium

Transmitting digital data as a square wave can be carried out, as we have seen, over relatively short lengths of cable only. Local area networks in factories and offices require serial transmission of data over much longer lengths of cable and so clearly a means of overcoming some of these problems is required.

10.1.4   Digital Signal Modulation

The use of broadband communication techniques significantly reduces length constraints and can also enable one cable to be used for other purposes in addition to computer networking. Broadband transmissions are used in many different commercial ventures: cable television companies transmit many channels on one cable as well as supplying a local telephone service.

If a pure sine wave is transmitted over the cable, then the major effects of the cable's low-pass filter characteristics, ignoring noise and interference, will be attenuation and a phase shift. The principle of carrying signals on a high frequency sine wave has been used with success for decades with radio and television broadcasts and the same method can be adapted for digital data transmission carried over a broadband medium. There are three ways in which data can be transmitted on a cable with a sine wave carrier and these are: *amplitude modulation, frequency modulation* and *phase modulation.* The latter can only be used for digital data on a local area network; the other two are similar in principle to radio transmission and are illustrated in Fig. 10.4.

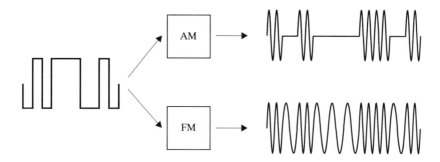

Figure 10.4 Amplitude and frequency modulation

With amplitude modulation the amplitude of the sine wave carrier is varied according to the transmitted signal. For digital transmission, one level of amplitude is used for logic 1 and another for logic 0. Frequency modulation, or *frequency shift keying* (FSK) as it is often called, works on the principle of using two frequencies of carrier wave for each of the logic states. In other words, a burst of lower frequency means logic 0 and a similar burst of higher frequency represents a logic 1.

Phase modulation, or *phase shift keying* (PSK), employs a method of coding two or three bits of data as a change in phase of the sine wave carrier. The circuitry receiving and decoding the signal must therefore be able to detect when the carrier wave phase or timing changes. This method is commonly used because the carrier wave frequency is far less dependent on the speed of transmission of digital data. Each phase change of the carrier represents the transmission of two or three bits per phase change and because of this, the speed of transmission is enhanced. If two bits are encoded per phase change then the modulation is said to be *DIBIT*, if three bits are encoded it is known as *TRIBIT* phase modulation. With DIBIT modulation, the carrier wave can change its phase in steps of 90 degrees depending on the pattern of two bits sent as shown in Table 10.1.

With TRIBIT modulation the carrier wave phase changes in steps of 45 degrees giving eight phases per 360 degrees and therefore the ability to represent a 3-bit number for each phase as shown in Table 10.2.

Table 10.1   DIBIT PSK

Data sent (2 bits)	Carrier wave phase (degs)
0 0	0
0 1	90
1 0	180
1 1	270

Table 10.2   TRIBIT PSK

Data sent (3 bits)	Carrier wave phase (degs)
0 0 0	0
0 0 1	45
0 1 0	90
0 1 1	135
1 0 0	180
1 0 1	225
1 1 0	270
1 1 1	315

Thus with DIBIT phase modulation, a byte of data can be encoded by four phase changes and with TRIBIT encoding nine bits can be transmitted in three phase changes.

Using co-axial cable, which is a common configuration for a number of local area networks, transmission rates in excess of 10 Mbps can be achieved. At such rates many devices can share a network, the basis of which is just a single co-axial cable accessed by all the devices, with good results.

10.2 LOCAL AREA NETWORKS

The basis for communications in a computer-integrated manufacturing environment is the local area network which enables all computing devices such as terminals, personal computers, workstations, factory floor controllers and peripherals to be interconnected. This gives access to the manufacturing database from any department using the relevant software for the design, planning, manufacture and distribution of a product. There are a number of proprietary local area networks available on the market for companies to install in their plant or offices and these are the results of years of development. It is because of this variety of development that there are many types, configurations, arrangements and topologies of local area network. All of them, in some form or another, rely on a connection being established between two or more *nodes* along the cable. A node is defined as a device which has been physically connected to the network. All nodes on a network have to share the transmission medium which requires a means of switching the messages or connections so that no transmission from one node collides or interferes with with that from another.

10.2.1 Types of Network Switching

There are a number of ways in which a transmission medium or network can be shared between the many devices connected to it. As mentioned above, this has to happen in order that no messages collide on the network and when a node transmits it must, for the duration of the transmission, have exclusive use of the medium. Three common methods of achieving this are time division multiplexing, circuit switching and packet switching.

Time division multiplexing or TDM gives each node on the network a slice of time, in a finite cycle, in which to transmit a frame of data. A master node controls the stream of frames and keeps a record of the connections between nodes. In any network, if a node wishes to transmit data to another, it must first establish the connection. In a TDM system when two nodes have such a *virtual connection*, they both transmit frames of data in their own time slots and read from those of the other node. This is illustrated in Fig. 10.5 where, if node A has established a connection to node C, then node A has to await its time slot before transmitting a frame of data onto the cable. Node C, knowing it is in communication with node A, awaits the arrival of the frame from node A and reads it. The same is true for the responses from node C to A.

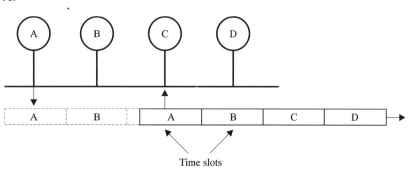

Time slots

Figure 10.5 Time division multiplexing

A TDM network invariably requires a manager node, or a scheduler, to keep track of the time cycles. In order for the cycle to be reasonably short so that the speed performance is acceptable, the number of nodes allowed on the network has a fixed upper limit. In the simplest configuration where each node has a fixed length time-slot there is a lot of wasted bandwidth when only a few of the connected nodes are actually using the network. More sophisticated TDM systems will dynamically allocate more time-slots to any remaining nodes on the network as others cease transmission and shut down.

Circuit switching is the most common way of managing network traffic. The most popular example of a circuit switched network is the early telephone system where someone making a call was physically connected to their destination by a switch at the telephone exchange. Circuit switching requires some form of switching bank or exchange so that connections between nodes are established by a hard-wired link which remains in force until either party request that it be broken. The reliability of a circuit switched network is therefore dependent on the switching exchange which is generally complex and hence more liable to develop faults.

Packet switching is used by many proprietary local area networks. Any connection between parties is virtual rather than physical and all data transmitted between them is broken down into a finite-sized packet. Each node in a packet switched network has a unique address and each packet is prefixed by the address of the transmitting node and that of the destination node. In many ways it is similar to time division multiplexing except that it is generally more stochastic in nature. That is, with TDM the transmission of the frames, which are essentially small packets, is fixed in time, whereas with many of the packet-switched networks available, the rules governing when a node can transmit a packet is more dependent on the state of the network's use in terms of traffic density.

10.2.2 Network Topologies

The topology of a network defines how it is physically laid out, which also determines how each node physically interacts with the network transmission medium. Figure 10.6 shows three major types of network topology.

The star topology is distinct from the other two in that it is the only configuration that can support circuit switching, having a central switching or exchange node through which all other nodes connect. Each node has exclusive use of the medium connecting it to the centre and the only difficulties with gaining a connection occur if the destination node is already connected to another node or if the exchange is at capacity. Because of this exclusivity, the use of cable in the star arrangement is more wasteful than in the others shown.

The ring topology connects all nodes in the network together in a physical ring and each node is an integral part of the ring circuit. This means that if a node breaks down or is removed then the ring is broken and all

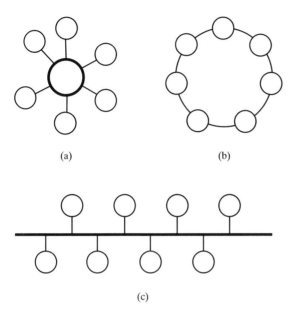

(a)   (b)

(c)

Figure 10.6   Network topologies: (a) star; (b) ring; and (c) bus

transmissions are interrupted. There are various methods of recovering from such an incident in proprietary rings including mercury switches in nodes which detect power-down and close the ring, drop cables and connectors which close switches as they are unplugged, and the use of a secondary ring as a back up. In the case of the latter, when a break in the ring is detected the network interfaces of the nodes either side of the break re-route the network onto the secondary ring thereby effecting a temporary repair as shown in Fig. 10.7. There are many proprietary ring networks which use packet switching as a means of message routeing and one of the ways in which nodes gain use of the medium to transmit a packet is by the *token ring* method. This is explained more fully later.

The bus topology   for a local area network is quite distinct in that the cable is not interrupted by the node itself but rather the node *taps onto* the transmission medium. This has advantages in that the reliability of the network is not dependent on the function of any one node and no additional measures need be taken into account for an inactive node. The bus topology is very popular among network suppliers because of its ease of installation. It is far easier to thread the cable from one end of a building to the other (with repeaters placed along the way) than it is to additionally have to return the cable back to the start for a ring or to thread cable from every node to a central hub for a star type configuration.

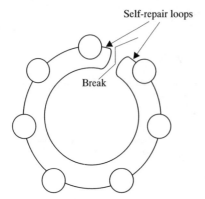

Figure 10.7   Self-repair of a ring network

10.2.3 Media Access Protocols

Regardless of topology, the major problem in managing network traffic is sharing the transmission medium among all the nodes wishing to transmit data, or the *contenders* as they are more commonly known. In a circuit switching system, it is less of a problem but if the exchange has limited switching capacity, priority has to be given to contenders on a fair and equitable basis. Packet-switched networks generally give the whole transmission medium over to one node at a time so that it can broadcast one packet which will be read by all nodes but only retained and used by the destination. A protocol is a system of rules governing communication between two or more parties so that there is no confusion and all have a fair share in the communications or negotiations. In a conference, if everyone spoke at once then there would be confusion resulting in one or more of the speaking parties being misunderstood. The normal procedure, or protocol, would be to raise your hand and address any questions and comments through the chair for all to hear.

A packet-switched network is operated on very much the same basis: there is a system of rules specifying how a node can gain exclusive use of the transmission medium for the period of time it takes to transmit one packet. That node must then go through the procedure for gaining access again before it can transmit the next packet. This, to the beginner, must seem very cumbersome especially as many of the ways in which the communication is carried out between individuals in the more helpful analogies, is slow. For example, the conference analogy given above is helpful in explaining the procedure or the need for a protocol, but does not give a real sense of the speed at which computer intercommunication takes place. In a conference situation, when a delegate has 'gained access' to the ears of audience in the session then he or she can 'transmit a packet' or make the speech—but at a human speech rate. In computer networks data can be transmitted at rates of around 10 Mbps, which means that a packet containing, say, 10 000 bytes (not all of it is actual data) will be broadcast in under 10 ms.

The most common forms of media access protocols, which are explained below, are for bus type topologies: carrier sense multiple access with collision detection (CSMA/CD) which is that used by the popular networks *ethernet* and *token passing bus* which is specified for General Motors manufacturing automation protocol (GM MAP). Ring-type networks generally use some form of token ring or token passing ring media access procedures.

Carrier sense multiple access with collision detection or CSMA/CD is a somewhat lengthy name but represents a fully adequate description. The protocol undergone by a contender is as follows:

1. *Carrier sense*. Any node wishing to transmit to another checks the electrical medium to see if there is a carrier. The presence of a sine wave carrier on the cable means that another node is in the process of transmitting and the contender must wait for the cable to be free before it can attempt to seize the medium for its use.
2. *Multiple access*. If or when there is no carrier, the node transmits its packet onto the cable but listens constantly while transmitting to ensure that no other node has also begun a transmission. As the freedom is there to attempt seizure of the medium when there is no carrier, any other node may have begun transmission at the same time. As both nodes will be constantly listening to (hopefully) their own transmission on the medium then any corruption will be detected.
3. *Collision detection*. When the two signals of the contenders meet and pass each other, they become corrupted as illustrated in Fig. 10.8. If such a bus contention or collision is detected then both nodes send a jamming signal onto the cable to warn off any other contenders and then they both back off for a random length of time. The random back-off times for each node have a high probability of being different which means that after this period the chances of another collision are diminished. On a busy network, however, there may be so many contenders that the medium is more dominated by collisions than pure packets. The collisions and recovery from them add a significant overhead to the performance of the network and so as usage increases, that is the number of contenders increases, then there will come a point where performance falls off very rapidly. CSMA/CD is defined by the internationally accepted standard IEEE 802.3

The token passing bus or token bus, as defined by the standard IEEE 802.4, was developed to overcome some of the contention problems of CSMA/CD

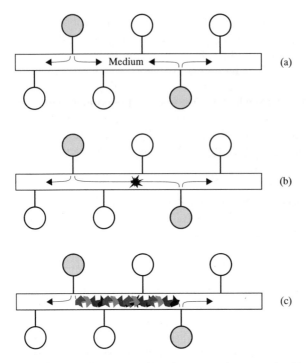

Figure 10.8 Collision detection: (a) two nodes transmit; (b) data collides; and (c) bus contention detected

protocols. Although CSMA/CD gives adequate performance even with relatively heavy loading, some companies, in particular General Motors, were concerned about the possibility of a node having to wait excessive amounts of time to transmit a packet. While this presents no great difficulties with activities which are not time-critical there may be, in an automated factory, the need to transmit data in real time and the CSMA/CD standard, IEEE 802.3, does not specify any mechanism for allocating priorities to particular nodes.

In a token bus all nodes are initially given equal priority to transmit a packet and the stochastic element of 802.3 is eliminated. As with all packet-switched networks, each node has a unique address and when the network is started up, the first node is sent a packet called the token. This is like a pass or permission for that node, and only that node, to broadcast a packet of data if it wishes to do so, in other words, if it *ready to send*. If the node has no data to transmit then it dispatches the token to its logical neighbour on the bus, that is the node with the next highest address numerically as depicted in Fig. 10.9. If it does have data to send then it transmits one packet-worth of the data, addressed to the destination, and then sends the token on the next node which then has exclusive use of the medium if

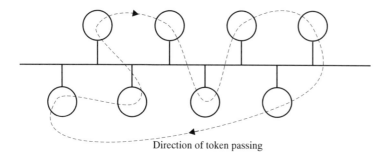

Direction of token passing

Figure 10.9   Token passing bus

required. The order in which the nodes are physically positioned on the bus is irrelevant because when the token is sent it is, as are all packets, broadcast to all nodes but only that node to which it is addressed is able to retain it.

The token passing ring   or token ring is also defined by an IEEE standard: IEEE 802.5. Many of the principles of the token bus apply in that there is one token and only the node in possession of the token can transmit. The distinctions between a ring and a bus are that the token ring has a physical ring topology, as described earlier, and the mechanism of passing on the token to the next station is point-to-point. This means that, unlike the token bus arrangement, it is not broadcast to all nodes and retained by the next contender but rather, if a node is ready to send, it seizes the token as it passes. The normal physical problems of arranging the cable in the ring apply which makes it less suitable for communications in a factory environment but more suited to an office. IBM have adopted the token ring media access protocol for its local area network.

Each node on a token ring receives all data circulating around the ring one bit at a time. As it receives each bit, it reads it and then copies it back onto the ring to be transmitted to the next node. This is often referred to as *single bit store and forward*. When no nodes are sending, the data circulating the ring is the token, which is a packet or frame with a special bit pattern. When a node becomes ready to send it must wait for the token to reach it and then it must seize it by removing it, bit by bit, from the ring. It can then place its packet of data on the ring which will pass through all subsequent nodes until it reaches its destination. The destination node reads the data and indicates its receipt by changing a bit in the header of the packet which then continues to circulate around the ring until it returns to the original sender. The sender can then verify that the data is an uncorrupted version of that sent, discard it and then regenerate the token for next contender to seize.

The problem with the single-bit store and forward approach of 802.5 is that because it takes a finite time for data to propagate along the medium, each bit occupies a physical length. If all nodes are powered down, which may occur at off-peak times during the day, it is possible that the token will not physically fit on the ring, whereas with all nodes functioning, the majority of the bits which make up the token will be stored one per node. The way this is overcome is to situate a device on the ring which simulates the presence of the shut down nodes.

The Cambridge ring   was one of the early types of ring local area network which uses a media access protocol often referred to as the *slotted ring*. Instead of there being only one token circulating around the ring to be seized by a contender, there may be a number of slots, in the form of small packets, which are either full or empty of data. The full or empty status is indicated by the state of a designated bit in the packet. Each packet is normally five bytes long, two of which are data, the remaining three bytes being given over to source and destination addresses and other relevant status information. There can be up to 254 user nodes on a ring, each having a unique 8-bit address, plus a *monitor node* which controls the circulation of packets. Any node which is ready to send has to wait for an empty packet to arrive and when it does, it marks it as full and puts into it its own address, that of the destination and the first two bytes of data it wants to send. The packet will circulate around the ring, being read and acknowledged by the destination node. The packet continues around the ring and back to the sender which will mark the packet as empty and remove the data. The sending node must then await the next empty packet before sending the next two bytes of data.

10.2.4 Network Performance

It is worth defining network performance here as from the user's point of view which is quite simply the measure of how quickly data gets through to its destination. In a computer-integrated manufacturing environment a large proportion of the data transmitted around the network is the transfer of files to and from the main database. In many instances, this does not place as heavy demands on a network as the case where many users require interactive access to mainframes or workstations using graphics. A major disadvantage of CSMA/CD protocols is that if the number of contenders for the bus is high then there may be relatively long periods of time when no node can transmit because of the large number of collisions occurring. This, as indicated earlier, can be unacceptable if some of the network traffic is of a high priority or is data requiring transfer in real-time applications.

Another problem with CSMA/CD which occurs significantly less with other protocols is that in order for collisions to be detected a node must not have finished transmitting a packet before the start of the packet has reached the extremes of the cable. If this were to occur then the node would assume that the packet or frame has been successfully transmitted without collision. Thus IEEE 802.3 states that a packet must be at least 64 bytes long from the start of the destination address to the end of the checksum (there are eight bytes of preamble and delimiter before this and the checksum is four bytes long and used for error checking). Thus if the node is sending only one byte of data in a frame there is a significant waste of transmission time and bandwidth. The only other network specification which gives constraints on the size of packet is the Cambridge ring where the proportion of actual data to packet size is 20 per cent or 40 per cent depending on whether one or two bytes of data are sent in the packet. The other systems (802.4 and 802.5) give very high or limitless sizes to their packets: the token bus allows up to about 8000 bytes of data in one packet and the token ring standard does not specify a limit. The general structure of a packet or frame specified in IEEE 802 standards is given in Fig. 10.10.

Number of bytes	3 to 8	2 or 6	2 or 6	to 1500, 8182 or ∞	4	0 or 2
	Preamble start delimiter and/or control	Destination address	Source or sender address	Data	Checksum	End delimiter

Figure 10.10   Generalized IEEE 802 frame/packet format

10.2.5 Connecting Equipment to Local Area Networks

Every local area network is highly specific in describing the type of cable, connectors, layout and means of incorporating equipment onto it. As regards cabling, the co-axial or twisted pair characteristics may be exactly specified. Ethernet specifies baseband or 50 ohm co-axial cable for what it calls *thin Ethernet*. This is used for short runs between equipment whereas *thick Ethernet* cable is more robust and used for longer lengths such as from a server or mainframe to the first group of personal computers or terminals. Thin Ethernet is connected with BNC-type plugs, sockets and T-connectors whereas a *tap* is made into a thick ethernet cable which cuts through the outer insulation to make contact with the inner cores. Token bus 802.4 specifies broadband 75 ohm co-axial cable such as that used for cable TV networks whereas 802.5 specifies shielded twisted pairs.

Any piece of equipment to be connected into a network, such as a terminal, personal computer, workstation or peripheral device, must have a suitable *interface card* installed. This printed circuit board plugs in to the bus inside the equipment and presents the correct type of connector to the outside for the chosen local area network. Interface cards for most networks can be purchased to suit most computing equipment and some printer manufacturers supply network cards for their devices so that a high quality printer can act as a shared resource.

The laying out of a local area network needs some care and planning. The cabling needs to be out of harm's way but also accessible for maintenance and addition of new nodes. Some networks such as Ethernet specify a maximum run of cabling between *repeaters*. A repeater is placed in line on the cable and receives the signal in both directions for amplification so that any attenuation in the signal does not lead to erroneous transmissions. Although it has a small delay time, a repeater is largely ignored by the software driving and controlling the network and a long run of cable with a number of repeaters on it will appear almost like one medium. A typical section of local area network layout is shown in Fig. 10.11.

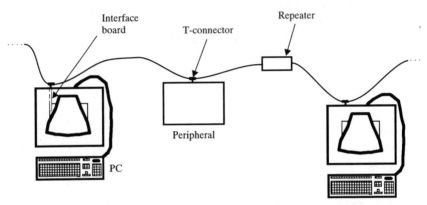

Figure 10.11   Typical local area network layout

10.3 NETWORK INTERCONNECTION

As we have seen from the preceding text, there is a wide range of local area network types, topologies and standards from which to choose when deciding on the most appropriate for factory communication. Each of the types has particular advantages and disadvantages for particular applications and some of these have already been examined. For example, for heavy real-time control traffic in an automated manufacturing shop, a CSMA/CD type of protocol may not be a suitable choice, whereas the General Motors manufacturing automation protocol which specifies IEEE 802.4 token bus has been specifically developed for this purpose. A CSMA/CD or IEEE 802.3 based network would be more suited to the engineering office where a significant amount of file transfer is carried out—that is if large data files are transferred between the mass storage media of workstations or personal computers. In fact CSMA/CD networks, and in particular

Ethernet, are very popular for linking personal computers and professional workstations to central file servers where the majority of usage is the transmission of applications programs and the data associated with them. The use of Ethernet can be quite wasteful, however, for connecting text terminals to a mainframe as much of the data transmission from the user to the mainframe is a single byte at a time—in this case it may be more appropriate to investigate the use of a token ring based system.

With these considerations in mind, it may be that a factory may have a variety of different network types installed so that the most appropriate is used in a particular area. In addition to this, the need to send and receive data to and from the outside world is almost certainly an important issue. Thus there will be a demand for transmitting data not only between nodes on any one network but also between nodes on distinctly different networks. As each network standard specifies its own cabling and connection requirements, media access protocols, addressing formats, frame or packet sizes, error recovery and other characteristics, some form of conversion will need to take place if data is to travel across a boundary between two networks. The structure and functionality of computer networks can be defined so that interconnection can take place and that all systems are potentially open to all types of user. The International Standards Organization (ISO) has developed a reference model for networks to follow and this is known as the ISO OSI (Open Systems Interconnection) seven-layer reference model. The ISO OSI model will be explained more specifically later but, in order to understand its philosophy, it would be more appropriate to examine the general requirements of all local area networks.

10.3.1 The Requirements of a Local Area Network

A local area network is more than a system of cabling for data to move around the areas within a factory or company. The definition must also include the facilities required by the users of the network and give guarantees of performance and reliability. The following requirements give a more complete definition, or specification, for a computer communications network and summarize some of the points made so far in this chapter.

1. A network must have a clearly defined, readily available, transmission medium and the means to connect computing equipment to the transmission medium with consistent reliability. The method of encoding data onto the medium should also be defined as well as the means by which data is transmitted from one node to another without interference from any other transmissions.

2. Transmissions should be free of errors and any data sent must be adequately acknowledged. The sharing out of the use of the

transmission medium should be appropriate to the application. The speed of data transmission should be such that it does not swamp a device which can only process data slowly, in other words there should be adequate data flow control mechanisms.

3. Each device connected to the network should be adequately identified and a means of tagging data with a destination device's identification or address must exist. There must be mechanisms for ensuring that all transmitted data reaches its destination.

4. One of the most important issues from a user's point of view is that all the above requirements, though absolutely necessary, should be transparent. The user is not concerned about how data flows or how the media is accessed but he or she is concerned about the reliability of the data transmission and what happens in the event of a breakdown. A local area network system should therefore provide a means to recover from a network crash and have good reporting procedures about what is happening to the user's connection and data.

5. The network must define the rules governing how two users will carry out communication, which user has priority over the connection and, during a dialogue, which user can send data first.

6. There must be a guarantee that the data sent by one user will be received and *understood* by another. If different devices have different ways of storing or coding data then the network must either define a common standard for all devices or provide conversion between them.

7. The network system must also include a number of facilities for the user such as file access, management and transfer, electronic mail, terminal emulators etc.

10.3.2 ISO OSI Seven-layer Reference Model

The above requirements have deliberately been ordered to correspond to the way in which the International Standards Organization has developed the universally accepted description of a local area network. The Open Systems Interconnection seven-layer reference model is a standard for defining various functional levels on a network. The model is shown diagrammatically in Fig. 10.12.

The ISO OSI model can be seen as describing a network in three different ways which correspond to the three different types of hierarchy discussed in Chapter 9. In one sense it is a stratified description, that is each layer is a level of abstraction or a way of viewing the network from a different point of view. For example, the *physical layer* is how an electrical engineer may view the installation of the network and the *application layer* is how users determine what it can do for them. In another sense it is a functional description with each layer having a clearly defined role in the overall operation of a successful networking system, fulfilling the requirements

7	Application
6	Presentation
5	Session
4	Transport
3	Network
2	Data link
1	Physical

Figure 10.12   Layers of the ISO OSI model

outlined above. In a third sense, which is also related to functionality, it is a hierarchy where, in varying degrees, each layer supplies information to the one below and reports status to the one above. It is largely with the functional aspects that we are concerned here.

The physical layer   describes the cabling and connection aspects of a network and how bits of data are transmitted onto the cable. Within the physical layer a description of medium access control or MAC is given as the *medium access sublayer*. We have already examined some of the physical layer descriptions for networks such as Ethernet's thick and thin baseband cable or MAP's broadband co-axial cable. From the reliability point of view, the physical layer demands that a digital signal introduced at one end of the transmission medium reaches the other end in a decipherable form, though it is not concerned with the correction of errors. This includes specifying such parameters as voltage levels and polarities for logic levels, signal modulation and how connections are made and broken.

The data link layer   builds on the function of the physical layer in that it assumes that raw data bits can be transmitted and so ensures that this is carried out with no errors. It is the data link layer which specifies not only the upper limit on the size of the data field in the packet or frame shown in Fig. 10.10, but also the actual amount during any one transmission. Making the sender of the data break it up into shorter frames ensures that any one frame is checked for errors, using the checksum, at the destination and acknowledgements are returned. If errors are found to have occurred, the software which carries out the data link function will either attempt to correct the error or request that the packet be sent again. Another function of the data link layer is flow control. The description of the layer for any one type of network specifies the type of flow control and the function of the software ensures that it is carried out. Flow control ensures that a device which cannot process received data very quickly, such as a printer, can request the sender to suspend transmission until it has carried out the processing.

The network layer The physical and data link layers describe how the foundational requirements of two nodes in communication are met. The network layer is concerned about how this can be done when there are many such dialogues on the one network. It is in the network layer description that addressing conventions are defined and it is the software carrying out the network layer function for any node which prefixes the source and destination addresses to the data. The role of the network layer is crucial for communication between networks of different types as it must take into account that addressing conventions may differ widely. Many establishments which operate a range of different networks in an open system use what is commonly known as TCP/IP. TCP stands for transmission control protocol and is a function of the transport layer discussed next. IP or internet protocol is a network layer standard which defines an internationally accepted addressing system for all devices worldwide. On each *subnet*, such as Ethernet, MAP, IBM ring, etc., local addressing conventions are used but each node requiring access across networks is given an IP address. Tables exist which map each IP address to each node specifying its subnet and local address. Each IP address is internationally unique.

The transport layer The main concern of a network user is that the messages and data sent arrive at the destination uncorrupted, in the right order and on time. The function of transport layer in a network system is to do just that, taking into account the size of the data to be sent and its priority. Different users have different requirements from any network; file transfer requires accuracy whilst real time control data requires speed. The transport layer takes the data to be transmitted and breaks it up into suitably sized pieces, known as transport protocol data units or TPDUs, to pass to the network layer and makes sure that all the TPDUs arrive at the destination intact. The data link layer may break them up even further for medium access control purposes but will always send them sequentially via the same route and on the same channel, treating each transport layer division as a separate entity. When the TPDUs arrive in a different order to that in which they were set, the transport layer software at the destination node must reassemble them correctly. This may occur if a different route is selected for each TPDU in a complex network, if multiple frequency channels are selected to speed up the transmission of urgent data on a broadband bus or if corrupted data has to be resent because there has been no acknowledgement that a TPDU has been successfully received after a predetermined time. TCP specifies one standard structure for its TPDUs which transport data in blocks not exceeding 64 kbytes.

The session layer allows the user of the network to establish the type of communication set up by the transport layer. A session defines a definitive period of communication such as logging on to a mainframe or transferring a file. Each of these activities and others which constitute a session require different types of data transport, dialogue priorities, security access and data synchronization. Some networks or applications require data to travel in both directions at the same time and others only in one direction and it is the session layer which establishes this. Another important function of the session layer is to provide a means whereby a lengthy data transmission task, such as the transfer of a large file, can be restarted after a network crash. Rather than having to start the task all over again, the session layer can continue from a checkpoint.

The presentation layer provides a number of facilities which ensure that data stored in different formats by different devices can be understood. The different ways in which some computers represent numbers and characters can be represented as a common format and converted at each node and this type of activity is a function of the presentation layer. In addition to this, other presentation activities include encryption of data so that it can be understood only by certain devices or users. Data security and confidentiality is a crucial issue in many areas where networks are used extensively.

The application layer provides all those facilities which allow a user to make full use of the network. These include terminals and terminal emulators, server services, file transfer programs and electronic mail. In a computer-integrated manufacturing environment, file transfer is important for accessing the files in the manufacturing database for transfer to a local personal computer or workstation for processing. Terminal emulation is useful for those users who wish to access and execute software on a remote host from a personal computer. Commonly used network applications are programs like FTP or file transfer protocol or Telnet for logging on to a remote host to execute programs. Electronic mail looks set to replace paper mail both within organizations and between them. For a company operating computer-integrated manufacturing, electronic mail is the future for order reception and processing. The transfer of a customer's order into a production planning system becomes a simple cut and paste exercise or, better still, the customer could mail an order in the precise format used by the order processing software.

In summary the ISO OSI reference model, in specifying functions in a layered structure, allows data transfer between the computing devices within an organization provided the networks on which those devices reside are adequately interconnected physically. Additionally, with the correct type of hardware, there can be interconnection of nodes on remote sites both interactively and for batch job submission. An example of this in the UK is

JANET or *Joint Academic NETwork* which allows any user in a university in the UK to interactively connect to the computer system in another or to exchange information via electronic mail. A diagrammatic summary of the ISO OSI seven-layer reference model is given in Fig. 10.13.

7	Application	User access to network functionality
6	Presentation	Common data formatting between parties, encryption
5	Session	Session type establishment and management
4	Transport	Transparent data transfer between parties
3	Network	Addressing messages on and between networks
2	Data link	Error-free bit transmission in frames
1	Physical	Encoding and decoding, cabling and modulation

Figure 10.13 Summary of the ISO OSI seven-layer reference model

10.3.3 Physical Network Interconnection

We have up to now confined the discussion of communication between networks of different types to the procedural aspects. In order to physically connect networks together, however, there are a number of devices which take on the role of protocol conversion. We have already discussed one such device: the repeater. The other devices are *bridges*, *routers* and *gateways*.

The repeater   is used to connect two segments of the same type of network together. Depending upon the characteristics of the cable, a segment has an upper length limit before the signals degrade. For the 50 ohm baseband cable specified for Ethernet, the maximum length between repeaters is 500 m, though in practice it is advisable to install repeaters at shorter intervals to this. Quite often it is more convenient to sight a repeater at the end of a floor, or at the start of a segment feeding a larger terminal room. The only function of a repeater is to amplify the signal in both directions—no protocol conversions take place and so the interface between one segment and the next can be said to only extend to the physical layer as shown in Fig. 10.14.

A bridge   is used to connect two networks together which have different physical and data link layers but which use the same specification for network layer. A CSMA/CD network can connect to a token bus or ring using a bridge if they are defined by IEEE 802 type protocols. With reference to the generalized IEEE 802 network frame shown in Fig. 10.10, it can be seen that the addressing conventions are similar but the preambles

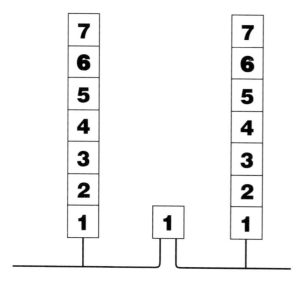

Figure 10.14 Data transfer across a repeater

and the data sizes are different. It is the task of the data link layer to break up data into manageable frames for the physical layer, and in many cases the size of the data fields in the frames is different from one network to another. Therefore a means of resizing frames is needed which means a protocol conversion up to and including the data link layer as depicted in Fig. 10.15.

If the transfer is from an 802.3 network to any of the other two then the size of the data portion need not be changed. From an 802.4 or 802.5 to a CSMA/CD network the data link layer in the bridge may have to break the frame down into smaller ones to correspond to 802.3 requirements. There will also be some conversion of the preamble presentation. A bridge is therefore a smart device in that it is controlled by software and because of this it introduces some delay in the transfer of data. The task of software therefore is to take the frame from the transmitting network and strip off the preamble, any start delimiters, control bytes and end delimiters which are particular to the data link of that network. It then evaluates the equivalent bytes for the receiving network and prefixes and appends them, as appropriate, to the whole of a portion of the data. If the data from the transmitting network is being divided up into a number of smaller frames, the bridge stores all remaining data in a buffer and continually adds prefixes and suffixes to acceptable-sized portions for transmission.

A router carries out protocol conversion to the the next layer up in the model, that is the network layer as depicted in Fig. 10.16. The router is therefore designed to connect networks which share a common transport

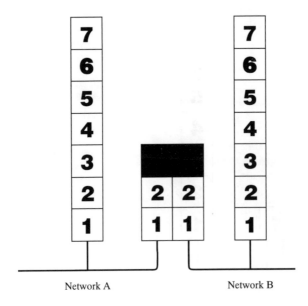

Network A   Network B

Figure 10.15   Protocol conversion for a bridge

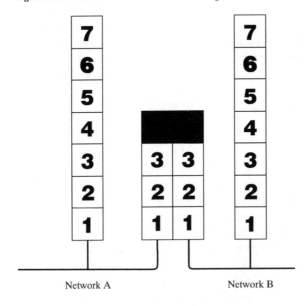

Network A   Network B

Figure 10.16   Protocol conversion in a router

layer definition but differ at the network layer. This means that there may be different addressing conventions for nodes and a different delimiter for frames or alternative checksum evaluation. A router is often used to interface an internal or local area network to a external, public network—a wide area network (WAN). While common transport conventions are used in this situation, the addressing notation has to take into account the wider perspective.

A gateway is the most complex of interconnection devices as it is designed to interface an ISO OSI based network to one which is not. In this case the protocol conversion nearly always occurs in the application layer, which generally means the gateway having to receive all the transmitted data, such as the complete file in a file transfer, before transmitting it onto the non-OSI network. This of course makes it very slow which limits the data transfer rates. Gateways are most commonly found linking new OSI networks with existing old networks or interconnecting WANs; in both these cases high speed is not an expectation.

EXERCISES

Assignment

Carry out a literature search for reports, journal or conference papers on the implementation of a local area network in two or more manufacturing companies. Write a report on your findings explaining the background of each case and the use of the network. Compare the experiences of the companies in using the network. If possible, draw out the problems they expected and those they actually met.

Questions

10.1 State the means of media access control used by the local area network system *Ethernet* and briefly explain its principles of operation.

10.2 List and explain the functions of the layers in the ISO OSI seven-layer reference model. What standard is used by the manufacturing automation protocol at the lower two layers?

10.3 What devices exist to enable the passage of network traffic when:

(a) two segments of a similar network type meet;
(b) a MAP segment connects to an Ethernet segment;
(c) two networks of completely dissimilar types meet.

Illustrate your answers with sketches or by written indication as to what layer protocol conversion takes place.

REFERENCES

Barnet, R. and S. Maynard-Smith. 1988, *Packet Switched Networks, Theory and Practice.* Sigma Press, Wilmslow.

Brey, B. B. 1984, *Microprocessor/Hardware Interfacing and Applications.* Merrill, Columbus, OH.

Dwyer, J. and A. Ioannou. 1987, *MAP and TOP, Advanced Manufacturing Communication.* Kogan Page, London.

Tanenbaum, A. S. 1989, *Computer Networks*, 2nd edn. Prentice-Hall, London.

INDEX